Y0-BRC-159

Rick Steves®

SNAPSHOT

Berlin

CONTENTS

INTRODUCTION

This Snapshot guide, excerpted from my guidebook *Rick Steves' Germany*, introduces you to the resurgent German capital. Once divided, now reunited, vibrant Berlin is racing into the future and re-emerging as one of Europe's leading cities. Walk under the Brandenburg Gate and stroll up the boulevard called Unter den Linden, pondering the layers of history beneath your feet. Relive the Cold War as you follow the course of the long-gone Berlin Wall, while towering cranes above you erect glittering new skyscrapers. Dip into art museums for a look at the Pergamon marbles and the famous bust of Queen Nefertiti. Take a day-trip to Frederick the Great's palaces and gardens in Potsdam or the sobering concentration camp memorial at Sachsenhausen.

I've also included a pair of nearby cities to round out your look at eastern Germany. Dresden—a glorious Baroque city of art, architecture, and culture, and home to some of the country's best museums—is finally being rebuilt after its notorious World War II firebombing. And laid-back Görlitz, a glossy textbook of architectural styles, offers a taste of the multiethnic region of Silesia.

To help you have the best trip possible, I've included the following topics in this book:

• **Planning Your Time,** with advice on how to make the most of your limited time

• **Orientation,** including tourist information (abbreviated as TI), tips on public transportation, local tour options, and helpful hints

• **Sights** with ratings:

▲▲▲—Don't miss

▲▲—Try hard to see

▲—Worthwhile if you can make it

No rating—Worth knowing about

• **Sleeping** and **Eating,** with good-value recommendations in every price range

• **Connections,** with tips on trains, buses, and driving

Practicalities, near the end of this book, has information on money, phoning, hotel reservations, transportation, and more, plus German survival phrases.

To travel smartly, read this little book in its entirety before you go. It's my hope that this guide will make your trip more meaningful and rewarding. Traveling like a temporary local, you'll get the absolute most out of every mile, minute, and dollar.

Gute Reise!

Rick Steves

BERLIN

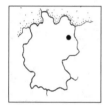

No tour of Germany is complete without a look at its historic and reunited capital. Over the last two decades, Berlin has been a construction zone. Standing on ripped-up tracks and under a canopy of cranes, visitors witnessed the rebirth of a great European capital. Although construction continues, today the once-divided city is thoroughly woven back together. Berlin has emerged as one of Europe's top destinations: captivating, lively, fun-loving, all-around enjoyable—and easy on the budget.

As you enjoy the thrill of walking over what was the Wall and through the well-patched Brandenburg Gate, it's clear that history is not contained in some book, but is an exciting story of which we are a part. In Berlin, the fine line between history and current events is excitingly blurry. But even for non-historians, Berlin is a city of fine experiences. Explore the fun and funky neighborhoods emerging in the former East, packed with creative hipster eateries and boutiques trying to one-up each other. Go for a pedal or a cruise along the delightful Spree riverfront. In the city's world-class museums, stroll up the steps of a classical Greek temple amid rough-and-tumble ancient statuary, and peruse canvases by Dürer, Rembrandt, and Vermeer. Nurse a stein of brew in a rollicking beer hall, or dive into a cheap *Currywurst* (arguably the most beloved food ever to come out of Berlin). On the outskirts of town, at Potsdam, glide like a swan through the opulent halls of an imperial palace, and ponder the darkest chapter of this nation's history at the Sachsenhausen Concentration Camp Memorial.

Of course, Berlin is still largely defined by its tumultuous 20th century. The city was Hitler's capital during World War II,

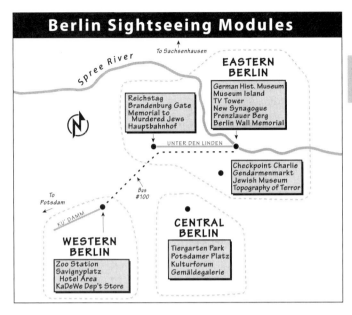

and in the postwar years, Berlin became the front line of a new global war—one between Soviet-style communism and American-style capitalism. The East-West division was set in stone in 1961, when the East German government boxed in West Berlin with the Berlin Wall. The Wall stood for 28 years. In 1990, less than a year after the Wall fell, the two Germanys—and the two Berlins—officially became one. When the dust settled, Berliners from both sides of the once-divided city faced the monumental challenge of reunification.

Berliners joke that they don't need to travel anywhere because their city's always changing. Spin a postcard rack to see what's new. A 10-year-old guidebook on Berlin covers a different city. City planners have seized on the city's reunification and the return of the national government to make Berlin a great capital once again. When the Wall fell, the East was a decrepit wasteland and the West was a paragon of commerce and materialism. More than 20 years later, the roles are reversed: It's eastern Berlin where you feel the vibrant pulse of the city, while western Berlin seems like yesterday's news.

Today, Berlin is like the nuclear fuel rod of a great nation. It's so vibrant with youth, energy, and an anything-goes-and-anything's-possible buzz that Munich feels spent in comparison. Berlin is both extremely popular and surprisingly affordable. As a booming tourist attraction, Berlin now welcomes more visitors than Rome.

BERLIN

The History of Berlin

Berlin was a humble, marshy burg—its name perhaps derived from an old Slavic word for "swamp"—until prince electors from the Hohenzollern dynasty made it their capital in the mid-15th century. Gradually their territory spread and strengthened, becoming the powerful Kingdom of Prussia in 1701. As the leading city of Prussia, Berlin dominated the northern Germanic world—both militarily and culturally—long before there was a united "Germany."

The only Hohenzollern ruler worth remembering was Frederick the Great (1712-1786). The ultimate enlightened despot, he was both a ruthless military tactician (he consolidated his kingdom's holdings, successfully invading Silesia and biting off a chunk of Poland) and a cultured lover of the arts (he actively invited artists, architects, and other thinkers to his lands). "Old Fritz," as he was called, played the flute, spoke six languages, and counted Voltaire among his friends. Practical and cosmopolitan, Frederick cleverly invited groups to Prussia who were being persecuted for their Protestantism elsewhere in Europe—including the French Huguenots and Dutch traders. Prussia became the beneficiary of these groups' substantial wealth and know-how. Frederick the Great left Berlin—and Prussia—a far more modern and enlightened place than he found it. Thanks largely to Frederick, Prussia was well-positioned to become a magnet of sorts for the German unification movement in the 19th century.

When Germany first unified, in 1871, Berlin (as the main city of its most powerful constituent state, Prussia) was its natural capital. After Germany lost World War I, although the country was in disarray, Berlin thrived as an anything-goes, cabaret-crazy cultural capital of the Roaring '20s. The city was Hitler's headquarters—and the place where the Führer drew his final breath—during World War II. When the Soviet Army reached Berlin, the protracted fighting (and vengeful postwar destruction) left the city in ruins.

Planning Your Time

On a three-week trip through Germany, I'd give Berlin three nights and at least two full days, and spend them this way:

Day 1: Begin your day getting oriented to this huge city. For a quick and relaxing once-over-lightly tour, jump on one of the many hop-on, hop-off buses that make a two-hour narrated orientation loop through the city. Use the bus as you like, to hop off and on at places of interest (such as Potsdamer Platz). Then walk from the Reichstag (reservations required), under the Brandenburg Gate, and down Unter den Linden. Tour the German History Museum, and cap your sightseeing day by catching the one-hour Spree River

In the years following World War II, Berlin was divided by the victorious Allied powers: The American, British, and French sectors became West Berlin, and the Soviet sector, East Berlin. In 1948 and 1949, the Soviet Union tried to starve the Western half (with approximately 2.2 million people) into submission in an almost medieval-style siege, blockading all roads into and out. But the siege was foiled by the Western Allies' Berlin Airlift, which flew in supplies from Frankfurt 24 hours a day for 10 months. With the overnight construction of the Berlin Wall—which completely surrounded West Berlin—in 1961, an Iron (or, at least, concrete) Curtain literally cut through the middle of the city. For details, see "The Berlin Wall (and Its Fall)" on page 68.

While the wild night when the Wall came down was inspiring, Berlin still faced a long and fitful transition to reunification. Two cities—and countries—became one at a staggering pace. Reunification had its negative side, and locals say, "The Wall survives in the minds of some people." Some "Ossies" (impolite slang for Easterners) miss their security. Some "Wessies" miss their easy ride (military deferrals, subsidized rent, and tax breaks offered to West Germans willing to live in an isolated city surrounded by the communist world). For free spirits, walled-in West Berlin was a citadel of freedom within the East.

But in recent years, the old East-West division has faded more and more into the background. Ossi-Wessi conflicts no longer dominate the city's political discourse. The city government has been eager to charge forward, with little nostalgia for anything that was associated with the East. Big corporations and the national government have moved in, and the dreary swath of land that was the Wall and its notorious "death strip" has been transformed. Berlin is a whole new city—ready to welcome visitors.

boat tour (or pedaling a rented bike) along the parklike banks of the Spree River from Museum Island to the Chancellery.

Day 2: Spend your morning touring the great museums on Museum Island (Pergamon Museum and the Egyptian collection at the Neues Museum—timed-entry tickets required for both, and Romantic German art in the Old National Gallery). Dedicate your afternoon to sights of the Third Reich and Holocaust: After lunch, hike via Potsdamer Platz to the Topography of Terror exhibit and along the surviving Zimmerstrasse stretch of the Wall to Checkpoint Charlie. You could also head up to the Berlin Wall Memorial for a more in-depth survey of that infamous barrier, or swing by the

Jewish Museum. Finish your day in the lively East—ideally in the once glum, then edgy, now fun-loving and trendy Prenzlauer Berg district.

Berlin merits additional time if you have it. There's much more in the city (such as the wonderful Gemäldegalerie art museum). And nearby are some very worthwhile side-trips: the concentration camp memorial at Sachsenhausen, the palaces at Potsdam, and the historic town of Wittenberg.

Orientation to Berlin

Berlin is huge, with 3.4 million people. The city is spread out and its sights numerous, so you'll need to be well-organized to experience the city smartly. The tourist's Berlin can be broken into three main digestible chunks:

1. Eastern Berlin has the highest concentration of notable sights and colorful neighborhoods. Near the landmark Brandenburg Gate, you'll find the Reichstag building, Pariser Platz, and the Memorial to the Murdered Jews of Europe. From Brandenburg Gate, the famous Unter den Linden boulevard runs eastward through former East Berlin, passing the German History Museum (a history lover's favorite) and Museum Island (Pergamon Museum, Neues Museum, and Berlin Cathedral) on the way to Alexanderplatz (TV Tower). The intersection of Unter den Linden and Friedrichstrasse has reclaimed its place as the center of the city. South of Unter den Linden are the delightful Gendarmenmarkt square, most Nazi sites (including the Topography of Terror), some good Wall-related sights (Museum of the Wall at Checkpoint Charlie and East Side Gallery), the Jewish Museum, and the colorful Turkish neighborhood of Kreuzberg. North of Unter den Linden are these worth-a-wander neighborhoods: Oranienburger Strasse (Jewish Quarter and New Synagogue), Hackescher Markt, and Prenzlauer Berg (several recommended hotels and a very lively restaurant/nightlife zone). Just west of Prenzlauer Berg is the Berlin Wall Memorial (with an intact surviving section of the Wall). Eastern Berlin's pedestrian-friendly Spree riverbank is also worth a stroll (or a river cruise).

2. Central Berlin is dominated by the giant Tiergarten park. South of the park are Potsdamer Platz and the Kulturforum museum cluster (including the Gemäldegalerie, New National Gallery, Musical Instruments Museum, and Philharmonic Concert Hall). To the north, the huge Hauptbahnhof (main train station) straddles the former Wall in what was central Berlin's no-man's-land.

3. Western Berlin centers on the Bahnhof Zoo (Zoo train station, often marked "Zoologischer Garten" on transit maps) and the grand Kurfürstendamm boulevard, nicknamed "Ku'damm" (transportation hub, tours, information, shopping, and recommended hotels). The East is all the rage. But the West, while staid in comparison, is bouncing back—with big-name stores and destination restaurants that keep the area buzzing. During the Cold War, this "Western Sector" was the hub for Western visitors. Capitalists visited the West, with a nervous side-trip beyond the Wall into the grim and foreboding East. (Cubans, Russians, Poles, and Angolans stayed behind the Wall and did their sightseeing in the East.) Remnants of this Iron Curtain-era Western focus have left today's visitors with a stronger focus on the Ku'damm and Bahnhof Zoo than the district deserves.

Tourist Information

With any luck, you won't have to use Berlin's TIs—they're for-profit agencies working for the city's big hotels, which colors the information they provide. TI branches, appropriately called "info-stores," are unlikely to have the information you need (tel. 030/250-025, www.visitberlin.de). You'll find them at the **Hauptbahnhof** train station (daily 8:00-22:00, by main entrance on Europaplatz), **Ku'damm** (Kurfürstendamm 22, in the glass-and-steel Neues Kranzler Eck building, Mon-Sat 9:30-20:00, Sun 9:30-18:00), and the **Brandenburg Gate** (daily 9:30-19:00).

Skip the TI's €1 map, and instead pick up any of the walking tour companies' brochures—they include nearly-as-good maps for free (most hotels also provide free city maps). While the TI does sell the three-day Museumspass (described next), it's also available at major museums. If you take a walking tour, your guide is likely a better source of nightlife or shopping tips than the TI.

Museum Passes: The three-day, €19 **Museumspass** is a great value. It gets you into more than 50 museums, including the national museums and most of the recommended biggies, on three consecutive days. As you'll routinely spend €6-10 per admission, this pays for itself in a hurry. And you'll enjoy the ease of popping in and out of museums that you might not otherwise want to pay for. Buy it at the TI or any participating museum. The pass generally lets you skip the line and go directly into the museum (though occasionally you may have to wait in line to get a printed free ticket). The €14 **Museum Island Pass** (Bereichskarte Museumsinsel, price can change with special exhibits) covers all the museums on Museum Island (otherwise €8-13 each) and is a fine value—but for just €5 more, the three-day Museumspass gives you triple the days and many more entries. TIs also sell the **WelcomeCard,** a transportation pass that also includes some museum discounts (described later, under "Getting Around Berlin").

Local Publications: Various magazines can help make your time in Berlin more productive (available at the TI and/or many newsstands). *Berlin Programm* is a comprehensive German-language monthly, especially strong in high culture, that lists upcoming events and museum hours (€2, www.berlin-programm.de). *Exberliner Magazine,* the only English monthly (published mostly by expat Brits who love to poke fun at expat Americans), is very helpful for curious travelers. It has an edgy, somewhat pretentious, youthful focus and gives a fascinating insider's look at this fast-changing city (€3 but often given away at theaters or on the street, www.exberliner.com).

Arrival in Berlin
By Train at Berlin Hauptbahnhof
Berlin's newest and grandest train station is Berlin Hauptbahnhof (main train station, a.k.a. simply "der Bahnhof", abbreviated Hbf). All long-distance trains arrive here, at Europe's biggest, mostly underground train station. This is a "transfer station"—unique for its major lines coming in at right angles—where the national train system meets the city's train system (S-Bahn).

The gigantic station can be intimidating on arrival, but it's laid

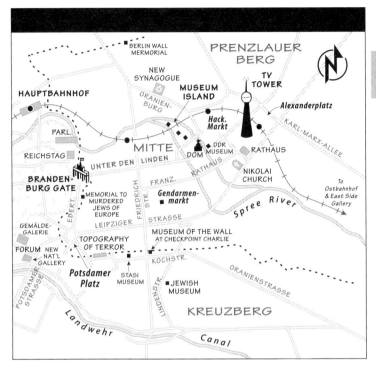

out logically on five floors (which, confusingly, can be marked in different ways). Escalators and elevators connect the **main floor** (*Erdgeschoss*, EG, a.k.a level 0); the two **lower levels** (*Untergeschoss*, UG1 and UG2, a.k.a. levels -1 and -2); and the two **upper levels** (*Obergeschoss*, OG1 and OG2, a.k.a. levels +1 and +2). Tracks 1-8 are in the lowest underground level (UG2), while tracks 11-16 (along with the S-Bahn) are on the top floor (OG2). Shops and services are concentrated on the three middle levels (EG, OG1, and UG1). The south entrance (toward the Reichstag and downtown, with a taxi stand) is marked *Washingtonplatz*, while the north entrance is marked *Europaplatz*.

Services: The **TI** is on the main floor (EG)—facing the north/*Europaplatz* entrance, look left; a 24-hour **pharmacy** is across the hall on the right (one floor above you, on OG1). The **"Rail & Fresh WC"** facility (public pay toilets) is on the main floor (EG) near the Burger King and food court. You can store your **luggage** at the Gepäck Center, an efficient and secure deposit service (€5/day per bag, daily 6:00-22:00, on upper level OG1 directly under track 14). Luggage lockers (€4) are difficult to find since they're in the parking garage (levels P-1, P-2, and P-3; look for the garage entrance near Kaisers supermarket on the underground shopping level UG1).

Train Information and Tickets: The station has two DeutscheBahn *Reisezentrum* information counters: one on the upper level (OG1/+1, daily 6:00-22:00), and the other on the lower level (UG1/-1, Mon-Fri 8:00-22:00, Sat-Sun 10:00-20:00; this branch also has the EurAide counter described next). If you're staying in western Berlin, keep in mind that the info center at the Bahnhof Zoo station is just as good and much less crowded.

EurAide is an English-speaking information desk with answers to your questions about train travel around Europe. It operates from a single counter in the underground shopping level *Reisezentrum* (follow signs to tracks 5-6 and *Reisezentrum -1*). It's American-run, so communication is simple. This is an especially good place to make fast-train and *couchette* reservations for later in your trip (April-Sept Mon-Fri 11:00-20:00—though May-July opens at 10:00, May-Aug also open Sat 10:00-16:00—otherwise closed Sat and always closed Sun; off-season Mon-Fri 11:00-18:30 only and closed Jan-Feb; www.euraide.com).

Shopping: In addition to all those trains, the Hauptbahnhof is also the home of 80 shops with long hours—some locals call the station a "shopping mall with trains" (daily 8:00-22:00, only stores selling travel provisions are open Sun). The Kaisers supermarket (on underground shopping level UG1, follow signs for tracks 1-2) is handy for assembling a picnic for your train ride.

Getting into Town: Taxis and buses wait outside the station, but the S-Bahn is probably the best means of connecting to your destination within Berlin. The cross-town express S-Bahn line connects the station with my recommended hotels in a few minutes. It's simple: All S-Bahn trains are on tracks 15 and 16 at the top of the station (level OG2/+2). All trains on track 15 go east, stopping at Friedrichstrasse, Hackescher Markt (with connections to Prenzlauer Berg), Alexanderplatz, and Ostbahnhof; trains on track 16 go west, toward Bahnhof Zoo and Savignyplatz. Your train ticket or railpass into the station covers your connecting S-Bahn ride into town (and your ticket out includes the transfer via S-Bahn to the Hauptbahnhof). U-Bahn rides are not covered by tickets or railpasses.

If you're sleeping at one of my recommended hotels in eastern Berlin's Prenzlauer Berg neighborhood, take any train on track 15 two stops to Hackescher Markt, then catch tram #M1 north.

If you're sleeping at one of my recommended hotels in western

BERLIN

Berlin, catch any train on track 16 to Savignyplatz, and you're a five-minute walk from your hotel. Savignyplatz is one stop after **Bahnhof Zoo** (rhymes with "toe"; a.k.a. Bahnhof Zoologischer Garten), the once-grand train hub now eclipsed by the Hauptbahnhof. Nowadays Bahnhof Zoo is useful mainly for its shops, uncrowded train-information desk, and BVG transit office (outside the entrance, amid the traffic).

The Berlin Hauptbahnhof is not well-connected to the city's U-Bahn (subway) system—yet. The station's sole U-Bahn line—U55—goes only two stops, to the Brandenburger Tor station, and doesn't really connect to the rest of the system. It's part of a planned extension of the U5 line to Alexanderplatz that's far from completion. But for transit junkies, it is an interesting ride on Europe's shortest subway line.

By Plane

For information on reaching the city center from Berlin's new airport, see "Berlin Connections" at the end of this chapter.

Helpful Hints

Medical Help: "**Call a doc**" is a nonprofit referral service designed for tourists (tel. 01805-321-303, phone answered 24 hours a day, www.calladoc.com). Payment is arranged between you and the doctor, and is likely far more affordable than similar care in the US. The US Embassy also has a list of local English-speaking doctors (tel. 030/83050, www.usembassy.de).

Museum Tips: Some major Berlin museums are closed on Monday—if you're in town on that day, review hours carefully before making plans. If you plan to see several museums, you'll save money with the Museumspass, which covers nearly all the city sights for three days—including everything covered by the one-day Museum Island Pass (see "Tourist Information—Museum Passes," earlier).

Addresses: Many Berlin streets are numbered with odd and even numbers on the same side of the street, often with no connection to the other side (for example, Ku'damm #212 can be across the street from #14). To save steps, check the white street signs on curb corners; many list the street numbers covered on that side of the block.

Cold War Terminology: Cold War history is important here, so it's helpful to learn a few key terms. What

Americans called "East Germany" was technically the German Democratic Republic—known here by its German name, the Deutsche Demokratische Republik. The initials **DDR** (day-day-AIR) are the shorthand you'll still see around what was once East Germany. The formal name for "West Germany" was the Federal Republic of Germany—the Bundesrepublik Deutschland (BRD)—and is the name now shared by all of reunited Germany.

Internet Access: You'll find Internet access in most hotels and hostels, as well as at small Internet cafés all over the city. Near Savignyplatz, **Internet-Terminal** is at Kantstrasse 38. In eastern Berlin, try **Hotdog World** in Prenzlauer Berg (Weinbergsweg 4, just a few steps from U8: Rosenthaler Platz toward Kastanienallee), or **Surf Inn** at Alexanderplatz 9. Bahnhof Zoo, Friedrichstrasse, and Hauptbahnhof train stations have coin-operated Internet terminals (though these unmanned machines can come with greater security risks).

Bookstore: Berlin Story, a big, cluttered, fun bookshop, has a knowledgeable staff and the best selection anywhere in town of English-language books on Berlin. They also stock an amusing mix of knickknacks and East Berlin nostalgia souvenirs (Mon-Sat 10:00-19:00, Sun 10:00-18:00, Unter den Linden 40, tel. 030/2045-3842, www.berlinstory.de). I'd skip the overpriced little museum in the back.

Other Berlin Souvenirs: If you're taken with the city's unofficial mascot, the *Ampelmännchen* (traffic-light man), you'll find a world of souvenirs slathered with his iconic red and green image at **Ampelmann Shops** (various locations, including near Gendarmenmarkt at Markgrafenstrasse 37, near Museum Island inside the DomAquarée mall, in the Hackeschen Höfe, and at Potsdamer Platz).

Laundry: Berlin has several self-service launderettes with long hours (wash and dry-€4-9/load). Near my recommended hotels in Prenzlauer Berg, try **Waschsalon 115** (daily 6:00-23:00, exact change required, free Wi-Fi, Torstrasse 115, around the corner from the recommended Circus hostel) or **Eco-Express Waschsalon** (daily 6:00-23:00, handy pizzeria next door, Danziger Strasse 7). The **Schnell & Sauber Waschcenter** chain has a location in Prenzlauer Berg (daily 6:00-23:00, exact change required, Oderberger Strasse 1).

Updates to this Book: For news about changes to this book's coverage since it was published, see www.ricksteves.com/update.

Getting Around Berlin

Berlin's sights spread far and wide. Right from the start, commit yourself to the city's fine public-transit system.

By Public Transit: Subway, Train, Tram, and Bus

Berlin's many modes of transportation are consolidated into one system that uses the same ticket: U-Bahn (*Untergrund-Bahn*, Berlin's subway), S-Bahn (*Stadtschnellbahn*, or "fast urban train," mostly aboveground and with fewer stops), *Strassenbahn* (streetcars, called "trams" by locals), and buses. For all types of transit, there are three lettered zones (A, B, and C). Most of your sightseeing will be in zones A and B (the city proper)—but you'll need to buy a ticket that also covers zone C if you're going to Potsdam, Sachsenhausen, the airport, or other outlying areas. Get and use the excellent *Discover Berlin by Train and Bus* map-guide published by the public transit operator BVG (at subway ticket windows).

Ticket Options: You have several options for tickets.

• The €2.30 **basic** ticket *(Einzelfahrschein)* covers two hours of travel in one direction on buses or subways. It's easy to make this ticket stretch to cover several rides...as long as they're all in the same direction.

• The €1.40 **short-ride** ticket *(Kurzstrecke)* covers a single ride of six bus stops or three subway stations (one transfer allowed).

• The €8.20 **four-trip** ticket *(4-Fahrten-Karte)* is the same as four basic tickets at a small discount.

• The **day pass** *(Tageskarte)* is good until 3:00 the morning after it expires (€6.30 for zones AB, €6.80 for zones ABC). For longer stays, consider a seven-day pass (*Sieben-Tage-Karte*; €27.20 for zones AB, €33.50 for zones ABC), or the WelcomeCard (described below), which is good for up to five days and also includes sightseeing discounts. The *Kleingruppenkarte* lets groups of up to five travel all day (€15 for zones AB, €15.50 for zones ABC).

• If you've already bought a ticket for zones A and B, and later decide that you also want to go to zone C, you can buy an "**extension ticket**" *(Anschlussfahrschein)* for €1.50 per ride in that zone.

• If you plan to cover a lot of ground using public transportation during a two- or three-day visit, the **WelcomeCard** (available at TIs) is usually the best deal. For longer stays, there's even a five-day option. It covers all public transportation and gives you up to 50 percent discounts on lots of minor and a few major museums (including Checkpoint Charlie), sightseeing tours (including 25 percent off the recommended Original Berlin Walks), and music and theater events (www.visitberlin.de/welcomecard). If you plan to stay inside the city, the Berlin-only option works best (covers transit zones AB, €17.90/48 hours, €23.90/72 hours). For trips beyond the city center, you might want to get the Berlin-with-Potsdam option (zones ABC, €19.90/48 hours, €25.90/72 hours). If you're a museum junkie, consider the **WelcomeCard+Museumsinsel** (€34/72 hours), which combines travel in zones A and B with unlimited access to the five museums on Museum Island. Families get an extra price break: The ABC version (€36/72 hours) is valid for one adult and up to three kids younger than 15.

Buying Tickets: You can buy U- and S-Bahn tickets from machines at stations. (They are also sold at BVG pavilions at train stations and the TI, and on board trams and buses—drivers give change.) *Erwachsener* means "adult"—anyone 14 or older. Don't be afraid of the automated machines: First select the type of ticket you want, then load the coins or paper bills. As you board the bus or tram, or enter the subway system, punch your ticket in a red or yellow clock machine to validate it (or risk a €40 fine—which may increase to €200 in 2013; for an all-day or multiday pass, stamp it only the first time you ride). Be sure to travel with a valid ticket. Tickets are checked frequently, often by plainclothes inspectors. Within Berlin, Eurailpasses are good only on S-Bahn connections from the train station when you arrive and to the station when you depart.

Transit Tips: The S-Bahn crosstown express is a river of public transit through the heart of the city, in which many lines converge on one basic highway. Get used to this, and you'll leap within a few minutes between key locations: Savignyplatz (hotels in western Berlin), Bahnhof Zoo (Ku'damm, bus #100), Hauptbahnhof (all major trains in and out of Berlin), Friedrichstrasse (a short walk north of the heart of Unter den Linden), Hackescher Markt (Museum Island, restaurants, nightlife, connection to Prenzlauer Berg hotels and eateries), and Alexanderplatz (eastern end of Unter den Linden).

Sections of the U- or S-Bahn sometimes close temporarily for repairs. In this situation, a bus route often replaces the train (*Ersatzverkehr*, or "replacement transportation"; *zwischen* means "between").

Berlin's public transit is operated by BVG (except the S-Bahn, run by the DeutscheBahn). Schedules, including bus timetables, are available on the helpful BVG website (www.bvg.de).

By Taxi

Taxis are easy to flag down, and taxi stands are common. A typical ride within town costs €8-10, and a crosstown trip (for example, Bahnhof Zoo to Alexanderplatz) will run about €15. Tariff 1 is for a *Kurzstrecke* (see below). All other rides are tariff 2 (€3.20 drop plus €1.65/kilometer). If possible, use cash—paying with a credit card comes with a hefty surcharge (about €4, regardless of the fare).

Money-Saving Taxi Tip: For any ride of less than two kilometers (about a mile), you can save several euros if you take advantage of the ***Kurzstrecke*** (short-stretch) rate. To get this rate, it's important that you flag the cab down on the street—not at or even near a taxi stand. Also, you must ask for the *Kurzstrecke* rate as soon as you hop in: Confidently say *"Kurzstrecke, bitte"* (KOORTS-shtreh-keh, BIT-teh), and your driver will grumble and flip the meter to a fixed €4 rate (for a ride that would otherwise cost €7).

By Bike

Flat Berlin is a very bike-friendly city, but be careful—Berlin's motorists don't brake for bicyclists (and bicyclists don't brake for pedestrians). Fortunately, some roads and sidewalks have special red-painted bike lanes. Don't ride on the regular sidewalk—it's *verboten*. Better yet, to get out of the city on two wheels, rent a bike, take it on the subway (requires extra €1.50 ticket) to the pleasant Potsdam/Wannsee parkland area west of town, then ride through forests and along skinny lakes to the vast Grünewald park, then back into the city. (Back during the Cold War, Grünewald was the Wessies' playground, while Ossies communed with nature at the Müggelsee east of town.) Good bike shops can suggest a specific route.

Fat Tire Bikes rents good bikes at two handy locations—East (at the base of the TV Tower near Alexanderplatz—facing the entrance to the tower, go around to the right) and West (at Bahnhof Zoo—leaving the station onto Hardenbergplatz, turn left and walk 100 yards to the big bike sign). Both locations have the same hours and rates (€7/4 hours, €12/day, cheaper rate for two or more days, free luggage storage and Internet access, daily May-Sept 9:30-20:00, March-April and Oct-Nov 9:30-18:00, shorter hours or by appointment only Dec-Feb, leave ID, tel. 030/2404-7991, www.berlinbikerental.com).

In eastern Berlin, **Take a Bike** near the Friedrichstrasse S-Bahn station is owned by a lovely Dutch-German couple who know a lot about bikes and have a huge inventory. They can help you find the perfect fit (3-gear bikes: €12.50/day, €19/2 days; more for better bikes, slightly cheaper for longer rentals; electric bikes-€29/day, helmets, daily 9:30-19:00, Neustädtische Kirchstrasse 8, tel. 030/2065-4730, www.takeabike.de). To find it, leave the S-Bahn station via the Friedrichstrasse exit, turn right, go through a triangle-shaped square, and hang a left on Neustädtische Kirchstrasse.

Tours in Berlin

▲▲▲Hop-on, Hop-off Bus Tours

Several companies offer the same routine: a €15 circuit of the city with unlimited hop-on, hop-off privileges all day (about 14 stops at the city's major sights) on buses with cursory narration in English and German by a live (but tired) guide or a boring recorded com-

Berlin at a Glance

▲▲▲German History Museum The ultimate swing through Germany's tumultuous story. **Hours:** Daily 10:00-18:00. See page 41.

▲▲▲Pergamon Museum World-class museum of classical antiquities on Museum Island, featuring the fantastic second-century B.C. Greek Pergamon Altar and frieze. **Hours:** Daily 10:00-18:00, Thu until 21:00. See page 45.

▲▲Reichstag Germany's historic parliament building, topped with a striking modern dome you can climb (reservations required). **Hours:** Daily 8:00-24:00, last entry at 23:00. See page 23.

▲▲Brandenburg Gate One of Berlin's most famous landmarks, a massive columned gateway, at the former border of East and West. **Hours:** Always open. See page 30.

▲▲Memorial to the Murdered Jews of Europe Holocaust memorial with almost 3,000 symbolic pillars, plus an exhibition about Hitler's Jewish victims. **Hours:** Memorial always open; information center open Tue-Sun 10:00-20:00, Oct-March until 19:00, closed Mon. See page 32.

▲▲Unter den Linden Leafy boulevard through the heart of former East Berlin, lined with some of the city's top sights. **Hours:** Always open. See page 35.

▲▲Neues Museum and Egyptian Collection Proud home (on Museum Island) of the exquisite 3,000-year-old bust of Queen Nefertiti. **Hours:** Daily 10:00-18:00, Thu-Sat until 20:00. See page 48.

▲▲Gendarmenmarkt Inviting square bounded by twin churches (one with a fine German history exhibit), a chocolate shop, and a concert hall. **Hours:** Always open. See page 57.

▲▲Topography of Terror Chilling exhibit documenting the Nazi perpetrators, built on the site of the former Gestapo/SS headquarters. **Hours:** Daily 10:00-20:00. See page 59.

▲▲Museum of the Wall at Checkpoint Charlie Kitschy but moving museum with stories of brave Cold War escapes, near the former site of the famous East-West border checkpoint; the surrounding street scene is almost as interesting. **Hours:** Daily 9:00-22:00. See page 63.

BERLIN

▲▲**Jewish Museum Berlin** Engaging, accessible museum celebrating Jewish culture, in a highly conceptual building. **Hours:** Daily 10:00-20:00, Mon until 22:00. See page 65.

▲▲**Gemäldegalerie** Germany's top collection of 13th- through 18th-century European paintings, featuring Holbein, Dürer, Cranach, Van der Weyden, Rubens, Hals, Rembrandt, Vermeer, Velázquez, Raphael, and more. **Hours:** Tue-Sun 10:00-18:00, Thu until 22:00, closed Mon. See page 82.

▲**Old National Gallery** German paintings, mostly from the Romantic Age. **Hours:** Tue-Sun 10:00-18:00, Thu until 22:00, closed Mon. See page 51.

▲**DDR Museum** Quirky collection of communist-era artifacts. **Hours:** Daily 10:00-20:00, Sat until 22:00. See page 54.

▲**New Synagogue** Largest prewar synagogue in Berlin, damaged in World War II, with a rebuilt facade and modest museum. **Hours:** March-Oct Sun-Mon 10:00-20:00, Tue-Thu 10:00-18:00, Fri 10:00-17:00—until 14:00 Oct and March-May, closed Sat; Nov-Feb Sun-Thu 10:00-18:00, Fri 10:00-14:00, closed Sat. See page 70.

▲**Berlin Wall Memorial** A "docu-center" with videos and displays, several outdoor exhibits, and lone surviving stretch of an intact Wall section. **Hours:** Visitor Center April-Oct Tue-Sun 9:30-19:00, Nov-March until 18:00, closed Mon; outdoor areas accessible 24 hours daily. See page 73.

▲**Potsdamer Platz** The "Times Square" of old Berlin, long a postwar wasteland, now rebuilt with huge glass skyscrapers, an underground train station, and—covered with a huge canopy—the Sony Center mall. **Hours:** Always open. See page 79.

▲**Deutsche Kinemathek Film and TV Museum** An entertaining look at German film and TV, from *Metropolis* to Dietrich to Nazi propaganda to the present day. **Hours:** Tue-Sun 10:00-18:00, Thu until 20:00, closed Mon. See page 80.

▲**Kaiser Wilhelm Memorial Church** Evocative destroyed church in heart of the former West Berlin, with modern annex. **Hours:** Church—daily 9:00-19:00; Memorial Hall in bombed tower—Mon-Sat 10:00-18:00, shorter hours Sun. See page 88.

▲**Käthe Kollwitz Museum** The black-and-white art of the Berlin artist who conveyed the suffering of her city's stormiest century. **Hours:** Daily 11:00-18:00. See page 89.

mentary in whatever language you want to dial up. In season, each company has buses running four times per hour. They are cheap and great for photography—and Berlin really lends itself to this kind of bus-tour orientation. You can hop off at any major tourist spot (Potsdamer Platz, Museum Island, Brandenburg Gate, the Kaiser Wilhelm Memorial Church, and so on). Go with a live guide rather than the recorded spiel (so you get a few current asides). When choosing seats, check the sun/shade situation—some buses are entirely topless, and others are entirely covered. My favorites are topless with a shaded covered section in the back (April-Oct daily 10:00-18:00, last bus leaves all stops at 16:00, 2-hour loop; for specifics, look for brochures in your hotel lobby or at the TI). Keep your ticket so you can hop off and on (with the same company) all day. In winter (Nov-March), buses come only twice an hour, and the last departure is at 15:00. Brochures explain extras offered by each company.

Other Bus Tours

City Bus #100—For do-it-yourselfers, Berlin's city bus #100 is a great alternative to the commercial hop-on, hop-off bus tours.

Full-Blown Bus Tours—BEX Sightseeing Berlin offers a long list of bus tours (not hop-on, hop-off) in and around Berlin; their three-hour "Berlin Classic Live" tour is a good introduction (€20; April-Oct daily at 10:00, Fri-Sun also at 14:00; Nov-March Wed-Sat at 10:00, no tours Sun-Tue; live guides in two languages, interesting historical photos displayed on bus monitors, departs from Ku'damm 216, buy ticket at bus, tel. 030/880-4190, www.berliner stadtrundfahrten.de).

▲▲▲Walking Tours

Berlin, with a fascinating recent history that can be challenging to appreciate on your own, is an ideal place to explore with a walking tour. The city is a battle zone of extremely competitive and creative walking-tour companies. Unlike many other European countries, Germany has no regulations controlling who can give city tours. This can make guide quality hit-or-miss, ranging from brilliant history buffs who've lived in Berlin for years while pursuing their PhDs, to new arrivals who memorize a script and start leading tours after being in town for just a couple of weeks. A good Berlin tour guide is equal parts historian and entertainer; the best tours make the city's dynamic story come to life. While upstart companies abound, in general you have the best odds of landing a great guide by using one of the more established companies I recommend in this section.

Most outfits offer walks that are variations on the same themes: general **introductory** walk, **Third Reich** (Hitler and

Nazi sites), and day trips to **Potsdam** and the **Sachsenhausen Concentration Camp Memorial**. Most tours cost about €12-15 and last about three to four hours (longer for the side-trips to Potsdam and Sachsenhausen); public-transit tickets and entrances to sights are extra. I've included some basic descriptions for each company, but for details—including prices and specific schedules—see the various websites or look for brochures in town (widely available at TIs, hotel reception desks, and many cafés and shops).

Vive Berlin—Formed by some of the city's most experienced guides, this "guiding collective" offers an introductory walk (Essential Berlin, Mon-Tue at 10:00), a Sachsenhausen visit (Tue, Fri, and Sun at 10:00), Third Reich and Cold War itineraries, and a Kreuzberg bike tour. Each tour is woven around the experiences of a real-life Berliner. Meet at Potsdamer Platz 10, in front of Balzac Coffee (U2/S-Bahn: Potsdamer Platz, use Stresemannstrasse exit; tel. 0157/845-46696, www.viveberlintours.de).

Insider Tour—This well-regarded company runs the full gamut of itineraries: introductory walk (daily), Third Reich, Cold War, Jewish Berlin, Sachsenhausen, and Potsdam, as well as bike tours, pub crawls, and a day trip to Dresden. Their tours have two meeting points (some tours convene at both, others at just one—check the schedule): in the West at the McDonald's across from Bahnhof Zoo, and in the East at AMT Coffee at the Hackescher Markt S-Bahn station (tel. 030/692-3149, www.insidertour.com).

Brewer's Berlin Tours—Specializing in longer, more in-depth walks, this company was started by Terry Brewer, who retired from the British diplomatic service in East Berlin. Today Terry's guides lead exhaustive—or, for some, exhausting—tours through the city (their Best of Berlin introductory tour, billed at 6 hours, can last 8 hours or more; daily at 10:30). Terry himself (who can be a bit gruff) leads a "six-hour" tour to some off-the-beaten-path hidden gems of Berlin twice weekly. They also do all-day Potsdam tours. Their tours depart from Bandy Brooks ice cream shop at the Friedrichstrasse S-Bahn station (tel. 030/2248-7435, mobile 0177-388-1537, www.brewersberlintours.com).

Original Berlin Walks—Aiming at a clientele that's curious about the city's history, their flagship introductory walk, Discover Berlin, offers a good overview in four hours (daily year-round, meet at 10:00 at Bahnhof Zoo, April-Oct also daily at 13:30). They offer a Third Reich walking tour (4/week in summer), tours to Potsdam and Sachsenhausen, and themed Jewish Life in Berlin and Nest of Spies walks (both 1/week April-Oct only). Readers of this book get a €1 discount per tour in 2013. You can buy tickets in advance at any S-Bahn service center, or just show up and buy a

BERLIN

ticket from the guide. All tours meet at the taxi stand in front of the Bahnhof Zoo train station; the Discover Berlin, Jewish Life, and Sachsenhausen tours also have a second departure point opposite East Berlin's Hackescher Markt S-Bahn station, outside the Weihenstephaner restaurant (tour info: tel. 030/301-9194, www.berlinwalks.de).

Sandeman's New Europe Berlin "Free" Tours—You'll see this company advertising supposedly "free" introductory tours, plus paid itineraries similar to those offered by competitors. But Sandeman's tours aren't really free—just misleading. Guides for the "free" tours pay the company a cut of €3 per person, so they hustle for tips. They expect to be "tipped in paper" (i.e., €5 minimum tip per person). This business model leads to high guide turnover, meaning that the guides are, overall, less experienced (though some are quite entertaining). They offer the standard Berlin itineraries, but target a younger crowd. Basic introductory city walks leave daily at 9:00, 11:00, 13:00, and 16:00 from outside the Starbucks on Pariser Platz, near the Brandenburg Gate. Paid tours include a wildly popular €12 pub crawl (nightly) and an excellent Alternative Berlin tour, which explores Berlin's gritty counterculture, squats, and urban life (€12, daily at 14:00; tel. 030/5105-0030, www.new-berlintours.com).

Berlin Underground Association (Berliner Unterwelten Verein)—Much of Berlin's history lies beneath the surface, and this group has an exclusive agreement with the city to explore and research what is hidden underground. Their one-of-a-kind Dark Worlds tour of a WWII air-raid bunker features a chilling explanation of the air war over Berlin (Wed-Mon at 11:00, also Mon at 13:00; Dec-Feb no tours on Wed). The From Flak Towers to Mountains of Debris tour enters the Humboldthain air defense tower (April-Oct Thu-Sun at 16:00). The Subways, Bunkers, Cold War tour visits a completely stocked and fully functional nuclear emergency bunker in former West Berlin (Tue-Sun at 13:00, March-Nov also Tue at 11:00, Dec-Feb no tours on Wed; each tour costs €10; meet in the hall of the Gesundbrunnen U-Bahn/S-Bahn station, follow signs to *Humboldthain/Brunnenstrasse* exit and walk up the stairs to their office, tel. 030/4991-0517, www.berliner-unterwelten.de).

Local Guides—**Nick Jackson** enjoys sharing the story of his adopted hometown with visitors (mobile 0171-537-8768, nick.jackson@berlin.de; also helps with Berlin Underground tours). If he's busy, try **Jennifer DeShirley** at Berlin and Beyond—this company has a crew of excellent, professional guides with an academic bent (tel. 030/8733-0584, mobile 0176-633-55565, info@berlinandbeyond.de). **Bernhard Wagner** is a young, enthusiastic historian with a particular passion for Germany's 20th-century history (mobile 0176-6422-9119, schlegelmilch@gmx.net).

Bike Tours

Fat Tire Bike Tours—Choose among five different tours (each €24, 4-6 hours, 6-10 miles): **City Tour** (March-Nov daily at 11:00, May-Sept also daily at 16:00, Dec-Feb Wed and Sat at 11:00), **Berlin Wall Tour** (April-Oct Mon, Thu, and Sat at 10:30), **Third Reich Tour** (April-Oct Wed, Fri, and Sun at 10:30), **"Raw" Tour** (covers countercultural, creative aspects of contemporary Berlin, April-Oct Tue, Fri, and Sun at 10:30), and **Gardens and Palaces of Potsdam Tour** (April-Oct Wed, Sat, and Sun at 10:00). For any tour, meet at the TV Tower at Alexanderplatz—but don't get distracted by the Russians pretending to be Fat Tire (reserve ahead for the Wall, Third Reich, Raw, and Potsdam tours, no reservations necessary for City Tour, tel. 030/2404-7991, www.fattirebiketours.com).

Finding Berlin Tours—This small, easygoing company offers tours that take you away from the mainstream sights and focus on Berlin's neighborhoods, people, and street art (€20-25/person, max 8 people, 3-5 hours, meet at Revaler Strasse 99, near intersection with Warschauer Strasse—look for gate with *RAW* sign and walk into courtyard to their shipping-container kiosk, S-Bahn: Warschauer Strasse, mobile 0176-9933-3913, see schedule at www.findingberlin-tours.com).

Boat Tours

Spree River Cruises— Several boat companies offer one-hour, €10 trips up and down the river. A relaxing hour on one of these boats can be time and money well-spent. You'll listen to excellent English audioguides, see lots of wonderful new  government-commissioned architecture, and enjoy the lively park action fronting the river. Boats leave from various docks that cluster near the bridge at the Berlin Cathedral (just off Unter den Linden). I enjoyed the Historical Sightseeing Cruise from **Stern und Kreisschiffahrt** (mid-March-Nov daily 10:30-18:30, leaves from Nikolaiviertel Dock—cross bridge from Berlin Cathedral toward Alexanderplatz and look right, tel. 030/536-3600, www.sternundkreis.de). Confirm that the boat you choose comes with English commentary.

Self-Guided Bus Tour

Bus #100 from Bahnhof Zoo to Alexanderplatz

While hop-on, hop-off bus tours are a great value, Berlin's city bus #100 laces together the major sights in a kind of poor man's bus tour. Bus #100 stops at Bahnhof Zoo, the Berlin Zoo, Victory Column, Reichstag, Unter den Linden, Brandenburg Gate, Pergamon Museum, and Alexanderplatz. A reader board inside the bus displays the upcoming stop. A basic €2.30 bus ticket is good for two hours of travel in one direction, and buses leave every few minutes.

Starting in the West from Bahnhof Zoo, here's a quick review of what you'll see: Leaving the train station, on your left and straight ahead, you'll spot the bombed-out hulk of the **Kaiser Wilhelm Memorial Church,** with its postwar sister church. Then, on the left, the elephant gates mark the entrance to the venerable and much-loved **Berlin Zoo** and its aquarium. After a left turn, you cross the canal and pass Berlin's **embassy row.** The first interesting embassy is Mexico's, with columns that seem to move when you're driving by (how do they do that?). The big turquoise wall marks the communal home of all five Nordic embassies. This building is very "green," run entirely on solar power.

The bus then enters the 400-acre **Tiergarten** park, packed with cycling paths, joggers, and—on hot days—nude sunbathers. Straight ahead, the **Victory Column** (Siegessäule; with the gilded angel), towers above this vast city park that was once a royal hunting grounds. A block beyond the Victory Column (on the left) is the 18th-century late-Rococo **Bellevue Palace.** Formerly the official residence of the Prussian (and later German) crown prince, and at one time a Nazi VIP guest house, it's now the residence of the federal president (whose power is mostly ceremonial—the chancellor wields the real clout). If the flag's out, he's in.

Driving along the Spree River (on the left), you'll see buildings of the **national government.** The huge brick "brown snake" complex (across the river) was built to house government workers—but it didn't sell, so now its apartments are available to anyone. A metal Henry Moore sculpture titled *Butterfly* (a.k.a. "The Drinker's Liver") floats in front of the slope-roofed House of World Cultures (Berliners have nicknamed this building "the pregnant oyster" and "Jimmy Carter's smile"). The modern tower (next, on the left) is a carillon with 68 bells (from 1987). Through the trees on the left you'll see Germany's **Chancellery**—essentially Germany's White House. The big open space is the **Platz der Republik,** where the Victory Column (which you passed earlier) stood until Hitler moved it. The Hauptbahnhof (Berlin's vast main train station, marked by its tall tower with the *DB* sign) is across the field between the Chancellery and the **Reichstag** (Germany's parliament—the old building with the new dome).

If you get off here, the "Sights in Eastern Berlin" descriptions in the following section cover the next string of attractions, which are best seen on foot. If you stay on the bus, you'll zip by them in this order:

Unter den Linden, the main east-west thoroughfare, stretches from the **Brandenburg Gate** (behind you) through Berlin's historic core (ahead) to the TV Tower in the distance (Alexanderplatz, where this bus finishes). You'll pass the **Russian Embassy** and the Aeroflot airline office (right). Crossing **Friedrichstrasse,** look right for a Fifth Avenue-style conga line of big, glitzy department stores. Later, on the left, are the **German History Museum, Museum Island** (with the **Pergamon Museum**), and the **Berlin Cathedral;** across from these (on the right) is the construction site of the new **Humboldt-Forum** (with the Humboldt-Box visitors center). Then you'll rumble to a final stop at what was the center of East Berlin in communist times: **Alexanderplatz.**

Sights in Eastern Berlin

The following sights are arranged roughly west to east, from the Reichstag down Unter den Linden to Alexanderplatz. It's possible to link these sights as a convenient self-guided orientation walk (I've included walking directions for this purpose)—allow about 1.5 hours without stops for sightseeing. Adding tours of several sights can easily fill a whole day. Remember that reservations are required for the Reichstag dome, and you'll need timed-entry tickets for the Pergamon and Neues Museums.

Also described here are sights to the south and north of Unter den Linden.

▲▲Reichstag

The parliament building—the heart of German democracy—has a short but complicated and emotional history. When it was inaugu-

rated in the 1890s, the last emperor, Kaiser Wilhelm II, disdainfully called it the "chatting home for monkeys" *(Reichsaffenhaus).* It was placed outside of the city's old walls—far from the center of real power, the imperial palace. But it was from the Reichstag that the German Republic was proclaimed in 1918.

In 1933, this symbol of democracy nearly burned down. The Nazis—whose influence on the German political scene was on the rise—blamed a communist plot. A Dutch communist, Marinus van der Lubbe, was eventually convicted and guillotined for the crime. Others believed that Hitler himself planned the fire, using it as a handy excuse to frame the communists and grab power. Even though Van der Lubbe was posthumously pardoned by the German government in 2008, most modern historians concede that he most likely was indeed guilty, and had acted alone—the Nazis were just incredibly lucky to have his deed advance their cause.

The Reichstag was hardly used from 1933 to 1999. Despite the fact that the building had lost its symbolic value, Stalin ordered his troops to take the Reichstag from the Nazis by May 1, 1945 (the date of the workers' May Day parade in Moscow). More than 1,500 Nazi soldiers made their last stand here—extending World War II by two days. On April 30, after fierce fighting on this rooftop, the Reichstag fell to the Red Army.

For the building's 101st birthday in 1995, the Bulgarian-American artist Christo wrapped it in silvery gold cloth. It was then wrapped again—in scaffolding—and rebuilt by British architect Lord Norman Foster into the new parliamentary home of the Bundestag (Germany's lower house, similar to the US House of Representatives). To many Germans, the proud resurrection of the Reichstag symbolizes the end of a terrible chapter in their country's history.

The **glass cupola** rises 155 feet above the ground. Its two sloped ramps spiral 755 feet to the top for a grand view. Inside the dome, a cone of 360 mirrors reflects natural light into the legislative chamber below. Lit from inside at night, this gives Berlin a memorable nightlight. The environmentally friendly cone—with an opening at the top—also helps with air circulation, drawing stale air out of the legislative chamber (no joke) and pulling in cool air from below.

Because of a terrorist plot discovered and thwarted in 2010, the building has tight security; getting in now requires a reservation.

Cost and Hours: Free but reservations highly recommended—see below, daily 8:00-24:00, last entry at 23:00, metal detectors, no big luggage allowed, Platz der Republik 1; S- or U-Bahn: Friedrichstrasse, Brandenburger Tor, or Bundestag; tel. 030/2273-2152, www.bundestag.de.

Reservations: To visit the dome, it's best to make a reservation (free); spots book up several days in advance. If you're in Berlin without a reservation, try dropping by the visitors center (on the Tiergarten side of Scheidemannstrasse, across from Platz der Republik) to ask if they have open slots (whole party must be present,

ID required, slots available no less than 2 hours and no more than 2 days out).

Your only way to guarantee a spot is to reserve further ahead **online.** The website is user-friendly, if (not surprisingly) a bit bureaucratic. Go to www.bundestag.de, click "English" at the top of the screen, and—under the "Visit the Bundestag" menu—select "Online registration." On this page, select "Visit the dome." Fill in the number of people in your party, ignore the "Comments" field, and click "Next." After entering the scrambled captcha code, you can select your preferred visit date and time (you can request up to three different time slots) and fill in your contact information. Once you complete the form and agree to their privacy policy, you'll be sent a confirmation email with a link to a website where you'll enter the name and birthdate for each person in your party and confirm your request. After completing this form, you'll receive a confirmation of your request (not a confirmation of your visit) by email. But you still have to wait for yet another email confirming your reservation. If the English page isn't working, you can try using the German version: Go to https://www.bundestag.de/besuche/besucherdienst/index.jsp and call up a German-speaking friend to help you out. Or, if you use Google's Chrome browser, simply click the "Translate" button to see the steps in English.

While they claim it's possible to **email** a reservation request (kuppelbesuch@bundestag.de), you won't receive a confirmation until the day before your visit—which can be stressful. Use the website instead.

Getting In: Once you have a reservation, simply report to the visitors center at the appointed time, and be ready to show ID. Give your name to the attendant, and you'll be let right in.

Tours: Pick up the English **"Outlooks" flier** just after the visitors center. The free GPS-driven **audioguide** explains the building and narrates the view as you wind up the spiral ramp to the top of the dome; the commentary starts automatically as you step onto the bottom of the ramp.

❺ Self-Guided Tour: As you approach the building, look above the door, surrounded by stone patches from WWII bomb damage, to see the motto and promise: *Dem Deutschen Volke* ("To the German People"). The open, airy lobby towers 100 feet high, with 65-foot-tall colors of the German flag. See-through glass doors show the **central legislative chamber.** The message: There will be no secrets in this government. Look inside. Spreading his wings behind the podium is a stylized German eagle: the *Bundestagsadler* (a.k.a. "the fat hen"), representing the Bundestag (each branch of government has its own symbolic eagle). Notice the doors marked *Ja* (Yes), *Nein* (No), and *Enthalten* (Abstain)...an homage to the Bundestag's traditional "sheep jump" way of counting votes

BERLIN

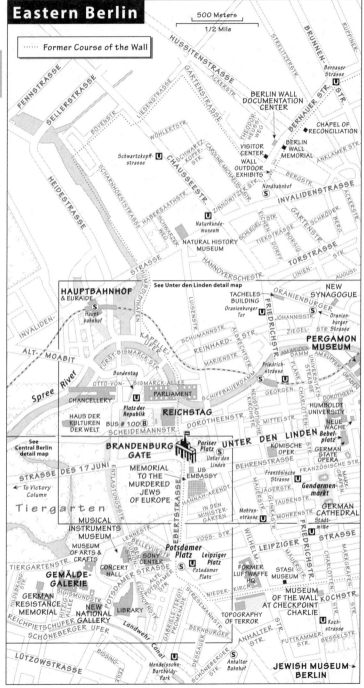

Eastern Berlin

500 Meters
1/2 Mile

...... Former Course of the Wall

FENNSTRASSE
SELLERSTRASSE
BOYENSTR.
HEIDESTRASSE
SCHARNHORSTSTRASSE
STRASSE
HUSSITENSTRASSE
GARTENSTRASSE
LIEBENWALDERSTR.
ACKERSTR.
WÖHLERTSTR.
SCHWARTZKOPFSTR.
CAROLINE-MICHAELIS-STR.
CHAUSSEESTR.
HABERSAATHSTR.
SCHWARZER WEG
ZINNOWITZERSTR.
THEODOR-HEUSS-WEG
STRELITZERSTR.
BRUNNEN
KUPPINER
Bernauer Strasse
BERNAUER STR.
ANKLAMER STR.
BERGSTR.

BERLIN WALL
DOCUMENTATION
CENTER

CHAPEL OF
RECONCILIATION

VISITOR
CENTER

BERLIN
WALL
MEMORIAL

WALL
OUTDOOR
EXHIBITS

Nordbahnhof

Schwartzkopff-
strasse

Naturkunde-
museum

NATURAL HISTORY
MUSEUM

SCHLEGELSTR.
EICHEN DORFF
TIEKSTR.
BORSIG
GARTENSTR.
SCHRÖDER BERG
ACKERSTR.
INVALIDENSTRASSE
TORSTRASSE
STR.
LINIEN STR.
AUGUST-

STRASSE
HANNOVERSCHESTR.

INVALIDEN-
ALT- MOABIT

HAUPTBAHNHOF
& EURAIDE

Haupt-
bahnhof

KAPELLE-UFER
FÜRST-BISMARCK-STR.
LUISENSTR.
SCHUMANNSTR.
REINHARDSTR.
ALBRECHTSTR.
MARIENSTR.

Bundestag

OTTO-VON- BISMARCK-ALLEE
CHANCELLERY
PARLIAMENT
Platz der
Republik
REICHSTAG
HAUS DER
KULTUREN
DER WELT
BUS # 100 B
SCHEIDEMANNSTR.
DOROTHEENSTR.

Spree River

See Unter den Linden detail map

TACHELES
BUILDING
Oranienburger
Tor
ORANIENBURGER
JOHANNISSTR.
FRIEDRICHSTR.
ZIEGEL-
AM WEIDEN
DAMM
Friedrich-
strasse
GEORGEN-
SCHIFFBAUERDAMM
NEUSTÄDTISCHE
KIRCHSTR.

NEW
SYNAGOGUE

Oranien-
burger
STR. Strasse

PERGAMON
MUSEUM

UNIVERSITÄTSSTRASSE
AM KUPFER-
GRABEN
DOROTHEEN-STR.
HUMBOLDT
UNIVERSITY
PLANCK STR.
CHARLOTTENSTR.

BRANDENBURG
GATE
Pariser
Platz
UNTER DEN LINDEN
Unter den
Linden
US
EMBASSY
BEHRENSTRASSE
MEMORIAL
TO THE
MURDERED
JEWS
OF EUROPE

KOMISCHE
OPER
NEUE
WACHE
Bebel-
platz
GERMAN
STATE
OPERA

See
Central Berlin
detail map

STRASSE DES 17 JUNI
ENTLASTUNGSSTR.
EBERTSTRASSE
HANNAH-ARENDT-STR.
IN DEN
MINISTER-
GÄRTEN
Mohren-
strasse
VOSS- STR.
Französische
Strasse
JÄGERSTR.
TAUBENSTR.
MOHRENSTR.
Gendarmen-
markt
GLINKASTR.
FRANZÖSISCHE STR.
MARK GRAFEN
GERMAN
CATHEDRAL

← To Victory
Column

Tiergarten

MUSICAL
INSTRUMENTS
MUSEUM

MUSEUM
OF ARTS &
CRAFTS

Potsdamer
Platz

Leipziger
Platz

Potsdamer
Platz

FORMER
LUFTWAFFE
HQ

KIRCH

STASI
MUSEUM

Stadt-
mitte
FRIEDRICHSTR.

MUSEUM
OF THE WALL
AT CHECKPOINT
CHARLIE

TIERGARTENSTR.
GEMÄLDE-
GALERIE
GERMAN
RESISTANCE
MEMORIAL
SIGISMUNDSTR.
HITZIG ALLEE
NEW
NATIONAL
GALLERY
LIBRARY
REICHPIETSCHUFER
SCHÖNEBERGER UFER
LÜTZOWSTRASSE
BELLEVUESTR.
LENNESTR.
CONCERT
HALL
SONY
CENTER
ALTE
POTSDAMER
EICHHORNSTR.
STRASSE
GABRIELE-TERGIT-
PROMENADE
Landwehr Canal
KÖTHENERSTR.
BERNBURGER
DESSAUER STR.
SCHÖNEBERGER STR.
BISSING ZEILE
Mendelssohn-
Bartholdy-
Park

WILHELM-STR.
LEIPZIGER STR.
MAUERSTR.
NIEDER-
KIRCHNERSTR.
STRESEMANNSTR.
TOPOGRAPHY
OF TERROR
ANHALTER
STR.
Anhalter
Bahnhof
SCHÜTZENSTR.
MARKGRAFEN-STR.
CHARLOTTEN STR.
STRASSE
KOCHSTR.
Koch-
strasse
PUTTKAMMER-
STR.
BESSELSTR.

JEWISH MUSEUM →
BERLIN

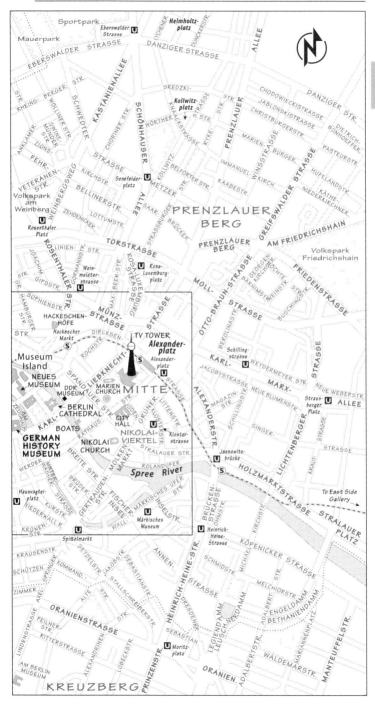

by exiting the chamber through the corresponding door (for critical votes, however, all 669 members vote with electronic cards).

Ride the elevator to the base of the glass **dome.** Pick up the free audioguide and take some time to study the photos and read the circle of captions—around the base of the central funnel—for an excellent exhibit telling the Reichstag story. Then study the surrounding architecture: a broken collage of new on old, torn between antiquity and modernity, like Germany's history. Notice the dome's giant and unobtrusive sunscreen that moves as necessary with the sun. Peer down through the skylight to look over the shoulders of the elected representatives at work. For Germans, the best view from here is down—keeping a close eye on their government.

Start at the ramp nearest the elevator and wind up to the top of the **double ramp.** Take a 360-degree survey of the city as you hike: The big park is the **Tiergarten,** the "green lungs of Berlin." Beyond that is the **Teufelsberg** ("Devil's Hill"): Built of rubble from the destroyed city in the late 1940s, it was famous during the Cold War as a powerful ear of the West—notice the telecommunications tower on top. Knowing the bombed-out and bulldozed story of their city, locals say, "You have to be suspicious when you see the nice, green park."

Find the **Victory Column** (Siegessäule), glimmering in the middle of the park. This was moved by Hitler in the 1930s from in front of the Reichstag to its present position in the Tiergarten, as the first step in creating a grandiose axis he envisioned for postwar Berlin. Next, scenes of the new Berlin spiral into your view—**Potsdamer Platz,** marked by the conical glass tower that houses Sony's European headquarters. Continue circling left, and find the green chariot atop the **Brandenburg Gate.** Just to its left is the curving fish-like roof of the **DZ Bank** building, designed by the unconventional American architect Frank Gehry. The **Memorial to the Murdered Jews of Europe** stretches south of the Brandenburg Gate. Next, you'll see **former East Berlin** and the city's next huge construction zone, with a forest of 300-foot-tall skyscrapers in the works. Notice the TV Tower, the Berlin Cathedral's massive dome, and the golden dome of the New Synagogue.

Follow the train tracks in the distance to the left toward Berlin's huge main train station, the **Hauptbahnhof.** Complete your spin-tour with the blocky **Chancellery,** nicknamed by Berliners "the washing machine." It may look like a pharaoh's tomb, but it's the office and home of Germany's most powerful person, the chancellor (currently Angela Merkel). To remind the chancellor who he or she works for, the Reichstag, at about 130 feet, is about six feet taller than the Chancellery.

Continue spiraling up. You'll pass all the same sights again, twice, from a higher vantage point.

Near the Reichstag

Memorial to Politicians Who Opposed Hitler—Near the road in front of the Reichstag, enmeshed in all the security apparatus, is a memorial of slate stones embedded in the ground. This row of slate slabs (which looks like a fancy slate bicycle rack) is a memorial to the 96 members of the Reichstag (the equivalent of our members of Congress) who were persecuted and murdered because their politics didn't agree with Chancellor Hitler's. They were part of the Weimar Republic, the weak and ill-fated attempt at post-WWI democracy in Germany. These were the people who could have stopped Hitler...so they became his first victims. Each slate slab remembers one man—his name, party (mostly KPD—Communists, and SPD—Social Democrats), and the date and location of his death—generally in concentration camps. (*KZ* stands for "concentration camp.") They are honored here, in front of the building in which they worked.

• *Facing the Reichstag, you can take a short side-trip to the river by circling around to the left of the building.*

Spree Riverfront—Admire the wonderful architecture incorporating the Spree River into the people's world. It's a poignant spot because this river was once a symbol of division—the East German regime put nets underwater to stymie those desperate enough for

freedom to swim to the West. When kings ruled Prussia, government buildings went right up to the water. But today, the city is incorporating the river thoughtfully into a people-friendly cityscape. From the Reichstag, a delightful riverside path leads around the curve, past "beach cafés," to the Chancellery. For a slow, low-impact glide past this zone, consider a river cruise (we'll pass the starting point—on Museum Island—later on this walk). The fine bridges symbolize the connection of East and West.

• *Leaving the Reichstag, return to the busy road, and cross the street at your first opportunity, to the big park. Walk (with the park on your right) to the corner. Along the railing at the corner of Scheidemannstrasse and Ebertstrasse is a small memorial of white crosses. This is the...*

Berlin Wall Victims Memorial—This monument—now largely  usurped by business promos and impromptu, wacko book stalls—commemorates some of the East Berliners who died trying to cross the Wall. Of these people, many perished within months of the Wall's construction on August 13, 1961. Most died trying to swim the river to freedom. The monument used to stand right on the Berlin Wall behind the Reichstag. Notice that the last person killed while trying to escape was 20-year-old Chris Gueffroy, who died nine months before the Wall fell. (He was shot through the heart in no-man's-land.)

Nearby: In the park just behind the memorial is the **Monument to the Murdered Sinti and Roma (Gypsies) of Europe.** The Sinti and Roma, as persecuted by the Nazis as the Jews were, lost the same percentage of their population to Hitler. Unveiled in 2012 after years of delays, the monument consists of a circular pool and an information wall.

• *From here, head to the Brandenburg Gate. Stay on the park side of the street for a better view of the gate ahead. As you cross at the light, notice the double row of* **cobblestones**—*it goes around the city, marking where the Wall used to stand.*

Brandenburg Gate and Nearby

▲▲**Brandenburg Gate (Brandenburger Tor)**—The historic Brandenburg Gate (1791) was the grandest—and is the last survivor—of 14 gates in Berlin's old city wall (this one led to the neighboring city of Brandenburg). The gate was the symbol of Prussian Berlin—and later the symbol of a divided Berlin. It's crowned by a majestic four-horse chariot, with the Goddess of Peace at the reins. Napoleon took this statue to the Louvre in Paris in 1806. After the Prussians defeated Napoleon and got it back (1813), she was renamed the Goddess of Victory.

The gate sat unused, part of a sad circle dance called the Wall, for more than 25 years. Now postcards all over town show the ecstatic day—November 9, 1989—when the world enjoyed the sight of happy Berliners jamming the gate like flowers on a parade float. Pause a minute and think about struggles for freedom—past and present. (There's actually a special room built into the gate for this purpose—see the sidebar.) Around the gate, look at the informa-

BERLIN

The Brandenburg Gate, Arch of Peace

Two hundred years ago, the Brandenburg Gate was designed as an arch of peace, crowned by the Goddess of Peace and showing Mars sheathing his sword. The Nazis misused it as a gate of triumph and aggression. Today a Room of Silence, built into the gate, is dedicated to the peaceful message of the original Brandenburg Gate (daily 11:00-18:00, shorter hours in winter). As you consider the history of Berlin in this room—which is carefully not dedicated to any particular religion—you may be inspired to read the prayer of the United Nations:

"Oh Lord, our planet Earth is only a small star in space. It is our duty to transform it into a planet whose creatures are no longer tormented by war, hunger, and fear, no longer senselessly divided by race, color, and ideology. Give us courage and strength to begin this task today so that our children and our children's children shall one day carry the name of man with pride."

tion boards with pictures of how this area changed throughout the 20th century. There's a TI within the gate (daily 9:30-19:00, S-Bahn: Brandenburger Tor).

The Brandenburg Gate, the center of old Berlin, sits on a major boulevard running east to west through Berlin. The western segment, called Strasse des 17 Juni (named for a workers' uprising against the DDR government on June 17, 1953), stretches for four miles from the Brandenburg Gate and Victory Column to the Olympic Stadium. But we'll follow this city axis in the opposite  direction, east, walking along a stretch called Unter den Linden—into the core of old imperial Berlin and past what was once the palace of the Hohenzollern family who ruled Prussia and then Germany. The palace—the reason for just about all you'll see—is a phantom sight, long gone. Alexanderplatz, which marks the end of this walk, is near the base of the giant TV Tower hovering in the distance.

• *Cross through the gate into...*

▲**Pariser Platz**—"Parisian Square," so named after the Prussians defeated Napoleon in 1813, was once filled with important government buildings—all bombed to smithereens in World War II. For decades, it was an unrecognizable, deserted no-man's-land—cut off from both East and West by the Wall. But now it's rebuilt, and the

BERLIN

banks, hotels, and embassies that were here before the bombing have reclaimed their original places—with a few additions: a palace of coffee (Starbucks) and the small Kennedys Museum (described later). The winners of World War II enjoy this prime real estate: The American, French, British, and Soviet (now Russian) embassies are all on or near this square.

Face the gate and look to your left. The **US Embassy** reopened in its historic location in 2008. The building has been controversial: For safety's sake, Uncle Sam wanted more of a security zone around the building, but the Germans wanted to keep Pariser Platz a welcoming people zone. (Throughout the world, American embassies are the most fortified buildings in town.) The compromise: The extra security the US wanted is built into the structure. Easy-on-the-eyes barriers keep potential car bombs at a distance, and its front door is on the side farthest from the Brandenburg Gate.

Just to the left, the **DZ Bank building** is by Frank Gehry, famous for Bilbao's organic Guggenheim Museum, Prague's Dancing House, Seattle's Experience Music Project, Chicago's Millennium Park, and Los Angeles' Walt Disney Concert Hall. Gehry fans might be surprised at the DZ Bank building's low profile. Structures on Pariser Platz are designed to be bland so as not to draw attention away from the Brandenburg Gate. (The glassy facade of the Academy of Arts, next to Gehry's building, is controversial for drawing attention to itself.) For your fix of the good old Gehry, step into the lobby and check out its undulating interior. It's a fish—and you feel like you're both inside and outside of it. The architect's vision is explained on a nearby plaque. The best view of the roof of Gehry's creation is from the Reichstag dome.

• Enter the Academy of Arts (Akademie der Kunst), next door to Gehry's building. Its doors lead to a lobby (with a small food counter, daily 10:00-20:00), which leads directly to the vast...

▲▲Memorial to the Murdered Jews of Europe (Denkmal für die Ermordeten Juden Europas)—
This Holocaust memorial, consisting of 2,711 gravestone-like pillars (called "stelae") and completed in 2005, is an essential stop for any visit to Berlin. It was the first formal, German government-sponsored Holocaust memorial. Jewish American architect Peter Eisenman won the competition for the commission (and built it on time and on budget—€27 million). It's been criticized for focusing on just one of the groups targeted by the Nazis,

but the German government has promised to erect memorials to other victims.

Cost and Hours: Free, memorial always open; information center open Tue-Sun 10:00-20:00, Oct-March until 19:00, closed Mon year-round; last entry 45 minutes before closing, S-Bahn: Brandenburger Tor or Potsdamer Platz, tel. 030/2639-4336, www.stiftung-denkmal.de. The €4 audioguide augments the experience.

Visiting the Memorial: The pillars are made of hollow concrete, each chemically coated for easy removal of graffiti. (Notably, the chemical coating was developed by a subsidiary of the former IG Farben group—the company infamous for supplying the Zyklon B gas used in Nazi death camps.) The number of pillars isn't symbolic of anything; it's simply how many fit on the provided land.

Once you enter the memorial, notice that people seem to appear and disappear between the columns, and that no matter where you are, the exit always seems to be up. Is it a labyrinth...a symbolic cemetery...and intentionally disorienting? It's entirely up to the visitor to derive the meaning, while pondering this horrible chapter in human history.

The pondering takes place under the sky. For the learning,

go under the field of concrete pillars to the state-of-the-art **information center** (there may be a short line because of the mandatory security check). Inside, a thought-provoking exhibit (well-explained in English) studies the Nazi system of extermination and humanizes the victims, while also providing space for silent reflection. In the Starting Hall, exhibits trace the historical context of the Nazi and WWII era, while six portraits—representing the six million Jewish victims—look out on the visitors. The Room of Dimensions has glowing boxes in the floor containing diaries, letters, and final farewells penned by Holocaust victims. The Room of Families presents case-studies of 15 Jewish families from around Europe, to more fully convey the European Jewish experience. Remember: Behind these 15 stories are millions more tales of despair, tragedy, and survival. In the Room of Names, a continually running soundtrack lists the names and brief biographical sketches of Holocaust victims; reading the names of all those murdered would take more than six and a half years. The Room of Sites documents some 220 different places of genocide. You'll also find exhibits about other Holocaust monuments and memorials, a searchable database of victims, and a video archive of interviews with survivors.

Imagining Hitler in the 21st Century

More than six decades after the end of World War II, the bunker where Hitler killed himself lies hidden underneath a Berlin parking lot. While the Churchill War Rooms are a major sight in London, no one wants to turn Hitler's final stronghold into a tourist attraction.

Germans tread lightly on their past. It took 65 years for the Germany History Museum to organize its first exhibit on the life of Hitler. Even then, the exhibit was careful not to give neo-Nazis any excuse to celebrate—even the size of the Hitler portraits was kept to a minimum.

The image of Hitler has been changing in Germany. No longer is he exclusively an evil mass murderer—sometimes he is portrayed as a nervous wreck, such as in the 2004 film *Downfall*, or as an object of derision. He's even a wax figure in the Berlin branch of Madame Tussauds.

But 21st-century Germans still treat the subject with extraordinary sensitivity. The Bavarian state government holds the copyright to Hitler's political manifesto—*Mein Kampf*—and won't allow any version to be published in German, even one annotated by historians (although it is readily available on the Internet and in the US). Any visit to Hitler's mountain retreat in Berchtesgaden includes a stop at the Nazi Documentation Center, where visitors see Nazi artifacts carefully placed in their historical context.

Many visitors to Berlin are curious about Hitler sites, but few artifacts of that dark period survive. The German Resistance Memorial is presented in German only and difficult for the tourist to appreciate (though it has a helpful audioguide in English; see page 78). Hitler's bunker is completely gone (near Potsdamer Platz). The best way to learn about Hitler sites is to take a Third Reich tour offered by one of the many local walking-tour companies (see "Tours in Berlin," page 15), or to visit the Topography of Terror, a fascinating exhibit located in a rebuilt hall on the same spot where the SS and Gestapo headquarters once stood (see page 59).

It's a balancing act, but when it comes to *der Führer,* Germans seem to be confronting their regrettable past.

The memorial's location—where the Wall once stood—is coincidental. Nazi propagandist Joseph Goebbels' bunker was discovered during the work and left buried under the northeast corner of the memorial. Hitler's bunker is just 200 yards away, under a nondescript parking lot. Such Nazi sites are intentionally left hidden to discourage neo-Nazi elements from creating shrines.

• Now backtrack to Pariser Platz (through the yellow building). Across the square (next to Starbucks), consider dropping into...

The Kennedys Museum—This crisp private enterprise facing the Brandenburg Gate recalls John F. Kennedy's Germany trip in 1963, with great photos and video clips as well as a photographic shrine to the Kennedy clan in America. It's a small, overpriced, yet delightful experience with interesting mementos—such as old campaign buttons and posters, and JFK's notes with the phonetic "Ish bin ein Bearleener." Jacqueline Kennedy commented on how strange it was that this—not even in his native language—was her husband's most quotable quote. Most of the exhibit consists of photographs that, if nothing else, spark a nostalgic longing for the days of Camelot.

    Cost and Hours: €7, includes special exhibits, reduced to €3.50 for a broad array of visitors—dream up a discount and ask for it, daily 10:00-18:00, Pariser Platz 4a, tel. 030/2065-3570, www.thekennedys.de.

• *Leave Pariser Platz and begin strolling...*

▲▲Unter den Linden

The street called Unter den Linden is the heart of former East Berlin. In Berlin's good old days, Unter den Linden was one of Europe's grand boulevards. In the 15th century, this carriageway

led from the palace to the hunting grounds (today's big Tiergarten). In the 17th century, Hohenzollern princes and princesses moved in and built their palaces here so they could be near the Prussian king.

    Named centuries ago for its thousand linden trees, this was the most elegant street of Prussian Berlin before Hitler's time, and the main drag of East Berlin after his reign. Hitler replaced the venerable trees—many 250 years old—with Nazi flags. Popular discontent actually drove him to replant the trees. Today, Unter den Linden is no longer a depressing Cold War cul-de-sac, and its pre-Hitler strolling café ambience has returned. Notice how it is divided, roughly at Friedrichstrasse, into a business section that stretches toward the Brandenburg Gate, and a culture section that spreads out toward Alexanderplatz. Frederick the Great wanted to have culture, mainly the opera and the university, closer to his palace, and to keep business (read: banks) farther away, near the city walls.

    ➋ Self-Guided Walk: As you walk toward the giant

BERLIN

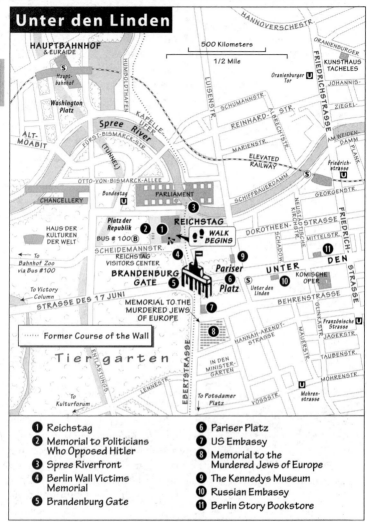

Unter den Linden

..... Former Course of the Wall

① Reichstag
② Memorial to Politicians Who Opposed Hitler
③ Spree Riverfront
④ Berlin Wall Victims Memorial
⑤ Brandenburg Gate
⑥ Pariser Platz
⑦ US Embassy
⑧ Memorial to the Murdered Jews of Europe
⑨ The Kennedys Museum
⑩ Russian Embassy
⑪ Berlin Story Bookstore

TV Tower, the big building you see jutting out into the street on your right is the **Hotel Adlon.** In its heyday, it hosted such notables as Charlie Chaplin, Albert Einstein, and Greta Garbo. This was the setting for Garbo's most famous line, "I vant to be alone," uttered in the film *Grand Hotel.* Damaged by the Russians just after World War II, the original hotel was closed with the construction of the nearby Wall in 1961 and later demolished. The grand Adlon was rebuilt in 1997. It was here that the late Michael Jackson shocked millions by dangling his baby, Blanket, over the railing (second balcony up, on the side of

BERLIN

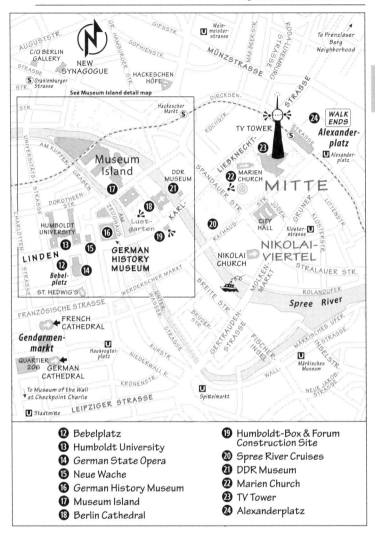

12	Bebelplatz	19	Humboldt-Box & Forum Construction Site
13	Humboldt University	20	Spree River Cruises
14	German State Opera	21	DDR Museum
15	Neue Wache	22	Marien Church
16	German History Museum	23	TV Tower
17	Museum Island	24	Alexanderplatz
18	Berlin Cathedral		

the hotel next to the Academy of Art). See how far you can get inside.

Descend into the Brandenburger Tor S-Bahn station ahead of you. It's one of Berlin's former **ghost subway stations.** During the Cold War, most underground train tunnels were simply blocked at the border. But a few Western lines looped through the East. To make a little hard Western cash, the Eastern government rented the use of these tracks to the West, but the stations (which happened to be in East Berlin) were strictly off-limits. For 28 years, the stations were unused, as Western trains slowly passed through and passengers saw only eerie DDR (East German) guards and lots of cobwebs. Literally within days of the fall of the Wall, these stations were reopened, and today they are a time warp (looking essentially as they did when built in 1931, with dreary old green tiles and original signage). Walk along the track (the walls are lined with historic photos of the Reichstag through the ages) and exit on the other side, following signs to *Russische Botschaft* (the Russian Embassy).

The **Russian Embassy** was the first big postwar building project in East Berlin. It's built in the powerful, simplified Neoclassical style that Stalin liked. While not as important now as it was a few years ago, it's as immense as ever. It flies the Russian white, blue, and red. Find the hammer-and-sickle motif decorating the window frames—a reminder of the days when Russia was the USSR.

Continuing past the Aeroflot airline offices, look across Glinkastrasse to the right to see the back of the **Komische Oper** (Comic Opera; program and view of ornate interior posted in window). While the exterior is ugly, the fine old theater interior—amazingly missed by WWII bombs—survives.

Back on the main drag, on the left at #40, is an entertaining bookstore, Berlin Story. In addition to a wide range of English-language books, this shop has a modest (but overpriced) museum and a wide range of nostalgic knickknacks from the Cold War. The West lost no time in consuming the East; consequently, some have felt a wave of *Ost*-**algia** for the old days of East Berlin. At election time, a surprising number of the former East Berlin's voters still opt for the extreme left party, which has ties to the bygone Communist Party, although the East-West divide is no longer at the forefront of most voters' minds.

One symbol of that communist era has been given a reprieve. As you continue to Friedrichstrasse, look at the DDR-style pedestrian lights, and you'll realize that someone had a sense of humor back then. The perky red and green men—*Ampelmännchen*—were recently under threat of replacement by far less jaunty Western-style signs. Fortunately, after a 10-year court battle, the DDR signals were kept after all.

At **Friedrichstrasse,** look right. Before the war, the Unter den Linden/Friedrichstrasse intersection was the heart of Berlin. In the 1920s,

Berlin was famous for its anything-goes love of life. This was the cabaret drag, a springboard to stardom for young and vampy entertainers like Marlene Dietrich. (Born in 1901, Dietrich starred in the one of the first German talkies—*The Blue Angel*—and then headed straight to Hollywood.) Over the last few years, this boulevard—lined with super department stores (such as Galeries Lafayette) and big-time hotels (such as the Hilton and Regent)—is attempting to replace Ku'damm as the grand commerce-and-café boulevard of Berlin. More recently, western Berlin is retaliating with some new stores of its own. And so far, Friedrichstrasse gets little more than half the pedestrian traffic that Ku'damm gets in the West. Why? Locals complain that this area has no daily life—no supermarkets, not much ethnic street food, and so on. Consider detouring to Galeries Lafayette, with its cool marble-and-glass, waste-of-space interior (Mon-Sat 10:00-20:00, closed Sun; check out the vertical garden on its front wall, belly up to its amazing ground-floor viewpoint, or have lunch in its recommended basement cafeteria).

If you continued down Friedrichstrasse, you'd wind up at Checkpoint Charlie (a 10-minute walk from here). But for now, continue along Unter den Linden. At the corner, the **VW Automobil Forum** shows off the latest models from the many car companies owned by VW (free, corner of Friedrichstrasse and Unter den Linden, VW art gallery and handy VW WC in the basement).

As you explore Berlin, you may see big, colorful **water pipes** running overground. Wherever there are big construction projects, streets are laced with these drainage pipes. Berlin's high water table means that any new basement comes with lots of pumping out.

Continue down Unter den Linden a few more blocks, past the large equestrian statue of Frederick the Great, and turn right into the square called **Bebelplatz.** Stand on the glass window set into the pavement in the center.

Frederick the Great—who ruled from 1740 to 1786—established Prussia not just as a military power, but as a cultural and intellectual heavyweight as well. This square was the center of the "new Athens" that Frederick envisioned. His grand palace was just down the street (explained later).

Look down through the glass you're standing on: The room of empty bookshelves is a memorial repudiating the notorious Nazi **book burning.** It was on this square in 1933 that staff and students from the university threw 20,000 newly forbidden books (like Einstein's) into a huge bonfire on the orders of the Nazi propaganda minister Joseph Goebbels. A plaque nearby reminds us of the prophetic quote by the German poet Heinrich Heine. In 1820, he wrote, "Where they burn books, at the end they also burn people." The Nazis despised Heine because he was Jewish before converting to Christianity. A century later, his books were among those that went up in flames on this spot.

Great buildings front Bebelplatz. Survey the square counterclockwise:

Humboldt University, across Unter den Linden, is one of Europe's greatest. Marx and Lenin (not the brothers or the sisters) studied here, as did the Grimms (both brothers) and more than two dozen Nobel Prize winners. Einstein, who was Jewish, taught here until taking a spot at Princeton in 1932 (smart guy). Used-book merchants set up their tables in front of the university, selling books by many of the authors whose works were once condemned to Nazi flames just across the street.

The former **state library** (labeled *Juristische Fakultät,* facing Bebelplatz on the right with your back to Humboldt University) is where Vladimir Lenin studied during much of his exile from Russia. If you climb to the second floor of the library and go through the door opposite the stairs, you'll see a 1968 vintage stained-glass window depicting Lenin's life's work with almost biblical reverence. On the ground floor is Tim's Espressobar, a great little café with light food, student prices, and garden seating (€3 plates, Mon-Fri 8:00-20:00, Sat 9:00-17:00, closed Sun, handy WC).

Between the library and the church, the square is closed by one of Berlin's swankiest lodgings—**Hotel de Rome,** housed in a historic bank building with a spa and lap pool fitted into the former vault.

The round, Catholic **St. Hedwig's Church,** nicknamed the "upside-down teacup," was built by the pragmatic Frederick the Great to encourage the integration of Catholic Silesians after his empire annexed their region in 1742. (St. Hedwig is the patron saint of Silesia, a region now shared by Germany, Poland, and the Czech Republic.) When asked what the church should look like, Frederick literally took a Silesian teacup and slammed it upside-down on a table. Like all Catholic churches in Berlin, St. Hedwig's is not on the street, but stuck in a kind of back lot—indicating inferiority to Protestant churches. You can step inside the church to see the cheesy DDR government renovation (generally daily until 17:00).

The **German State Opera** was bombed in 1941, rebuilt to bolster morale and to celebrate its centennial in 1943, and bombed again in 1945. Now it's being renovated (through 2013).

Cross Unter den Linden to the university side. The Greek-temple-like building set in the small chestnut-tree-filled park is the **Neue Wache** (the emperor's "New Guardhouse," from 1816). Converted to a memorial to the victims of fascism in 1960, the structure was transformed again, after the Wall fell, into a national memorial. Look inside, where a replica of the Käthe Kollwitz statue, *Mother with Her Dead Son,* is surrounded by thought-provoking silence. This marks the tombs of Germany's unknown soldier and an unknown concentration camp victim. The inscription in front reads, "To the victims of war and tyranny." Read the entire statement in English (on wall, left of entrance). The memorial, open to the sky, incorporates the elements—sunshine, rain, snow—falling on this modern-day *pietà.*

• *After the Neue Wache, the next building you'll see is Berlin's pink-yet-formidable Zeughaus (arsenal). Dating from 1695, it's considered the oldest building on the boulevard, and now houses the...*

▲▲▲German History Museum (Deutsches Historisches Museum)

This fantastic museum is a two-part affair: the pink former Prussian arsenal building and the I. M. Pei-designed annex. The main building (fronting Unter den Linden) houses the permanent collection, offering the best look at German history under one roof, anywhere. The modern annex features good temporary exhibits surrounded by the work of a great contemporary architect. While this city has more than its share of hokey "museums" that slap together WWII and Cold War bric-a-brac, then charge too much for admission, this thoughtfully presented museum—with more than 8,000 artifacts telling not just the story of Berlin, but of all Germany—is clearly the top history museum in town.

Cost and Hours: €8, daily 10:00-18:00, Unter den Linden 2, tel. 030/2030-4751, www.dhm.de.

Audioguide: For the most informative visit, invest in the excellent €3 audioguide, with six hours of info to choose from.

Visiting the Museum: The permanent collection packs two huge rectangular floors of the old arsenal building with historical objects, photographs, and models—all well-described in English and intermingled with multimedia stations to help put everything in context. From the lobby, head upstairs (to the "**first floor**") and work your way chronologically down. This floor traces German history from 1 B.C. to 1918, with exhibits on early cultures, the Middle Ages, Reformation, Thirty Years' War, German Empire, and World War I. You'll see a Roman floor mosaic, lots of models of higgledy-piggledy medieval towns and castles, tapestries, suits of armor, busts of great Germans, a Turkish tent from the Ottoman siege of Vienna (1683), flags from German unification in 1871 (the first time "Germany" existed as a nation), exhibits on everyday life in the tenements of the Industrial Revolution, and much more.

History marches on through the 20th century on the **ground floor,** including the Weimar Republic, Nazism, World War II, Allied occupation, and a divided Germany. Propaganda posters trumpet Germany's would-be post-WWI savior, Adolf Hitler. Look for the model of the impossibly huge, 950-foot-high, 180,000-capacity domed hall Hitler wanted to erect in the heart of Berlin, which he planned to re-envision as Welthauptstadt Germania, the "world capital" of his far-reaching Third Reich. Another model shows the sobering reality of Hitler's grandiosity: a crematorium at Auschwitz-Birkenau concentration camp in occupied Poland. The exhibit wraps up with chunks of the Berlin Wall, reunification, and a quick look at Germany today.

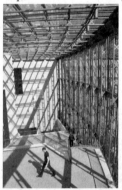

For architecture buffs, the big attraction is the **Pei annex** behind the history museum, which complements the museum with often-fascinating temporary exhibits. From the old building, cross through the courtyard (with the Pei glass canopy overhead) to reach the annex. A striking glassed-in spiral staircase unites four floors with surprising views and lots of light. It's here that you'll experience why Pei—famous for his glass pyramid at Paris' Louvre—is called the "perfector of classical modernism," "master of light," and a magician of uniting historical buildings with new ones. (If the museum is closed, or you don't have a ticket, venture down the street—Hinter dem Giesshaus—to the left of the museum to see the Pei annex from the outside.)

• *Back on Unter den Linden, head toward the Spree River. Just before the bridge, wander left along the canal through a tiny but colorful arts-and-crafts market (weekends only; a larger flea market is just outside the Pergamon Museum). Continue up the riverbank two blocks and cross the footbridge over the Spree. This takes you to...*

Museum Island (Museumsinsel)

This island is filled with some of Berlin's most impressive museums (all part of the Staatliche Museen zu Berlin). The first building—the Altes Museum—went up in the 1820s, and the rest of the complex began development in the 1840s under King Fried-

rich Wilhelm IV, who envisioned the island as a place of culture and learning. The island's imposing Neoclassical buildings host five grand museums: the **Pergamon Museum** (classical antiquities, including the top-notch Pergamon Altar, with its temple and frieze); the **Neues Museum** ("New Museum," famous for its Egyptian collection with the bust of Queen Nefertiti); the **Old National Gallery** (Alte Nationalgalerie, 19th-century art, mostly German Romantic and Realist paintings); the **Altes Museum** ("Old Museum," more antiquities); and the **Bode Museum** (European statuary and paintings through the ages, coins, and Byzantine art).

• *The museums of Museum Island, worth the better part of a sightseeing day, are described in more detail below.*

The Museums of Museum Island

A formidable renovation is under way on Museum Island. When

complete, a grand entry and unified visitors center will serve the island's five venerable but separate museums; tunnels will lace the complex together; and this will become one of the grandest museum zones in Europe (intended completion date: 2015, www.museumsinsel-berlin.de). In the meantime, pardon their dust.

Cost: The €14 Museum Island Pass combo-ticket—covering all five museums—is a far better value than buying individual entries ranging from €8 to €13 (prices can vary depending on special exhibits). All five museums are also included in the city's €19 Museumspass. Special exhibits are extra.

Hours: Pergamon—daily 10:00-18:00, Thu until 21:00. Neues Museum—daily 10:00-18:00, Thu-Sat until 20:00. Old National Gallery and Bode Museum—Tue-Sun 10:00-18:00, Thu until 22:00, closed Mon; same hours for Altes Museum except closes Thu at 20:00. Tel. 030/266-424-242, www.smb.museum.

Required Reservation for Pergamon and Neues Museums: Visiting either the Pergamon Museum or Neues Museum requires a *Zeitfensterticket* ("time-window ticket") that gives you

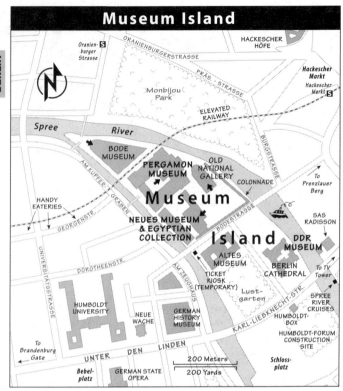

Museum Island

a 30-minute time slot for entering the museum (included with admission; separate appointments required for each museum). Once inside, you can stay as long as you like. Reserve your time online (www.smb.museum) or in person at any Museum Island ticket office. (At less busy times, tickets are sometimes sold without any particular time slot.)

You can usually get a time slot within about an hour, often sooner—except at the busiest times (Sat and Sun mornings), when you may have to wait longer. The least-crowded times are evenings when the museums are open late (Thu for Pergamon, Thu-Sat for Neues).

Buying Tickets: The temporary kiosk on Bodestrasse functions as the ticket booth for the Neues Museum and comes with avoidable lines. Long ticket-buying lines also plague the Pergamon Museum. Avoid them by purchasing your museum pass (and getting your assigned entry time) at one of the island's three never-crowded museums: Altes, Bode, or Old National Gallery. (From Unter den Linden, Altes is most convenient; if coming from Prenzlauer Berg, try the Bode.)

Planning Your Time: I'd start at the Bode, where I'd ask for an entry time to the Pergamon Museum in about an hour, and a ticket to the Neues Museum for 1.5 hours after that. Tickets and appointments in hand, spend any time left before your Pergamon time slot browsing the Bode. Then enjoy the Pergamon collection, where the art is earth-shaking but easy to see in an hour. If you have any extra time before your Neues appointment, nip into the time-tunnel Old National Gallery. Step into the Neues Museum within 30 minutes of your entry time, and be prepared to linger. I'd skip the Altes Museum. For lunch nearby, follow the elevated train tracks away from the Pergamon down Georgenstrasse.

Getting There: The nearest S-Bahn station is Hackescher Markt, about a 10-minute walk away. From hotels in the Prenzlauer Berg, ride tram #M-1 to the end of line, and you're right at the Pergamon Museum.

▲▲▲Pergamon Museum (Pergamonmuseum)

The star attraction of this world-class museum, part of Berlin's Collection of Classical Antiquities (Antikensammlung), is the fantastic and gigantic Pergamon Altar. The Babylonian Ishtar Gate (slathered with glazed blue tiles from the 6th century B.C.) and the museum's many ancient Greek, Mesopotamian, Roman, and early Islamic treasures are also impressive.

Audioguide: Make ample use of the superb audioguide (included with admission)—it will broaden your experience. Punching #10 on the audioguide gets you the "Pergamon in 30 Minutes" general tour. Or follow my quicker, more succinct self-guided tour.

◐ Self-Guided Tour: With your timed entry and museum pass, walk boldly by the long line of people who don't have or read guidebooks, and go directly in.

There's a lot to see in this museum (everything is well-described by posted English information and the included audioguide). The best plan for the casual visitor is to focus on a few highlights.

From the entrance, walk straight ahead to find the museum's namesake, the **Pergamon Altar.** Actually a 65-foot-wide temple, this "altar" comes from the second-century B.C. Greek city of Pergamon (near the west coast of today's Turkey). The Pergamon Altar was just one component of a spectacular hilltop ensemble—temples, sanctuaries, palaces, theaters, and other buildings erected to honor the gods—modeled after the Acropolis in Athens. (See a model of the complete Pergamon Acropolis to the right, as you face the stairs.)

Pergamon was excavated from 1878 to 1886 by German archaeologist Carl Humann, who unearthed fragments of the temple's frieze all over the site (many pieces had been "recycled" as building materials in later structures). The bits and pieces were brought here to Berlin, reassembled on this replica of the temple, and put on display in this purpose-built museum in 1930.

The temple replica re-creates the western third of the original building. Stairs lead up to a chamber with a small sacrificial altar, where priests and priestesses sacrificed and burned animals, while toga-clad Greeks assembled in awe at the foot of the stairs below.

Surviving pieces of a 269-foot-long frieze that wrapped around the entire temple dramatically spill onto the stairs and around the room. Called the **Gigantomachy Frieze,** it shows the Greek gods under Zeus and Athena defeating the giants in a dramatic pig pile of mythological mayhem. Imagine how much more evocative these sculptures once were, slathered in colorful paint, gold, and silver trim.

So what's the fight about? Long before the time of man, an epic struggle pitted the titans against the gods. When the gods won, they thrust their foes into a miserable underworld (the mythological equivalent of purgatory) and settled in for a comfy period of rule atop Mount Olympus. But the troublesome race of giants—children of the earth goddess Gaia, mother of the titans—sought revenge. The giants had legs of slithering snakes that kept them in contact with the ground, allowing Gaia to make them immortal. This frieze captures a pivotal event, when the giants Alkyoneus and Porphyrion led a rebellion of their race against the gods. (The people of Pergamon appreciated the parallels between this story and their own noble struggle against unenlightened barbarians.)

With your back to the altar steps, look at the right end of the frieze to find panels with Zeus and Athena, locked in combat with

the giants. Faint surviving labels on the cornice above the statues—in Greek, of course—help identify the combatants; the modern English letters below may prove more helpful.

Find the **Athena** panel. Athena (faceless, in the center, with the shield) and Nike (all that's left are

her wings, right arm, and left leg) pull the chief giant Alkyoneus (his snake legs curling around his bicep) up by his hair—breaking his connection to the earth, the source of his immortality. Below them, Gaia—the mother of the giants—rises up from her subterranean realm to lend a hand. (See the fear in Gaia's and Alkyoneus' tortured eyes.) Alkyoneus would survive this brush with Athena, only to be killed soon after by Hercules. (The statue of Hercules is missing—all that survives is one pathetic paw of his lion pelt.)

The **Zeus** panel shows the (headless) king of the gods raining lightning bolts down on his enemies—including the snake-legged Porphyrion, with his back(side) toward us. Notice Zeus' disembodied right hand up above, ready to pitch some serious heat. Fans of Greek mythology can take a slow walk along the entire length of the frieze, identifying their favorite gods and giants...the gang's all here. Before long, the giants will be history, and the gods can go back about their usual business of conspiring against each other and impregnating mortals.

Facing the altar stairs, go through the door to your left. The intricate, ancient Greek **mosaic floor** is finely assembled from miniscule pebbles, with a particularly impressive floral motif decorating the border. In the otherwise undecorated box in the middle, in what looks like an ancient Post-It note, you can see where the artist "signed" his work. The Athena statue standing in the middle of the room is a replica of one that once stood at the center of Athens' Acropolis. Turn around to see the doorway you just came through, surrounded by the original, double-decker ornamental entryway to the Pergamon Acropolis. Ancient pilgrims who had come from far and wide to worship the gods in Pergamon passed through here on their way to the altar.

Return to the altar room, cross straight through it, and go out the door on the far side. From Pergamon, flash-forward 300 years (and travel south 110 miles) to the ancient Roman city of Miletus. Dominating this room (on your right) is the

BERLIN

95-foot-wide, 55-foot-high **Market Gate of Miletus,** destroyed by an earthquake centuries ago and now painstakingly reconstructed here in Berlin. The exquisite mosaic floor from a Roman villa in Miletus has two parts: In the square panel, the musician Orpheus strokes his lyre to charm the animals; in stark contrast, in the nearby rectangular mosaic (from an adjacent room), hunters pursue wild animals.

Step through the market gate and all the way back to 575 B.C., to the Fertile Crescent—Mesopotamia (today's Iraq). The Assyrian ruler Nebuchadnezzar II, who amassed a vast empire and enormous wealth, wanted to build a suitably impressive processional entryway to his capital city, Babylon, to honor the goddess Ishtar. His creation, the **Ishtar Gate,** inspired awe and obedience in anyone who came to his city. This is a reconstruction, using some original components. The gate itself is embellished with two animals: a bull and a mythical dragon-like combination of lion, cobra, eagle, and scorpion. The long hall leading to the main gate—designed for a huge processional of deities to celebrate the new year—is decorated with a chain of blue and yellow glazed tiles with 120 strolling lions (representing the goddess Ishtar). To get the big picture, find the model of the original site in the center of the hall.

These main exhibits are surrounded by smaller galleries. Upstairs is the **Museum of Islamic Art.** It contains fine carpets, tile work, the Aleppo Room (with ornately painted wooden walls from an early 17th-century home in today's Syria; since it was commissioned by a Christian, it incorporates Arabic, Persian, and biblical themes), and the Mshatta Facade (walls and towers from one of the early eighth-century Umayyad "desert castles," from today's Jordan).

▲▲Neues (New) Museum and Egyptian Collection

Oddly, Museum Island's so-called "new" museum features the oldest stuff around. There are three collections here: the Egyptian Collection (with the famous bust of Queen Nefertiti; floor 0 and parts of floors 1-2), the Museum of Prehistory and Early History (floor 3 and parts of floors 1-2), and some items from the Collection of Classical Antiquities (artifacts from ancient Troy—famously excavated by German adventurer Heinrich Schliemann—and Cyprus, just off the entrance).

The top draw here is the Egyptian art—clearly one of the world's best collections. But let's face it: The main reason to visit is to enjoy one of the great thrills in art appreciation—gazing into the still-young-and-beautiful face of Queen Nefertiti. If you're in a pinch for time, make a beeline to her (floor 2, far corner of Egyptian Collection in room 210; for more on the museum, see www.neues-museum.de).

Audioguide: The fine audioguide (included with admission) celebrates new knowledge about ancient Egyptian civilization and offers fascinating insights into workaday Egyptian life as it describes the vivid papyrus collection, slice-of-life artifacts, and dreamy wax portraits decorating mummy cases.

Visiting the Museum: After being damaged in World War II and sitting in ruins for some 40 years, the Neues Museum was recently rebuilt. Everything is well-described by posted English information and the audioguide.

To tour the whole collection, begin by going all the way to the top (floor 3) where you'll find the **prehistory section.** The entire floor is filled with Stone Age, Ice Age, and Bronze Age items. You'll see early human remains, tools, spearheads, and pottery.

The most interesting item on this floor (in corner room 305) is the tall, conehead-like **Golden Hat,** made of paper-thin hammered gold leaf. Created by an early Celtic civilization in Central Europe, it's particularly exquisite for something so old (from the Bronze Age, around 1000 B.C.). The circles on the hat represent the sun, moon, and other celestial bodies—leading archaeologists to believe that this headwear could double as a calendar, showing how the sun and moon sync up every 19 years.

Down on floor 2, you'll find **early history** exhibits on migrations, barbarians, and ancient Rome (including larger-than-life statues of Helios and an unidentified goddess) as well as a fascinating look at the Dark Ages after the fall of Rome.

Still on floor 2, cross to the other side of the building for the **Egyptian** section. On the way, you'll pass through the impressive Papyrus Collection—a large room of seemingly empty glass cases. Press a button to watch a 3,000-year-old piece of primitive "paper" (made of aquatic reeds) imprinted with primitive text trundle out of its protective home.

Then, finally, in a room all her own, is the 3,000-year-old bust of **Queen Nefertiti** (the wife of King Akhenaton, c. 1340 B.C.)—the most famous piece of Egyptian art in Europe. Called "Berlin's most beautiful woman," Nefertiti has all the right beauty marks: long neck, symmetrical face, and the perfect amount of makeup. And yet, she's not completely idealized. Notice the fine wrinkles that show she's human (though these only enhance her beauty). Like a movie star discreetly sipping a glass of wine at a sidewalk café, Nefertiti seems somehow more dignified in person. The bust never left its studio, but served as a master model for all other portraits of the queen. (That's probably why the left eye was never inlaid.) Stare at her long enough, and you may get the sensation that she's winking at you. Hey, beautiful!

How the queen arrived in Germany is a tale out of *Indiana Jones.* The German archaeologist Ludwig Borchardt uncovered her in the Egyptian desert in 1912. The Egyptian Department of Antiquities had first pick of all the artifacts uncovered on their territory. After the first takings, they divided the rest 50/50 with the excavators. When Borchardt presented Nefertiti to the Egyptians, they passed her over, never bothering to examine her closely.

Unsubstantiated rumors persist that Borchardt misled the Egyptians in order to keep the bust for himself—rumors that have prompted some Egyptians to call for the return of Nefertiti (just as the Greeks are lobbying the British to return the Parthenon frieze currently housed in the British Museum). Although this bust is not particularly representative of Egyptian art in general—and despite increasing claims that her long neck suggests she's a Neoclassical fake—Nefertiti has become a symbol of Egyptian art by popular acclaim.

The Egyptian Collection continues with other sculptures, including kneeling figures holding steles (stone tablets inscribed with prayers). On floor 1, a fascinating exhibit examines how depictions of the human image evolved during the 3,000-year span of ancient

Egyptian culture. You'll also see entire walls from tombs and (in the basement—floor 0) a sea of large sarcophagi.

▲Old National Gallery (Alte Nationalgalerie)

This gallery, behind the Neues Museum and Altes Museum, is designed to look like a Greek temple. Spanning three floors, it focuses on art (mostly paintings) from the 19th century: Romantic German paintings (which I find most interesting) on the top floor, and French and German Impressionists and German Realists on the first and second floors. You likely won't recognize any specific paintings, but it's still an enjoyable stroll through German culture from the century in which that notion first came to mean something. The included audioguide explains the highlights.

Visiting the Museum: Start on the third floor, with Romantic canvases and art of the Goethe era (roughly 1770-1830), and work your way down. Use the audioguide to really delve into these romanticized, vivid looks at life in Germany in the 19th century and before. As you stroll through the Romantic paintings—the museum's strength—keep in mind that they were created about the time (mid-late 19th century) that Germans were first working toward a single, unified nation. By glorifying pristine German landscapes and a rugged, virtuous people, these painters evoked the region's high-water mark—the Middle Ages, when "Germany" was a patchwork of powerful and wealthy merchant city-states. Linger over dreamy townscapes with Gothic cathedrals and castles that celebrate medieval German might. Still lifes, idealized portraits of tow-headed children, and genre paintings (depicting everyday scenes, often with subtle social commentary) strum the heartstrings of anyone with Teutonic blood. The Düsseldorf School excelled at Romantic landscapes (such as Carl Friedrich Lessing's *Castle on a Rock*). Some of these canvases nearly resemble present-day fantasy paintings. Perhaps the best-known artist in the collection is Caspar David Friedrich, who specialized in dramatic scenes celebrating grandeur and the solitary hero. His *The Monk by the Sea (Der Mönch am Meer)* shows a lone figure standing on a sand dune, pondering a vast, turbulent expanse of sea and sky.

On the second floor, you'll find one big room of minor works by bigger-name French artists, including Renoir, Cézanne, Manet, Monet, and Rodin. Another room is devoted to the Romantic Hans von Marées, the influential early Symbolist Arnold Böcklin, and other artists of the "German Roman" (Deutschrömer) movement—Germans who lived in, and were greatly influenced by, Rome. Artists of the Munich School are represented by naturalistic canvases of landscapes or slice-of-life scenes.

On the first floor, 19th-century Realism reigns. While the Realist Adolph Menzel made his name painting elegant royal gatherings and historical events, his *Iron Rolling Mill (Das Eisenwalzwerk)* captures the gritty side of his moment in history—the emergence of the Industrial Age—with a warts-and-all look at steelworkers toiling in a hellish factory. The first floor also hosts a sculpture collection, with works by great sculptors both foreign (the Italian Canova, the Dane Thorvaldsen) and German (Johann Gottfried Schadow's delightful *Die Prinzessinnen*, showing the dynamic duo of Prussian princesses Louise and Frederike).

Bode Museum

At the "prow" of Museum Island, the Bode Museum (designed to appear as if it's rising up from the river), is worth a brief stop. Just inside, a grand statue of Frederick William of Brandenburg on horseback, curly locks blowing in the wind, welcomes you into the lonely halls of the museum. This fine building contains a hodge-podge of collections: Byzantine art, historic coins, ecclesiastical art, sculptures, and medals commemorating the fall of the Berlin Wall and German reunification. For a free, quick look at its lavish interior, climb the grand staircase to the charming café on the first floor.

Altes (Old) Museum

The least interesting of the five museums, this building features the rest of the Collection of Classical Antiquities (the best of which is in the Pergamon Museum)—namely, Etruscan, Roman, and Greek art. I'd pass it up.

Other Sights on and near Museum Island

In addition to the five museums just described, Museum Island is home to the following sights. One more sight (the DDR Museum) sits just across the river.

Lustgarten—For 300 years, the island's big central square has flip-flopped between being a military parade ground and a people-friendly park, depending upon the political tenor of the time. During the revolutions of 1848, the Kaiser's troops dispersed a protesting crowd that had assembled here, sending demonstrators onto footpaths. Karl Marx later commented, "It is impossible to have a revolution in a country where people stay off the grass."

Until recently, it was *verboten* to relax or walk on the Lustgarten's grass. But in 1999, the Lustgarten was made into a park (read the history posted in the corner opposite the church). On a sunny day, it's packed with relaxing locals and is one of Berlin's most enjoyable public spaces.

BERLIN

Berlin Cathedral (Berliner Dom)—This century-old church towers over Museum Island. Inside, the great reformers (Luther, Calvin, and company) stand around the brilliantly restored dome like stern saints guarding their theology. Frederick I rests in an ornate tomb (right transept, near entrance to dome). The 270-step climb to the outdoor dome gallery is tough but offers pleasant, breezy views of the city at the finish line. The crypt downstairs is not worth a look.

Cost and Hours: €7 includes access to dome gallery, €10 with audioguide, not covered by Museum Island ticket, Mon-Sat 9:00-20:00, Sun 12:00-20:00, until 19:00 Oct-March, closes early—around 17:30—on some days for concerts, interior closed but dome open during services, tel. 030/2026-9136, www.berliner-dom.de. The cathedral hosts many organ concerts (often on weekends, tickets from about €10 always available at the door).

Humboldt-Forum Construction Site (Former Site of Hohenzollern Palace)—Across Unter den Linden from Berlin Cathedral is a big lawn that for centuries held the Baroque palace of the Hohenzollern dynasty of Brandenburg and Prussia. Much of that palace actually survived World War II but was replaced by the communists with a blocky, Soviet-style "Palace" of the Republic—East Berlin's parliament building/entertainment complex and a showy symbol of the communist days. The landmark building fell into disrepair after reunification and was eventually dismantled in 2007. After much debate about how to use this prime real estate, the German parliament decided to construct the Humboldt-Forum, a huge public venue filled with museums, shops, galleries, and concert halls behind a facade constructed in imitation of the original Hohenzollern palace. With a €1.2 billion price tag, many Berliners consider the reconstruction plan a complete waste of money.

The temporary **Humboldt-Box** has been set up to help the public follow the construction of the new Humboldt-Forum. The multiple floors of the futuristic "box" display building plans and models for the project (€4, daily 10:00-20:00, after that, free entry to terrace-café until 23:00, tel. 01805-030-707, www.humboldt-box.com). On the top floor, the terrace-café with unobstructed views over Berlin serves coffee, desserts, and light food until 18:00, and a dinner menu after that (€5-15 lunch dishes, €15-22 dinners).

Spree River Cruises—The recommended Spree River boat tours depart from the riverbank near the bridge by the Berlin Cathedral.
• *Directly across the bridge from Museum Island, down along the riverbank, look for the...*

▲**DDR Museum**—Although this exhibit began as a tourist trap, it has expanded and matured into a genuinely interesting look at life in former East Germany (DDR). It's well-stocked with kitschy everyday items from the communist period, plus photos, video clips, and concise English explanations. The exhibits are interactive—you're encouraged to pick up and handle anything that isn't behind glass. You'll crawl through a Trabant car (designed by East German engineers to compete with the West's popular VW Beetle) and pick up some DDR-era jokes ("East Germany had 39 newspapers, four radio stations, two TV channels...and one opinion.") The reconstructed communist-era home lets you tour the kitchen, living room, bedrooms, and more. You'll learn about the Russian-imported *Dacha*—the simple countryside cottage (owned by one in six East Germans) used for weekend retreats from the grimy city. (Others vacationed on the Baltic Coast, where nudism was all the rage, as a very revealing display explains.) Lounge in DDR movie chairs as you view a subtitled propaganda film or clips from beloved-in-the-East TV shows (including the popular kids' show *Sandmännchen*—"Little Sandman"). Even the meals served in the attached restaurant are based on DDR-era recipes.

Cost and Hours: €6, daily 10:00-20:00, Sat until 22:00, just across the Spree from Museum Island at Karl-Liebknecht-Strasse 1, tel. 030/847-123-731, www.ddr-museum.de.

Museum Island to Alexanderplatz

• *Continue walking down Unter den Linden. Before crossing the bridge (and leaving Museum Island), look across the river. The pointy twin spires of the 13th-century Nikolai Church mark the center of medieval Berlin. This* **Nikolaiviertel** *(Viertel means "quarter") was restored by the DDR and trendy in the last years of communism. Today, it's a lively-at-night riverside restaurant district.*

As you cross the bridge, look left in the distance to see the gilded **New Synagogue** dome, rebuilt after WWII bombing (described later on this walk).

Across the river to the left of the bridge, directly below you, is the **DDR Museum** (described earlier). Just beyond that is the giant **SAS Radisson Hotel** and shopping center, with a huge aquarium in the center. The elevator goes right through the middle of a deep-sea world. (You can see it from the unforgettable Radisson hotel lobby—tuck in your shirt and walk past the guards with the confidence of a guest who's sleeping there.) Here in the center of the old communist capital, it seems that capitalism has settled in with a spirited vengeance.

In the park immediately across the street (a big jaywalk from the Radisson) are grandfatherly statues of **Marx and Engels** (nicknamed "the old pension-ers"). Surrounding them are stainless-steel monoliths with evocative photos that show the struggles of the workers of the world.

Walk toward **Marien Church** (from 1270), just left of the base of the TV Tower. An artist's rendering helps you follow the interesting but very faded old "Dance of Death" mural that wraps around the narthex inside the door.

The big red-brick building past the trees on the right is the **City Hall,** built after the revolutions of 1848 and arguably the first dem-ocratic building in the city.

The 1,200-foot-tall **TV Tower** (Fern-sehturm) has a fine view from halfway up (€12, daily March-Oct 9:00-24:00, Nov-Feb 10:00-24:00, www.tv-turm.de). The tower of-fers a handy city orientation and an interest-ing view of the flat, red-roofed sprawl of Ber-lin—including a peek inside the city's many courtyards *(Höfe).* Consider a kitschy trip to the observation deck for the view and lunch in its revolving restaurant (mediocre food, €12 plates, horrible lounge music, reservations smart for dinner, tel. 030/242-3333). The retro tower is quite trendy these days, so it can be crowded (your ticket comes with an assigned entry time). Built (with Swedish know-how) in 1969 for the 20th anniversary of the communist govern-ment, the tower was meant to show the power of the atheistic state at a time when DDR leaders were having the crosses removed from church domes and spires. But when the sun shined on their tower—the greatest spire in East Berlin—a huge cross was reflected on the mirrored ball. Cynics called it "The Pope's Revenge." East Berlin-ers dubbed the tower the "Tele-Asparagus." They joked that if it fell over, they'd have an elevator to the West.

Farther east, pass under the train tracks into **Alexanderplatz.** This area—especially the former Kaufhof department store (now Galeria Kaufhof)—was the commercial pride and joy of East Ber-lin. Today, it's still a landmark, with a major U- and S-Bahn sta-tion. The once-futuristic, now-retro "World Time Clock," installed in 1969, is a nostalgic favorite and a popular meeting point. Stop in the square for a coffee and to people-watch. It's a great scene.

• *Our orientation stroll or bus ride (this is the last stop for bus #100) is finished. From here, you can hike back a bit to catch the riverboat tour, take in the sights south of Unter den Linden, venture into the colorful Prenzlauer Berg neighborhood, or consider extending this foray into eastern Berlin.*

Karl-Marx-Allee

The buildings along Karl-Marx-Allee in East Berlin (just beyond Alexanderplatz) were completely leveled by the Red Army in 1945. As an expression of their adoration to the "great Socialist Father" (Stalin), the DDR government decided to rebuild the street better than ever (the USSR provided generous subsidies). They intentionally made it one meter wider than the Champs-Elysées, named it Stalinallee, and lined it with "workers' palaces" built in the bold "Stalin Gothic" style so common in Moscow in the 1950s. Now renamed after Karl Marx, the street and its restored buildings provide a rare look at Berlin's communist days. Distances are a bit long for convenient walking, but you can cruise Karl-Marx-Allee by taxi, or ride the U-Bahn to Strausberger Platz (which was built to resemble an Italian promenade) and walk to Frankfurter Tor, reading the good information posts along the way. Notice the Social Realist reliefs on the buildings and the lampposts, which incorporate the wings of a phoenix (rising from the ashes) in their design. Once a "workers' paradise," the street now hosts a two-mile-long capitalist beer festival the first weekend in August.

The **Café Sibylle,** just beyond the Strausberger Platz U-Bahn station, is a fun spot for a coffee, traditional DDR ice-cream treats, and a look at its free informal museum that tells the story of the most destroyed street in Berlin. While the humble exhibit is nearly all in German, it's fun to see the ear (or buy a €10 plaster replica) and half a moustache from what was the largest statue of Stalin in Germany (the centerpiece of the street until 1961). It also provides a few intimate insights into apartment life in a DDR flat. The café is known for its good coffee and *Schwedeneisbecher mit Eierlikor*—an ice-cream sundae with a shot of egg liqueur, popular among those nostalgic for communism (Mon-Fri 10:00-20:00, Sat-Sun 12:00-20:00, Karl-Marx-Allee 72, at intersection with Koppenstrasse, a block from U-Bahn: Strausberger Platz, tel. 030/2935-2203).

Heading out to Karl-Marx-Allee (just beyond the TV Tower), you're likely to notice a giant colorful **mural** decorating a blocky communist-era skyscraper. This was the Ministry of Education, and the mural is a tile mosaic trumpeting the accomplishments of the DDR's version of "No Child Left Behind."

South of Unter den Linden

The following sights—heavy on Nazi and Wall history—are listed roughly north to south (as you reach them from Unter den Linden).

▲▲Gendarmenmarkt

This delightful, historic square is bounded by twin churches, a tasty

chocolate shop, and the Berlin Symphony's concert hall (designed by Karl Friedrich Schinkel, the man who put the Neoclassical stamp on Berlin and Dresden). In summer, it hosts a few outdoor cafés, *Biergartens*, and sometimes concerts. Wonderfully symmetrical, the square is considered by Berliners to be the finest in town (U6: Französische Strasse; U2 or U6: Stadtmitte).

The name of the square—part French and part German (after the *Gens d'Armes,* Frederick the Great's royal guard, who were headquartered here)—reminds us that in the 17th century, a fifth of all Berliners were French émigrés—Protestant Huguenots fleeing Catholic France. Back then, Frederick the Great's tolerant Prussia was a magnet for the persecuted (and for their money). These émigrés vitalized Berlin with new ideas and know-how...and their substantial wealth.

Of the two matching churches on Gendarmenmarkt, the one to the south (bottom end of square) is the **German Cathedral** (Deutscher Dom). This cathedral (not to be confused with the Berlin Cathedral on Museum Island) was bombed flat in the war and rebuilt only in the 1980s. It houses the thought-provoking Milestones, Setbacks, Sidetracks *(Wege, Irrwege, Umwege)* exhibit, which traces the history of the German parliamentary system—worth ▲. The parliament-funded exhibit—while light on actual historical artifacts—is well done and more interesting than it sounds. It takes you quickly from the revolutionary days of 1848 to the 1920s, and then more deeply through the tumultuous 20th century. As the exhibit is designed for Germans rather than foreign tourists, there are no English descriptions—but you can follow the essential, excellent, and free 1.5-hour English audioguide or buy the wonderfully detailed €10 guidebook. If you think this museum is an attempt by the German government to develop a more sophisticated and educated electorate in the interest of stronger democracy, you're exactly right. Germany knows (from its own troubled history) that a dumbed-down electorate, manipulated by clever spin-meisters and sound-bite media blitzes, is a dangerous thing (free, Tue-Sun May-Sept 10:00-19:00, Oct-April 10:00-18:00, closed Mon year-round, tel. 030/2273-0431).

The **French Cathedral** (Französischer Dom), at the north end of the square, offers a humble museum on the Huguenots (€2, Tue-Sat 12:00-17:00, Sun 11:00-17:00, closed Mon, enter around the right side) and a viewpoint in the dome up top (€3, daily 10:30-19:00, last entry at 18:00, 244 steps, enter through door facing square). Fun fact: Neither of these churches is a true cathedral, as they never contained a bishop's throne; their German title of *Dom*

(cathedral) is actually a mistranslation from the French word *dôme* (cupola).

Fassbender & Rausch, on the corner near the German Cathedral, claims to be Europe's biggest chocolate store. After 150 years of chocolate-making, this family-owned business proudly displays its sweet delights—250 different kinds—on a 55-foot-long buffet. Truffles are sold for about €0.60 each; it's fun to compose a fancy little eight-piece box of your own for about €5. Upstairs is an elegant hot chocolate café with fine views. The window displays feature giant chocolate models of Berlin landmarks—Reichstag, TV Tower, Kaiser Wilhelm Memorial Church, and so on. If all this isn't enough to entice you, I have three words: erupting chocolate volcano (Mon-Sat 10:00-20:00, Sun 11:00-

20:00, corner of Mohrenstrasse at Charlottenstrasse 60, tel. 030/2045-8440).

Gendarmenmarkt is buried in what has recently emerged as Berlin's "Fifth Avenue" shopping district. For the ultimate in top-end shops, find the corner of Jägerstrasse and Friedrichstrasse and wander through the **Quartier 206** (Mon-Fri 11:00-20:00, Sat 10:00-18:00, closed Sun, www.quartier206.com). The adjacent, middlebrow **Quartier 205** has more affordable prices.

Nazi and Cold War Sites on Wilhelmstrasse

Fragment of the Wall—Surviving stretches of the Wall are virtually nonexistent in downtown Berlin. One of the most convenient places to see a bit is at the intersection of Wilhelmstrasse and Zimmerstrasse/ Niederkirchnerstrasse, a few blocks southwest of Gendarmenmarkt. Many visitors make the short walk over here from the Checkpoint Charlie sights (described later), then drop into the museum listed next.

▲▲Topography of Terror (Topographie des Terrors)— Coincidentally, the patch of land behind the surviving stretch of Wall was closely associated with a different regime: It was once the nerve center for the most despicable elements of the Nazi government, the Gestapo and the SS. This stark-gray, boxy building is one of the few memorial sites that focuses on the perpetrators rather than the victims of the Nazis. It's chilling but thought-provoking to

see just how seamlessly and bureaucratically the Nazi institutions and state structures merged to become a well-oiled terror machine. There are few actual artifacts; it's mostly written explanations and photos, like reading a good textbook standing up. And, while you could read this story anywhere, to take this in atop the Gestapo headquarters is a powerful experience. The exhibit's a bit dense, but WWII historians (even armchair ones) will find it fascinating.

Cost and Hours: Free, daily 10:00-20:00, outdoor exhibit closes at sunset in winter, Niederkirchnerstrasse 8, tel. 030/254-5090, www.topographie.de.

Background: This location marks what was once the most feared address in Berlin: the headquarters of the Reich Main Security Office *(Reichssicherheitshauptamt)*. These offices served as the engine room of the Nazi dictatorship, as well as the command center of the SS *(Schutzstaffel,* whose members began as Hitler's personal bodyguards), the Gestapo *(Geheime Staatspolizei,* secret state police), and the SD *(Sicherheitsdienst,* the Nazi intelligence agency). This trio (and others) were ultimately consolidated under Heinrich Himmler to become a state-within-a-state, with talons in every corner of German society. This elite militarized branch of the Nazi machine was also tasked with the "racial purification" of German-held lands, especially Eastern Europe—the Holocaust. It was from these headquarters that the Nazis administered concentration camps, firmed up plans for the "Final Solution to the Jewish Question," and organized the domestic surveillance of anyone opposed to the regime. The building was also equipped with dungeons, where the Gestapo detained and tortured thousands of prisoners.

The Gestapo and SS employed intimidation techniques to coerce cooperation from the German people. The general public knew that the Gestapo was to be feared: It was considered omnipotent, omnipresent, and omniscient. Some political prisoners underwent "enhanced interrogation" right here in this building. The threat of *Schutzhaft* ("protective custody," usually at a concentration camp) was used to terrify any civilians who stepped out of line—or who might make a good example. But Hitler and his cronies also won people's loyalties through propaganda. They hammered home the idealistic notion of the *Volksgemeinschaft* ("people's community") of a purely Germanic culture and race, which empowered Hitler to create a pervasive illusion that "We're all in this together." Anyone who was not an Aryan was *Untermensch*—subhuman—and must be treated as such.

Visiting the Museum: The complex has two parts: indoors, in the modern boxy building; and outdoors, in the trench that runs along the surviving stretch of Wall. Visit the indoor exhibit first.

Inside, you'll find a visitors center with an information desk and an extensive **Topography of Terror** exhibit about the SS and Gestapo, and the atrocities they committed in Berlin and across Europe. A model of the government quarter, circa 1939, sets the stage of Nazi domination in this area. A timeline of events and old photographs, documents, and newspaper clippings illustrates how Hitler and his team expertly manipulated the German people to build a broadly supported "dictatorship of consent."

The exhibit walks you through the evolution of Hitler's regime: the Nazi takeover; institutions of terror (Himmler's "SS State"); terror, persecution, and extermination; atrocities in Nazi-occupied countries; and the war's end and postwar. Some images here are indelible, such as photos of SS soldiers stationed at Auschwitz, gleefully yukking it up on a retreat in the countryside (even as their helpless prisoners were being gassed and burned a few miles away).  The exhibit profiles specific members of the various reprehensible SS branches, as well as the groups they targeted: Jews, Roma, and Sinti (Gypsies); the unemployed or homeless; homosexuals; and the physically and mentally ill (considered "useless eaters" who consumed resources without contributing work).

Downstairs is a WC and a library with research books on these topics. Before heading outside, ask at the information desk to borrow the free audioguide that describes the outdoor exhibits.

Outside, in the trench along the Wall, you'll find the exhibit **Berlin 1933-1945: Between Propaganda and Terror,** which overlaps slightly with the indoor exhibit but focuses on Berlin. The chronological survey begins with the post-WWI Weimar Republic and continues through the ragged days just after World War II. One display explains how Nazis invented holidays (or injected new Aryan meaning into existing ones) as a means of winning over the public. Other exhibits cover the "Aryanization" of Jewish businesses (they were simply taken over by the state and handed over to new Aryan owners); Hitler's plans for converting Berlin into a gigantic "Welthauptstadt (World Capital) Germania"; and the postwar Berlin Airlift, which brought provisions to some 2.2 million West Berliners whose supply lines were cut off by East Berlin.

With more time, explore the grounds around the blocky building on a **"Site Tour."** Posted signs explain 15 different locations, including the scant remains of the prison cellars.

German Finance Ministry (Bundesministerium der Finanzen)—Across the street (facing the Wall chunk) are the former headquarters of the Nazi Luftwaffe (Air Force), the only major Hitler-era government building that survived the war's bombs. Notice how the whole building gives off a monumental feel, making the average person feel small and powerless. Walk into the stark courtyard. After the war, this was the headquarters for the Soviet occupation. Later the DDR was founded here, and the communists used the building to house their—no joke—Ministry of Ministries. Walk up Wilhelmstrasse (to the north) to see an entry gate (on your left) that looks much like it did when Germany occupied nearly all of Europe. On the north side of the building (farther

up Wilhelmstrasse, at corner with Leipziger Strasse) is a wonderful example of communist art. The mural, Max Lingner's *Aufbau der Republik* (*Building the Republic,* 1953), is classic Socialist Realism, showing the entire society—industrial laborers, farm workers, women, and children—all happily singing the same patriotic song. Its subtitle: "The importance of peace for the cultural development of humanity and the necessity of struggle to achieve this goal." This was the communist ideal. For the reality, look at the ground in the courtyard in front of the mural to see an enlarged photograph from a 1953 uprising here against the communists...quite a contrast. Placards explain the events of 1953 in English.

Stasi Museum—This modest exhibit, roughly between the Topography of Terror and Checkpoint Charlie, tells the story of how the communist-era Ministry for State Security (*Staatssicherheit*, a.k.a. Stasi) infiltrated all aspects of German life. Soon after the Wall fell, DDR authorities scrambled to destroy the copious illicit information their agents and informants had collected about the people of East Germany. But the government mandated that these records be preserved as evidence of DDR crimes, and the documents are now managed by the Federal Commissioner for Stasi Records. A timeline traces the history of the archives, and wraparound kiosks profile individual "subversive elements" who were targeted by the Stasi. There are a few actual artifacts, but the exhibit is mostly dryly written texts and reproduced photographs that don't do much to personalize the victims—making this museum worth a visit only for those with a special interest in this period. Temporary exhibits are upstairs.

Cost and Hours: Free, daily 10:00-18:00, Zimmerstrasse 90-91, tel. 030/232-450, www.bstu.bund.de.

Other Stasi Sites: If you're interested in this chapter of East German history, you may find it more satisfying (but time-consuming) to visit two other sites affiliated with the Stasi: a different **Stasi Museum,** in the former State Security headquarters (€5, Mon-Fri 11:00-18:00, Sat-Sun 12:00-18:00, Ruscherstrasse 103, U-5: Magdalenenstrasse, tel. 030/553-6854, www.stasimuseum.de); and the **Stasi Prison,** where "enemies of the state" served time (€4, visits possible only with a tour; English tours daily at 14:30—call to confirm before making the trip; German tours Mon-Fri at 11:00, 13:00, and 15:00, Sat-Sun hourly 10:00-16:00; Genslerstrasse 66, reachable on various trams from downtown—see website for specifics, tel. 030/9860-8230, www.stiftung-hsh.de). There's also a good Stasi Museum in the former State Security branch in Leipzig.

Checkpoint Charlie

This famous Cold War checkpoint was not named for a person, but for its checkpoint number—as in Alpha (#1, at the East-West German border, a hundred miles west of here), Bravo (#2, as you enter Berlin proper), and Charlie (#3, the best known because most foreigners passed through here). While the actual

checkpoint has long since been dismantled, its former location is home to a fine museum and a mock-up of the original border crossing. The area has become a Cold War freak show and—as if celebrating the final victory of crass capitalism—is one of Berlin's worst tourist-trap zones. A McDonald's stands defiantly over-looking the former haunt of East German border guards. You can even pay an exorbitant €10 for a full set of Cold War-era stamps in your passport. (For a more sober and intellectually redeeming look at the Wall's history, head for the out-of-the-way Berlin Wall Memorial at Bernauer Strasse, north of here near the Prenzlauer Berg neighborhood. Local officials, likely put off by the touristy crassness of the Checkpoint Charlie scene, have steered local funding to that area.)

▲**Checkpoint Charlie Street Scene**—Where Checkpoint Char-

lie once stood, notice the thought-provoking post with larger-than-life **posters** of a young American soldier facing east and a young Soviet soldier facing west. The rebuilt **guard station** now hosts two actors playing American guards who pose for photos. (Across the street is Snack Point Charlie.) A **photo exhibit** stretches down the street, with great English descriptions telling the story of the Wall. While you could get this information from a book, it's poignant to stand here in person and ponder the gripping history of this place.

A few yards away (on Zimmerstrasse), a **glass panel** describes the former checkpoint. From there, a double row of **cobbles** in Zimmerstrasse traces the former path of the Wall. These innocuous cobbles run throughout the city, even through some buildings.

Farther down on Zimmerstrasse, before Charlottenstrasse, find the **Memorial to Peter Fechter** (set just off the sidewalk, barely inside the Wall marker), who was shot and left for dead here in the early days of the Wall. For more on his sad story, see "The Berlin Wall (and Its Fall)" sidebar.

▲▲**Museum of the Wall at Checkpoint Charlie (Mauermuseum Haus am Checkpoint Charlie)**—While the famous border checkpoint between the American and Soviet sectors is long gone, its memory is preserved by one of Europe's most cluttered museums. During the Cold War, the House at Checkpoint Charlie stood defiantly—spitting distance from the border guards—showing off all the clever escapes over, under, and through the Wall. Today, while the drama is over and hunks of the Wall stand like trophies at its door, the museum survives as a living artifact of the Cold War days. The yellowed descriptions, which have scarcely changed since that time, tinge the museum with nostalgia. It's dusty, disorganized, and overpriced, with lots of reading involved, but all that just adds to this museum's borderline-kitschy charm. If you're pressed for time, this is a decent after-dinner sight.

Cost and Hours: €12.50, assemble 20 tourists and get in for €8.50 each, €3.50 audioguide, discount with WelcomeCard but not covered by Museumspass, daily 9:00-22:00, U6 to Kochstrasse or—better from Zoo—U2 to Stadtmitte, Friedrichstrasse 43-45, tel. 030/253-7250, www.mauermuseum.de.

Visiting the Museum: Exhibits narrate a gripping history of the Wall, with a focus on the many ingenious **escape attempts** (the early years—with a cruder wall—saw more escapes). You'll see the actual items used to smuggle would-be Wessies—a VW bug whose trunk hid a man, two side-by-side suitcases into which a woman squeezed, a makeshift zip line for crossing over (rather than through) the border, a hot-air balloon in which two families  floated to safety (immortalized in the Disney film *Night Crossing*), an inflatable boat that puttered across the dangerous Baltic Sea, primitive homemade aircraft, two surfboards hollowed out to create just enough space for a refugee, and more. One chilling exhibit lists some 43,000 people who died in "Internal Affairs" internment camps during the transition to communism (1945-1950). Profiles personalize various escapees and their helpers, including John P. Ireland, an American who posed as an eccentric antiques collector so he could transport 10 different refugees to safety in his modified Cadillac.

You'll also see **artwork** inspired by the Wall and its fall, and a memorial to Rainer Hildebrandt, who founded this museum shortly after the Wall went up in 1961 (he died in 2004, but the museum lives on as a shrine to his vision). On the **top floor** (easy to miss), that vision broadens to the larger themes of freedom and persecution, including exhibits on Eastern European rebellions (the 1956 uprising in Hungary, 1968's Prague Spring, and the Solidarity movement in 1980s Poland) and Gandhi's protests in India—plus a hodgepodge of displays on world religions and Picasso's *Guernica*. Fans of "the Gipper" appreciate the room honoring President Ronald Reagan, displaying his actual cowboy hat and boots. The small movie theater shows various Wall-related films (a schedule is posted), and the displays include video coverage of those heady days when people power tore down the Wall.

▲▲Jewish Museum Berlin (Jüdisches Museum Berlin)

BERLIN

This museum is one of Europe's best Jewish sights. The highly conceptual building is a sight in itself, and the museum inside—an overview of the rich culture and history of Europe's Jewish community—is excellent, particularly if you take advantage of the informative and engaging audioguide. Rather than just reading dry texts, you'll feel this museum as fresh and alive—an exuberant celebration of the Jewish experience that's accessible to all. Even though the museum is in a nondescript residential neighborhood, it's well worth the trip.

Cost and Hours: €5, sometimes extra for special exhibits, discount with WelcomeCard, daily 10:00-20:00, Mon until 22:00, last entry one hour before closing, closed on Jewish holidays. Tight security includes bag check and metal detectors. The excellent €3 audioguide—with four hours of commentary on 151 different items—is essential to fully appreciate the exhibits. Tel. 030/2599-3300, www.jmberlin.de.

Getting There: Take the U-Bahn to Hallesches Tor, find the exit marked *Jüdisches Museum,* exit straight ahead, then turn right on Franz-Klühs-Strasse. The museum is a five-minute walk ahead on your left, at Lindenstrasse 9.

Eating: The museum's restaurant, Liebermanns, offers good Jewish-style meals, albeit not kosher (€9 daily specials, lunch served 12:00-16:00, snacks at other times, tel. 030/2593-9760).

Visiting the Museum: Designed by American architect Daniel Libeskind (the master planner for the redeveloped World Trade Center in New York), the zinc-walled building has a zigzag shape pierced by voids symbolic of the irreplaceable cultural loss caused by the Holocaust. Enter the 18th-century Baroque building next door, then go through an underground tunnel to reach the museum interior.

Before you reach the exhibit, your visit starts with three **memorial spaces.** Follow the Axis of Exile to a disorienting slanted garden with 49 pillars (evocative of the Memorial to the Murdered Jews of Europe, across town). Next, the Axis of Holocaust, lined with artifacts from Jews imprisoned and murdered by the Nazis, leads to an eerily empty tower shut off from the outside world. The Axis of Continuity takes you to stairs and the main exhibit. A detour partway up the long stairway leads to the Memory Void, a compelling space of "fallen leaves": heavy metal faces that you walk on, making unhuman noises with each step.

Finish climbing the stairs to the top of the museum, and stroll chronologically through the 2,000-year **story of Judaism** in Germany. The exhibit, on two floors, is engaging, with lots of actual artifacts. Interactive bits (you can, for example, spell your name in Hebrew, or write a prayer and hang it from a tree) make it lively for kids. English explanations interpret both the exhibits and the design of the very symbolic building.

The top floor focuses on everyday life in Ashkenaz (medieval German-Jewish lands). The nine-minute movie "A Thousand Years Ago" sets the stage for your journey through Jewish history. You'll learn what garlic had to do with early Jews in Germany (hint: It's not just about cooking). The Middle Ages were a positive time for Jewish culture, which flourished then in many areas of Europe. But around 1500, many Jews were expelled from the countryside and moved into cities. Viewing stations let you watch nine short, lively videos that pose provocative questions about faith. Moses Mendelssohn's role in the late-18th-century Jewish Enlightenment, which gave rise to Reform Judaism, is highlighted. The Tradition and Change exhibit analyzes how various subgroups of the Jewish faith modified and relaxed their rules to adapt to a changing world.

Downstairs, on the middle floor, exhibits detail the rising tide of anti-Semitism in Germany through the 19th century—ironically, at a time when many Jews were so secularized that they celebrated Christmas right along with Hanukkah. Berlin's glory days (1890-1933) were a boom time for many Jews, though it was at times challenging to reconcile the reformed ways of the more assimilated western (German) Jews with the more traditional Eastern European Jews. The exhibit segues into the **dark days** of Hitler—the collapse of the relatively tolerant Weimar Republic, the rise of the Nazis, and the horrific night of November 9-10, 1938, when, throughout Germany, hateful mobs destroyed Jewish-owned businesses, homes, synagogues, and even entire villages—called "Crystal Night" (Kristallnacht) for the broken glass that glittered in the streets.

The thought-provoking conclusion brings us to the present day, with the question: How do you keep going after six million of your people have been murdered? You'll see how German society has reacted to the Holocaust blood on its hands (one fascinating exhibit has footage of a 1975 sit-in of German Jews to protest a controversial play with a stereotypical Jewish villain), and listen to headphone commentary of Jewish people describing their experiences growing up in postwar Germany, Austria, and Switzerland.

More Sights South of Unter den Linden

East Side Gallery—The biggest remaining stretch of the Wall is now "the world's longest outdoor art gallery." It stretches for nearly a mile and is covered with murals painted by artists from around the world. The murals (classified as protected monuments) got a facelift in 2009, when the city invited the original artists back to re-create their work for the 20th anniversary of the fall of the Wall. This segment of the Wall makes a poignant walk. For a quick look, take the S-Bahn to the Ostbahnhof station (follow signs to Stralauerplatz exit; once outside, TV Tower will be to your right; go left and at next corner look to your right—the Wall is across the busy street). The gallery is slowly being consumed by developers. If you walk the entire length of the East Side Gallery, you'll find a small Wall souvenir shop at the end and a bridge crossing the river to a subway station at Schlesisches Tor (in Kreuzberg). The bridge, a fine example of Brandenburg Neo-Gothic brickwork, has a fun neon "rock, paper, scissors" installment poking fun at the futility of the Cold War (visible only after dark).

Kreuzberg—This district—once abutting the dreary Wall and inhabited mostly by poor Turkish guest laborers and their families—is still run-down, with graffiti-riddled buildings and plenty of student and Turkish street life. It offers a gritty look at melting-pot Berlin, in a city where original Berliners are as rare as old buildings. Berlin is the largest Turkish city outside of Turkey itself, and Kreuzberg is its "downtown." But to call it a "little Istanbul" insults the big one. You'll see *Döner Kebab* stands, shops decorated with spray paint, and mothers wrapped in colorful scarves. But lately, an influx of immigrants from many other countries has diluted the Turkish-ness of Kreuzberg. Berliners come here for fun ethnic eateries. For an easy dose of Kreuzberg, joyride on bus #129 (catch it near Jewish Museum). For a colorful stroll, take the U-Bahn to Kottbusser Tor and wander—ideally on Tuesday and Friday between 12:00 and 18:00, when the Turkish Market sprawls along the Maybachufer riverbank.

North of Unter den Linden

There are few major sights to the north of Unter den Linden, but this area has some of Berlin's trendiest, most interesting neighborhoods. I've listed these roughly from south to north, as you'd approach them from the city center and Unter den Linden. On a sunny day, a stroll (or tram ride) through these bursting-with-life areas can be as engaging as any museum in town.

The Berlin Wall (and Its Fall)

The 96-mile-long "Anti-Fascist Protective Rampart," as it was called by the East German government, was erected almost overnight in 1961 to stop the outward flow of people from East to West (3 million had leaked out between 1949 and 1961). The Wall (*Mauer*) was actually two walls; the outer was a 12-foot-high concrete barrier whose rounded, pipe-like top (to discourage grappling hooks) was adorned with plenty of barbed wire. Sandwiched between the walls was a no-man's-land (or "death strip") between 30 and 160 feet wide. More than 100 sentry towers kept a close eye on the Wall. On their way into the death strip, would-be escapees would trip a silent alarm, which alerted sharpshooters.

During the Wall's 28 years, border guards fired 1,693 times and made 3,221 arrests, and there were 5,043 documented successful escapes (565 of these were East German guards). Officially, 136 people were killed at the Wall while trying to escape. One of the first, and most famous, was 18-year-old Peter Fechter. On August 17, 1962, East German soldiers shot and wounded Fechter as he was trying to climb over the Wall. For more than an hour, Fechter lay bleeding to death while soldiers and bystanders on both sides of the Wall did nothing. In 1997, a German court sentenced three former border guards to two years in prison for manslaughter.

As a tangible, almost too-apt symbol for the Cold War, the Berlin Wall got a lot of attention from politicians both East and West. Two of the 20th century's most repeated presidential quotes were uttered within earshot of the death strip. In 1963, US President John F. Kennedy stood in front of the walled-off Brandenburg Gate and professed American solidarity with the struggling people of Berlin: *Ich bin ein Berliner.* A generation later in 1987, with the stiff winds of change already blowing westward from Moscow, President Ronald Reagan came here to issue an ultimatum to his Soviet counterpart: "Mr. Gorbachev, tear down this wall."

The actual fall of the Wall had less to do with presidential proclamations than with the obvious failings of the Soviet system, a general thawing in Moscow (where Gorbachev introduced *perestroika* and *glasnost,* and declared that he would no longer employ force to keep Eastern European satellite states under Soviet rule)—and a bureaucratic snafu.

By November of 1989, it was clear that change was in the air. Hungary had already opened its borders to the West that summer, making it next to impossible for East German authorities to keep people in. A series of anti-regime protests had swept nearby Leipzig a few weeks earlier, attracting hundreds of thousands of supporters. On October 7, 1989—on the 50th anniversary of the official creation of the DDR—East German premier Erich Honecker said, "The Wall will be standing in 50 and even in 100 years." He was only off by 99 years and 11 months. A similar rally in East Berlin's Alexanderplatz on November 4—with a half-million protesters chanting, *Wir wollen raus!* (We want out!)—persuaded the East German politburo to begin a gradual process of relaxing travel restrictions.

The DDR's intention was to slightly crack the door to the West, but an inarticulate spokesman's confusion inadvertently threw it wide open. The decision was made on Thursday, November 9, to tentatively allow a few more Easterners to cross into the West—a largely symbolic reform that was intended to take place gradually, over many weeks. Licking their wounds, politburo members left town early for a long weekend. The announcement about travel restrictions was left to a spokesman, Günter Schabowski, who knew only what was on a piece of paper handed to him moments before he went on television for a routine press conference. At 18:54, Schabowski read the statement dutifully, with little emotion, seemingly oblivious to the massive impact of his own words: "exit via border crossings...possible for every citizen." Reporters, unable to believe what they were hearing, began to prod him about when the borders would open. Schabowski looked with puzzlement at the brief statement, shrugged, and offered his best guess: *Ab sofort, unverzüglich.* ("Immediately, without delay.")

Schabowski's words spread like wildfire through the streets of both Berlins, its flames fanned by West German TV broadcasts (and Tom Brokaw, who had rushed to Berlin when alerted by NBC's bureau chief). East Berliners began to show up at Wall checkpoints, demanding that border guards let them pass. As the crowds grew, the border guards could not reach anyone who could issue official orders. (The politburo members were effectively hiding out.) Finally, around 23:30, a border guard named Harald Jäger at the Bornholmer Strasse crossing decided to simply open the gates. Easterners flooded into the West, embracing their long-separated cousins, unable to believe their good fortune. Once open, the Wall could never be closed again.

The carnival atmosphere of those first years after the Wall fell is gone, but hawkers still sell "authentic" pieces of the Wall, DDR flags, and military paraphernalia to gawking tourists. When it fell, the Wall was literally carried away by the euphoria. What managed to survive has been nearly devoured by decades of persistent "Wall-peckers."

Americans—the Cold War victors—have the biggest appetite for Wall-related sights, and a few bits and pieces remain for us to seek out. Berlin's best Wall-related sights are the Berlin Wall Memorial along Bernauer Strasse, with a long stretch of surviving Wall (near S-Bahn: Nordbahnhof; page 73) and the Museum of the Wall at Checkpoint Charlie (see page 63). Other stretches of the Wall still standing include the short section at Zimmerstrasse/Wilhelmstrasse (near the Topography of Terror exhibit; page 59) and the longer East Side Gallery (near the Ostbahnhof; page 67).

Hackescher Markt

This area, in front of the S-Bahn station of the same name, is a great people scene day and night. The brick trestle supporting the train track is another classic example of the city's Brandenburg Neo-Gothic brickwork. Most of the brick archways are now filled with hip shops, which have official—and newly trendy—addresses such as "S-Bahn Arch #9, Hackescher Markt." Within 100 yards of the S-Bahn station, you'll find Hackeschen Höfe (described next), recommended Turkish and Bavarian restaurants, walking-tour and pub-crawl departure points, and tram #M1 to Prenzlauer Berg.

Hackeschen Höfe (a block in front of the Hackescher Markt S-Bahn station) is a series of eight courtyards bunny-hopping through a wonderfully restored 1907 *Jugendstil* (German Art Nouveau) building. Berlin's apartments are organized like this—courtyard after courtyard leading off the main roads. This complex is full of trendy restaurants (including the recommended Turkish eatery, Hasir), theaters, and cinemas (playing movies in their original languages). This is a wonderful example of how to make huge city blocks livable. Two decades after the Cold War, this area has reached the final evolution of East Berlin's urban restoration. (These courtyards also serve a useful lesson for visitors: Much of Berlin's charm hides off the street front.)

Oranienburger Strasse

Oranienburger Strasse is anchored by an important and somber sight, the New Synagogue. But the rest of this zone (roughly between the synagogue and Torstrasse) is colorful and quirky—especially after dark. The streets behind Grosse Hamburger Strasse flicker with atmospheric cafés, *Kneipen* (pubs), and art galleries. At night (from about 20:00), techno-prostitutes line Oranienburger Strasse. Prostitution is legal throughout Germany. Prostitutes pay taxes and receive health care insurance like anyone else. On this street, they hire security guards (lingering nearby) for safety—and they all seem to buy their Barbarella wardrobes at the same place.

▲**New Synagogue (Neue Synagogue)**—A shiny gilded dome marks the New Synagogue, now a
museum and cultural center. Consecrated in 1866, this was once the biggest and finest synagogue in Germany, with seating for 3,200 worshippers and a sumptuous Moorish-style interior modeled after the Alhambra. It was desecrated by Nazis on Crystal Night (Kristall-
nacht) in 1938, bombed in 1943, and partially rebuilt in 1990. Only the dome and facade have been restored—a window overlooks the

vacant field marking what used to be the synagogue. On its facade, a small plaque—added by East Berlin Jews in 1966—reads "Never forget" *(Vergesst es nie)*. At that time East Berlin had only a few hundred Jews, but now that the city is reunited, the Jewish community numbers about 12,000.

Inside, past tight security, the small but moving permanent exhibit called Open Ye the Gates describes the Berlin Jewish community through the centuries (filling three big rooms on the ground floor and first floor, with some good English descriptions). Examine the cutaway model showing the entire synagogue (pre-destruction) and an exhibit of religious items. Stairs lead up (past temporary exhibits, with a separate entry fee) to the dome, where there's not much to see except the unimpressive-from-the-inside dome itself and ho-hum views—not worth the entry price or the climb.

Cost and Hours: Main exhibit-€3.50, dome-€2, temporary exhibits-€3, €7 combo-ticket covers everything, audioguide-€3; March-Oct Sun-Mon 10:00-20:00, Tue-Thu 10:00-18:00, Fri 10:00-17:00—until 14:00 in Oct and March-May, closed Sat; Nov-Feb Sun-Thu 10:00-18:00, Fri 10:00-14:00, closed Sat; Oranienburger Strasse 28/30, enter through the low-profile door in the modern building just right of the domed synagogue facade, S-Bahn: Oranienburger Strasse, tel. 030/8802-8300 and press 1, www.cjudaicum.de.

Nearby: A block from the synagogue (to the right as you face it), walk 50 yards down **Grosse Hamburger Strasse** to a little park. This street was known for 200 years as the "street of tolerance" because the Jewish community donated land to Protestants so they could build a church. Hitler turned it into the "street of death" *(Todesstrasse)*, bulldozing 12,000 graves of the city's oldest Jewish cemetery and turning a Jewish nursing home into a deportation center. Because of the small but growing radical Islamic element in Berlin, and a smattering of persistent neo-Nazis, several police officers and an Israeli secret agent keep watch over this park and the Jewish high school nearby.

Other Sights on Oranienburger Strasse—This is an enjoyable zone to explore by day or night. Spice up your stroll with these stops.

Next door to the New Synagogue (to the left as you face it) is every local kid's favorite traditional candy shop, **Bonbonmacherei,** where you can see candy being made the old-fashioned way (Wed-Sat 12:00-20:00, closed Sun-Tue, at Oranienburger Strasse 32, in the Heckmann Höfe—another classic Berlin courtyard).

Just beyond the candy shop, across Tucholskystrasse, is the stately old red-brick facade of the former Imperial Post Office. Today this complex hosts an innovative avant-garde photography

Stolpersteine (Stumbling Stones)

As you wander through the Hackeschen Höfe and Oranien-burger Strasse neighborhoods—and throughout Germany—you might stumble over small brass plaques in the sidewalk called *Stolpersteine*. *Stolpern* means "to stumble," which is what you are meant to do. These plaques are placed in front of former homes of residents who were killed during World War II. The *Stolpersteine* serve not only to honor the victims, but also to stimulate thought and discussion on a daily basis (rather than only during visits to memorial sites) and to put an individual's name on the mass horror.

More than 25,000 of these plaques have been installed across Germany. They're made of brass so they stay polished as you walk over them, instead of fading into the sidewalk. On each plaque is the name of the victim who lived in that spot, and how and where that person died. While some Holocaust memorials formerly used neutral terminology like "perished," now they use words like "murdered"—part of the very honest way in which today's Germans are dealing with their country's past. The city of Munich, however, has banned *Stolpersteine*, saying that the plaques were insulting and degrading to vic-tims of persecution, who would continue to be trod on by "Nazi boots." Installation of a *Stolperstein* can be sponsored for €95 and has become popular in schools, where students research the memorialized person's life as a class project.

gallery called **C/O Berlin,** with pricey rotating exhib-its on two floors (usually one big-name exhibit plus lesser-known, more out-there pho-tographers) and occasional in-stallations outside the building (€10—but price can vary with exhibits, daily 11:00-20:00, Oranienburger Strasse 35-36, tel. 030/2844-4160, www.co-berlin.com).

Two blocks farther down (across from the intersection with Auguststrasse) is the run-down, graffiti-slathered **Tacheles build-ing.** This building—which may be gone by the time you read this—until recently hosted an arts collective called Kunsthaus Tacheles. Severely damaged in World War II, the condemned building was taken over by a community of squatters in 1990, shortly before its planned demolition. They managed to secure landmark status for the place and proceeded to convert the damaged husk of a build-ing into living and studio space for artists. The bank that owns the building (now eager to develop this prime real estate into a fancy hotel) tried to evict the artists in early 2011, but they were spared thanks to a €1 million donation from an anonymous supporter. Next, the bank cut the unwanted tenants off from the outside world by—no joke—surrounding the entrances with a 10-foot-high wall (a bold move in a city that knows a thing or two about the divisiveness of a wall). The artists finally left peacefully in 2012.

BERLIN

▲Prenzlauer Berg

Young, in-the-know locals agree that Prenzlauer Berg (PRENTS-low-er behrk) is one of Berlin's most colorful neighborhoods (roughly between Helmholtzplatz and Kollwitzplatz and along Kastanienallee, U2: Senefelderplatz and Eberswalder Strasse; or take the S-Bahn to Hackescher Markt and catch tram #M1 north). Tourists call it "Prenzl'berg" for short, while Berliners just call it "der Berg." This part of the city was largely untouched during World War II, but its buildings slowly rotted away under the communists. After the Wall fell, it was overrun with laid-back hipsters, energetic young families, and clever entrepreneurs who breathed life back into its classic old apartment blocks, deserted factories, and long-forgotten breweries. Ten years of rent control kept things affordable for its bohemian residents. But now landlords are free to charge what the market will bear, and the vibe is changing. This is ground zero for Berlin's baby boom: Tattooed and pierced young moms and dads, who've joined the modern rat-race without giving up their alternative flair, push their youngsters in designer strollers past trendy boutiques and restaurants. You'll count more kids here than just about anywhere else in town. Locals complain that these days the cafés and bars cater to yuppies sipping prosecco, while the working class and artistic types are being pushed out. While it has changed plenty, I still find Prenzlauer Berg a celebration of life and a joy to stroll through. Though it's a few blocks farther out than the neighborhoods described previously, it's a fun area to explore and have a meal or spend the night.

▲Berlin Wall Memorial (Gedenkstätte Berliner Mauer)

While tourists flock to Check-point Charlie, local authorities have been investing in this site to develop Berlin's most substantial attraction relating to its gone-but-not-forgotten Wall. Exhibits line up along a two-block stretch of Bernauer Strasse, stretching northeast from the Nordbahnhof S-Bahn station. You can enter two different

museums; see several fragments of the Wall, plus various open-air exhibits and memorials; and peer from an observation tower down into a preserved, complete stretch of the Wall system (as it was during the Cold War).

Cost and Hours: Free; Visitor Center and Documentation Center open April-Oct Tue-Sun 9:30-19:00, Nov-March until 18:00, closed Mon year-round; outdoor areas accessible 24 hours daily; last English movie starts at 18:00, memorial chapel closes at 17:00; Bernauer Strasse 111, tel. 030/4679-86666, www.berliner-mauer-gedenkstaette.de.

Getting There: Take the S-Bahn (line S-1, S-2, or S-25—all handy from Potsdamer Platz, Brandenburger Tor, or Friedrichstrasse) to the Nordbahnhof. The Nordbahnhof's underground hallways have history exhibits in English (explained later). Exit by following signs for *Bernauer Strasse*, and you'll pop out across the street from a long chunk of Wall and kitty-corner from the Visitor Center.

Background: The Berlin Wall, which was erected virtually overnight in 1961, ran right along Bernauer Strasse. People were suddenly separated from their neighbors across the street. This stretch was particularly notorious because existing apartment buildings were incorporated into the structure of the Wall itself. Film  footage and photographs from the era show Berliners worriedly watching workmen seal off these buildings from the West, brick by brick. Some people attempted to leap to freedom from upper-story windows, with mixed results. One of the unfortunate ones was Ida Siekmann, who fell to her death from her third-floor apartment on August 22, 1961, and is considered the first casualty of the Berlin Wall.

Visiting the Memorial: From the Nordbahnhof station (which has some interesting Wall history in itself), head first to the Visitor Center to get your bearings, then explore the assorted Wall fragments and other sights in the park across the street. Work your way up Bernauer Strasse to the Documentation Center, Wall System, and memorial chapel.

Nordbahnhof—This S-Bahn station was one of the "ghost stations" of Cold War Berlin. As it was a dogleg of the East mostly surrounded by the West, Western subway trains had permission to use the underground tracks to zip through this station (without stopping, of course) en route between stops in the West. Posted information boards show photos comparing 1989 with 2009, and explain that East German border guards, who were stationed here to ensure that nobody got on or off those trains, were literally locked into their surveillance rooms to prevent them from escaping. (But one subway employee and his family used the tunnels to walk to the West and freedom.)

Follow signs down a long yellow hall to Bernauer Strasse. Climbing the stairs up to the Bernauer Strasse exit, ponder that the doorway at the top of these stairs (marked by the *Sperrmauer 1961-1989* plaque) was a bricked-off no-man's-land just 25 years ago. Stepping outside, you'll see the Wall park directly across the street, and the Visitor Center in a low rust-colored building kitty-corner across the street.

Visitor Center (Bezucherzentrum)—This new, small complex has a helpful information desk, a bookstore, and two good movies that provide context for a visit (they run in English at the top of each hour, about 30 minutes for the whole spiel): *History of the Wall* offers a great 12-minute overview of why the Wall was built and how it fell. That's followed by *Walled In!*, an animated 12-minute film illustrating the Wall as it functioned here at Bernauer Strasse (Wall wonks will find it fascinating). Before leaving, pick up the brochure explaining the outdoor exhibits, and ask about any new exhibits.

Wall Fragments and Other Sights—Across the street from the Visitor Center is a long stretch of Wall. The park behind it is scattered with a few more Wall chunks as well as monuments and memorials honoring its victims. To get your bearings, find the small model of the entire area when the Wall still stood (just across the street from the Nordbahnhof). While most items are explained by English plaques, the brochure from the Visitor Center helps you better appreciate what you're seeing. The rusty "Window of Remembrance" monument honors slain would-be escapees with their names, dates of death, and transparent photos viewable from both sides. Before it was the no-man's-land between the walls, this area was the parish graveyard for a nearby church; ironically, DDR officials had to move a thousand graves from here to create a "death strip."

Berlin Wall Documentation Center (Dokumentationszentrum Berliner Mauer)—This "Doku-Center" has two movies, a small exhibit, and a viewpoint tower overlooking the preserved Wall section. The two **films** shown on the ground floor are different from those screened at the Visitor Center: *The View*, dating from 1965, tells the story of an elderly West Berlin woman who lived near the Wall, and could look into the death strip and the East from her window (in German only). *Mauerflug* features aerial photography of Berlin from the spring of 1990—after the Wall had opened, but while most of the 96-mile-long barricade still stood, offering an illuminating look at a divided city (English subtitles).

Upstairs is an **exhibit** with photos and videos detailing the construction of the Wall that began August 13, 1961. At the model of the Wall along Bernauer Strasse, notice how existing buildings were incorporated into the structure. Headphones let you listen to propagandistic, high-spirited oompah music from East Germany that celebrated the construction of the Wall: "It was high time!" There's also a list of the 163 people who died attempting to cross the Wall. From the top-floor **viewpoint** look down at the Wall itself (described next).

Wall System—This is the last surviving intact bit of the complete "Wall system" (with both sides of its Wall—capped by the round pipe that made it tougher for escapees to get a grip—and its

no-man's-land, or death strip). The guard tower came from a different part of the Wall; it was actually purchased on that great capitalist invention, eBay (over in Moscow, Stalin spins in his grave). A strip of photos and descriptions explains what you're seeing. Plaques along the sidewalk below you mark the locations of escapes or deaths.

Just beyond the Wall section (to the left), and also viewable from the tower, is a modern, cagelike church (described next).

Chapel of Reconciliation (Kapelle der Versöhnung)—This marks the spot of the late-19th-century Church of Reconciliation, which survived WWII bombs...but did not survive the communists. When the Wall was built, this church wound up, unusable,

right in the middle of the death strip. It was torn down in 1985, supposedly because it got in the way of the border guards' sight lines. (This coincided with a period in which anti-DDR opposition movements were percolating in Christian churches, prompting the nonbeliever regime to destroy several houses of worship.) If

you're interested, walk around the chapel for a closer look (it closes at 17:00). Notice the larger footprint of the original church in the field around it. The chapel hosts daily prayer services for the victims of the Wall.

More Wall Sights—Over the next few years, the Memorial plans to gradually add more open-air exhibitions about the Berlin Wall farther along Bernauer Strasse. Eventually the chain of sights will stretch all the way to Eberswalder Strasse and Oderberger Strasse, near the heart of Prenzlauer Berg.

Natural History Museum (Museum für Naturkunde)

This museum is worth a visit just to see the largest dinosaur skeleton ever assembled. While you're there, meet "Bobby" the stuffed ape, and tour the new Wet Collections, displaying shelf after shelf of animals preserved in ethanol (about a million all together). The museum is a magnet for the city's children, who love the interactive displays, the "History of the Universe in 120 Seconds" exhibit, and the cool virtual-reality "Jurascope" glasses that put meat and skin on all the dinosaur skeletons.

Cost and Hours: €6, €3.50 for kids, Tue-Fri 9:30-18:00, Sat-Sun 10:00-18:00, closed Mon, last entry 30 minutes before closing, Invalidenstrasse 43, U6: Naturkundemuseum, tel. 030/2093-8591, www.naturkundemuseum-berlin.de.

Sights in Central Berlin

Tiergarten Park and Nearby

Berlin's "Central Park" stretches two miles from Bahnhof Zoo to the Brandenburg Gate.

Victory Column (Siegessäule)—The Tiergarten's newly restored centerpiece, the Victory Column, was built to commemorate the Prussian defeat of Denmark in 1864...then reinterpreted after the defeat of France in 1870. The pointy-helmeted Germans rubbed it in, decorating the tower with French cannons and paying for it all with francs received as war reparations. The three lower rings commemorate Bismarck's victories. I imagine the statues of Moltke and other German military greats—which lurk in the trees nearby—goose-stepping around the floodlit angel at night.

Originally standing at the Reichstag, in 1938 the tower was moved to this position and given a 25-foot lengthening by Hitler's architect Albert Speer, in anticipation of the planned re-envisioning of Berlin as "Germania"—the capital of a worldwide Nazi empire. Streets leading to the circle are flanked by surviving Nazi guardhouses, built in the stern style that fascists loved. At the memorial's first level, notice how WWII bullets chipped the fine marble columns. From 1989 to 2003, the column was the epicenter of the Love Parade (Berlin's city-wide techno-hedonist street party), and it was the backdrop for Barack Obama's summer 2008 visit to Germany as a presidential candidate. (He asked to speak in front of the Brandenburg Gate, but German Chancellor Angela Merkel wanted to save that symbol from "politics.")

Climbing its 270 steps earns you a breathtaking Berlin-wide view and a close-up of the gilded bronze statue of the goddess Victoria (go ahead, call her "the chick on a stick"—everybody here

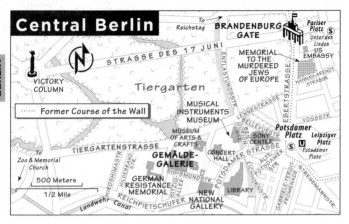

does). You might recognize Victoria from Wim Wenders' 1987 art-house classic *Wings of Desire*, or the *Stay (Faraway, So Close!)* video he directed for the rock band U2.

Cost and Hours: €2.20; April-Oct Mon-Fri 9:30-18:30, Sat-Sun 9:30-19:00; Nov-March Mon-Fri 10:00-17:00, Sat-Sun 10:00-17:30; closes in the rain, WCs for paying guests only, no elevator, bus #100, tel. 030/8639-8560. From the tower, the grand Strasse des 17 Juni leads east to the Brandenburg Gate.

Flea Market—A colorful flea market thrives weekends on Strasse des 17 Juni, with great antiques, more than 200 stalls, collector-savvy merchants, and fun German fast-food stands (Sat-Sun 6:00-16:00, right next to S-Bahn: Tiergarten).

German Resistance Memorial (Gedenkstätte Deutscher Widerstand)—This memorial and museum, located in the former Bendlerblock military headquarters just south of the Tiergarten, tells the story of several organized German resistance movements and the more than 42 separate assassination attempts against Hitler. An ill-fated scheme to kill Hitler was plotted in this building (the actual attempt occurred in Rastenburg, eastern Prussia; the event was dramatized in the 2009 Tom Cruise film *Valkyrie*). The conspirators, including Claus Schenk Graf von Stauffenberg, were shot here in the courtyard. While there are no real artifacts, the spirit that haunts the place is multilingual.

Cost and Hours: Free, Mon-Fri 9:00-18:00, Thu until 20:00, Sat-Sun 10:00-18:00, free and good English audioguide—passport required, €3 printed English translation, no crowds, near Kulturforum at Stauffenbergstrasse 13, enter in courtyard, door on left, main exhibit on third floor, bus #M29, tel. 030/2699-5000, www.gdw-berlin.de.

Potsdamer Platz and Nearby

The "Times Square of Berlin," and possibly the busiest square in Europe before World War II, Potsdamer Platz was cut in two by the Wall and left a deserted no-man's-land for 40 years. Today, this immense commercial/residential/entertainment center, sitting on a futuristic transportation hub, is home to the European corporate headquarters of several big-league companies.

BERLIN

▲Potsdamer Platz

The new Potsdamer Platz was a vision begun in 1991, when it was announced that Berlin would resume its position as the capital of Germany. Sony, Daimler, and other major corporations have turned the square once again into a center of Berlin. Like great Christian churches built upon pagan holy grounds, Potsdamer Platz—with its corporate logos flying high and shiny above what was the Wall—trumpets the triumph of capitalism.

While Potsdamer Platz tries to give Berlin a common center, the city has always been—and remains—a collection of towns. Locals recognize 28 distinct neighborhoods that may have grown together but still maintain their historic orientation. While Munich has the single dominant Marienplatz, Berlin will always have Charlottenburg, Savignyplatz, Kreuzberg, Prenzlauer Berg, and so on. In general, Berliners prefer these characteristic neighborhoods to an official city center. They're unimpressed by the grandeur of Potsdamer Platz, simply considering it a good place to go to the movies, with overpriced, touristy restaurants.

While most of the complex just feels big (the arcade is like any huge, modern, American mall), the entrance to the complex and Sony Center are worth a visit, and German-film buffs will enjoy the Deutsche Kinemathek museum (described later).

For an overview of the new construction, and a scenic route to the Sony Center, start at the Bahnhof Potsdamer Platz (east end of Potsdamer Strasse, S- and U-Bahn: Potsdamer Platz, exit following *Leipziger Platz* signs to see the best view of skyscrapers as you emerge). Find the green hexagonal **clock tower** with the traffic lights on top. This is a replica of the first automatic traffic light in Europe, which once stood at the six-street intersection of

Potsdamer Platz. On either side of Potsdamer Strasse, you'll see enormous cubical entrances to the underground Potsdamer Platz train station. Near these entrances, notice the slanted **glass cylinders** sticking out of the ground. The mirrors on the tops of the tubes move with the sun to collect light and send it underground (saving piles of euros in energy costs). A line in the pavement indicates where the **Berlin Wall** once stood. On the right side of the street, notice the re-erected slabs of the Wall. Imagine when the first piece was cut out (see photo and history on nearby panel). These hang like scalps at the gate of Fort Capitalism...look up at the towering corporate headquarters: Market forces have won a clear victory. Now descend into one of the train station entrances and follow signs to *Sony Center.* As you walk through the passage, notice the wall panels with historical information.

You'll come up the escalator into the **Sony Center** under a grand canopy (designed to evoke Mount Fuji). At night, multicolored floodlights play on the underside of this tent. Office workers and tourists eat here by the fountain, enjoying the parade of people. The modern Bavarian Lindenbräu beer hall—the Sony boss wanted a *Bräuhaus*—serves traditional food (€11-17, daily 11:00-24:30, big €8 salads, three-foot-long taster boards of eight different beers, tel. 030/2575-1280). Across the plaza, Josty Bar is built around a surviving bit of a venerable hotel that was a meeting place for Berlin's rich and famous before the bombs (€10-17 meals, daily 10:00-24:00, tel. 030/2575-9702). CineStar is a rare cinema that plays mainstream movies in their original language (www.cinestar.de).

Sights near Potsdamer Platz

▲Deutsche Kinemathek Film and TV Museum—This exhibit is the most interesting place to visit in the Sony Center. The early pioneers in filmmaking were German (including Fritz Lang, F. W. Murnau, Ernst Lubitsch, and the Austrian-born Billy Wilder), and many of them also became influential in Hollywood—making this a fun visit for cinephiles. Your admission ticket gets you into several floors of exhibits (including temporary exhibits on floors 1 and 4) made meaningful by the included, essential English audioguide.

Cost and Hours: €6, includes 1.5-hour audioguide, Tue-Sun 10:00-18:00, Thu until 20:00, closed Mon, tel. 030/2474-9888, www.deutsche-kinemathek.de.

Nearby: The Kino Arsenal theater downstairs shows offbeat art-house films in their original language.

BERLIN

Visiting the Museum: From the ticket desk, ride the elevator up to the third floor, where you can turn left (into the film section, floors 3 and 2) or right (into the TV section, floors 3 and 4).

In the **film section,** you'll walk back in time through a fun mirrored entryway. The exhibit starts with the German film industry's beginnings, with an emphasis on the Weimar Republic period in the 1920s, when Berlin rivaled Hollywood. Influential films included the early German Expressionist masterpiece *The Cabinet of Dr. Caligari* (1920) and Fritz Lang's seminal *Metropolis* (1927). Three rooms are dedicated to Marlene Dietrich, who was a huge star both in Germany and, later, in Hollywood. (Dietrich, who performed at USO shows to entertain Allied troops fighting against her former homeland, once said, "I don't hate the Germans, I hate the Nazis.") Another section examines Nazi use of film as propaganda, including Leni Riefenstahl's masterful documentary of the 1936 Berlin Olympics and her earlier, chillingly propagandistic *Triumph of the Will* (1935). The postwar period was defined by two separate East and West German film industries. The exhibit's finale reminds us that German filmmakers are still highly influential and successful—including Wolfgang Petersen *(Das Boot, Air Force One, The Perfect Storm)* and Werner Herzog (the documentary *Grizzly Man* and the drama *Rescue Dawn*). (If this visit gets you curious about German cinema, see the recommendations in the Appendix.)

The **TV section** tells the story of *das Idioten Box* from its infancy (when it was primarily used as a Nazi propaganda tool) to today. The 30-minute kaleidoscopic review—kind of a frantic fast-forward montage of greatest hits in German TV history, both East and West—is great fun even if you don't understand a word of it (it plays all day long, with 10-minute breaks). Otherwise, the TV section is a little more challenging for non-German speakers to appreciate. Upstairs (on the fourth floor) is a TV archive where you can dial through a wide range of new and classic German TV standards.

Panoramapunkt—Across Potsdamer Strasse from the Film and TV Museum, you can ride what's billed as "the fastest elevator in Europe" to skyscraping rooftop views. You'll travel at nearly 30 feet per second to the top of the 300-foot-tall Kollhoff Tower. Its sheltered but open-air view deck provides a fun opportunity to survey Berlin's ongoing construction from above.

Cost and Hours: €5.50, €9.50 VIP ticket lets you skip the line, audioguide-€2.50, daily 10:00-20:00, until 22:00 in summer, last elevator 30 minutes before closing, in red-brick building at Potsdamer Platz 1, tel. 030/2593-07080, www.panoramapunkt.de.

Kulturforum

Just west of Potsdamer Platz, Kulturforum rivals Museum Island as the city's cultural heart, with several top museums and Berlin's concert hall—home of the world-famous Berlin Philharmonic orchestra (admission to all Kulturforum sights covered by a single €8 Bereichskarte Kulturforum combo-ticket—a.k.a. Quartier-Karte—and also by the Museumspass; info for all museums: tel. 030/266-424-242, www.kulturforum-berlin.de). Of its sprawling museums, only the Gemäldegalerie is a must (S- or U-Bahn to Potsdamer Platz, then walk along Potsdamer Platz; or from Bahnhof Zoo, take bus #200 to Philharmonie).

▲▲Gemäldegalerie—Literally the "Painting Gallery," Germany's top collection of 13th- through 18th-century European paintings (more than 1,400 canvases) is beautifully displayed in a building that's a work of art in itself. The North Wing starts with German paintings of the 13th to 16th centuries, including eight by Albrecht Dürer. Then come the Dutch and Flemish—Jan van Eyck, Pieter Brueghel, Peter Paul Rubens, Anthony van Dyck, Frans Hals, and Jan Vermeer. The wing finishes with German, English, and French 18th-century artists, such as Thomas Gainsborough and Antoine Watteau. An octagonal hall at the end features an impressive stash of Rembrandts. The South Wing is saved for the Italians—Giotto, Botticelli, Titian, Raphael, and Caravaggio.

Cost and Hours: Covered by €8 Kulturforum combo-ticket, Tue-Sun 10:00-18:00, Thu until 22:00, closed Mon, audioguide included with entry, clever little loaner stools, great salad bar in cafeteria upstairs, Matthäikirchplatz 4.

❺ Self-Guided Tour: I'll point out a few highlights, focusing on Northern European artists (Germans, Dutch, and Flemish), with a few Spaniards and Italians thrown in. To go beyond my selections, make ample use of the excellent audioguide.

The collection spreads out on one vast floor surrounding a central hall. Inner rooms have Roman numerals (I, II, III), while adjacent outer rooms are numbered (1, 2, 3). After showing your ticket, turn right into room I and work your way counterclockwise (and roughly chronologically) through the collection.

Rooms I-III/1-4 kick things off with early German paintings (13th-16th centuries). In room 1, look for the 1532 portrait of wealthy Hanseatic cloth merchant Georg Gisze by **Hans Holbein the Younger** (1497-1543). Gisze's name appears on several of the notes stuck to the wall behind him. And, typical of detail-rich Northern European art, the canvas is bursting with highly symbolic tidbits. Items scattered on the tabletop and on the shelves be-

hind the merchant represent his lofty status and aspects of his life story. In the vase, the carnation represents his recent engagement, and the herbs symbolize his virtue. And yet, the celebratory flowers are already beginning to fade and the scales behind him are unbalanced, reminders of the fleetingness of happiness and wealth.

BERLIN

In room 2 are fine portraits by the remarkably talented **Albrecht Dürer** (1471-1528), who traveled to Italy during the burgeoning days of the early Renaissance and melded the artistic harmony and classical grandeur he discovered there with a Northern European attention to detail. In his *Portrait of Hieronymus Holzschuher* (1526), Dürer skillfully captured the personality of a friend from Nürnberg, right down to the sly twinkle in his sidelong glance. Technically the portrait is perfection: Look closely and see each individual hair of the man's beard and fur coat, and even the reflection of the studio's windows in his eyes. Also notice Dürer's little pyramid-shaped, D-inside-A signature. Signing one's work was a revolutionary assertion of Dürer's renown, at a time when German artists were considered anonymous craftsmen.

Lucas Cranach the Elder (1472-1553), whose works are in room III, was a court painter for the prince electors of Saxony and a close friend of Martin Luther (and his unofficial portraitist). But *The Fountain of Youth* (1546) is a far cry from Cranach's solemn portrayals of the Reformer. Old women helped to the fountain (on the left) emerge as young ladies on the right. Newly nubile, the women go into a tent to dress up, snog with noblemen in the bushes (right foreground), dance merrily beneath the trees, and dine grandly beneath a landscape of phallic mountains and towers. This work is flanked by Cranach's Venus nudes. I sense a pattern here.

Netherlandish painters (rooms IV-VI/4-7) were early adopters of oil paint (as opposed to older egg tempera), whose flexibility allowed them to brush the super-fine details for which they are famous. **Rogier van der Weyden** (room IV) was a virtuoso handler of the new medium. In *Portrait of a Young Woman* (c. 1400-1464), the subject wears a typical winged bonnet, addressing the viewer directly with her fetching blue eyes. The subjects (especially women) of most portraits of the time look off to one side; some art historians guess that the confident woman shown here is Van

BERLIN

der Weyden's wife. In the same room is a remarkable, rare trio of three-panel altarpieces by Van der Weyden: The *Marienaltar* shows the life of the Virgin Mary; the *Johannesaltar* narrates the life of John the Baptist—his birth, baptizing Christ (with God and the Holy Spirit hovering overhead), and his gruesome death by decapitation; and the *Middelburger Altar* tells the story of the Nativity. Savor the fine details in each panel of these altarpieces.

Flash forward a few hundred years to the 17th century and Flemish (Belgian) painting (rooms VII-VIII/9-10), and it's appar-

ent how much the Protestant Reformation—and resulting Counter-Reformation—changed the tenor of Northern European art. In works by **Peter Paul Rubens** (1577-1640)—including *Jesus Giving Peter the Keys to Heaven*—calm, carefully studied, detail-oriented seriousness gives way to an exuberant Baroque trumpeting of the greatness of the Catholic Church. In the Counter-Reformation world, the Catholic Church had serious competition for the hearts and minds of its congregants. Exciting art like this became a way to keep people in the pews. Notice the quivering brushstrokes and almost too-bright colors. (In the same room are portraits by Rubens' student, Anthony van Dyck, as well as some hunting still lifes from Frans Snyders and others.) In the next rooms (VIII and 9) are more Rubens, including the mythological *Perseus Freeing Andromeda* and *The Martyrdom of St. Sebastian by Arrows* (loosely based on a more famous rendition by Andrea Mantegna).

Dutch painting from the 17th century (rooms IX-XI/10-19) is dominated by the convivial portraits by **Frans Hals** (c. 1582-1666). His 1620 portrait of Catharina Hooft (far corner, room 13) presents a startlingly self-possessed baby (the newest member of a wealthy merchant family) dressed with all the finery of a queen, adorned with lace and jewels, and clutching a golden rattle. The smiling nurse supporting the tyke offers her a piece of fruit, whose blush of red perfectly matches the nanny's apple-fresh cheeks.

But the ultimate Dutch master is **Rembrandt van Rijn** (1606-1669), whose powers of perception and invention propelled him to fame in his lifetime. Displayed here are several storytelling scenes (room 16), mostly from classical mythology or biblical stories, all employing Rembrandt's trademark chiaroscuro technique (with

a strong contrast between light and dark). In *The Rape of Persephone*, Pluto grabs Persephone from his chariot and races toward the underworld, while other goddesses cling to her robe, trying to save her. Cast against a nearly black background, the almost overexposed, action-packed scene is shockingly emotional. In the nearby *Samson and Delilah* (1628), Delilah cradles Samson's head in her lap while silently signaling to a goon to shear Samson's hair, the secret to his strength. A self-portrait (room X) of a 28-year-old Rembrandt wearing a beret is paired with the come-hither 1637 *Portrait of Hendrickje Stoffels* (the two were romantically linked). *Samson Threatens His Father-in-Law* (1635) captures the moment just after the mighty Samson (with his flowing hair, elegant robes, and shaking fist) has been told by his wife's father to take a hike. I wouldn't want to cross this guy.

Although **Johannes Vermeer** (1632-1675) is today just as admired as Rembrandt, he was little known in his day, probably because he painted relatively few works for a small circle of Delft collectors. Vermeer was a master at conveying a complicated story through a deceptively simple scene with a few poignant details—whether it's a woman reading a letter at a window, a milkmaid pouring

milk from a pitcher into a bowl, or (as in *The Glass of Wine*, room 18) a young man offering a drink to a young lady. The young man had been playing her some music on his lute (which now sits, discarded, on a chair) and is hoping to seal the deal with some alcohol. The woman is finishing one glass of wine, and her would-be suitor stands ready—almost *too* ready—to pour her another. His sly, somewhat smarmy smirk drives home his high hopes for what will come next. Vermeer has perfectly captured the exact moment of "Will she or won't she?" The painter offers some clues—the coat of arms in the window depicts a woman holding onto the reigns of a horse, staying in control—but ultimately, only he (and the couple) know how this scene will end.

Shift south to Italian, French, and Spanish painting of the 17th and 18th centuries (rooms XII-XIV/23-28). Venetian cityscapes by Canaletto (who also painted Dresden) and lots of bombastic Baroque art hang in room XII. Room XIII features big-name Spanish artists Murillo, Zurbarán, and the great **Diego Velázquez** (1599-

1660). He gave the best of his talents to his portraits, capturing warts-and-all likenesses that are effortlessly real. His 1630 *Portrait of a Lady* conveys the subject's subtle, sly Mona Lisa smile. Her figure and face (against a dull gray background) are filtered through a pleasant natural light. Notice that if you stand too close, the brushstrokes get muddy—but when you back up, the scene snaps into perfectly sharp relief.

From here, the collection itself takes a step backwards—into Italian paintings of the 13th-16th centuries (rooms XV-XVIII/29-41). This section includes some lesser-known works by great Italian Renaissance painters, including Raphael (rooms XVII and 29, including five different Madonnas, among them the *Terranuova Madonna*, in a round frame) and Sandro Botticelli (room VIII).

New National Gallery (Neue Nationalgalerie)—This gallery features 20th-century art, with ever-changing special exhibits.

Cost and Hours: Covered by €8 Kulturforum combo-ticket, Tue-Fri 10:00-18:00, Thu until 22:00, Sat-Sun 11:00-18:00, closed Mon, café downstairs, Potsdamer Strasse 50.

Museum of Decorative Arts (Kunstgewerbemuseum)— Wander through a mazelike floor plan displaying a thousand years of applied arts—porcelain, fine *Jugendstil* (German Art Nouveau) furniture, Art Deco, and reliquaries. There are no English descriptions and no crowds.

Cost and Hours: Covered by €8 Kulturforum combo-ticket, Tue-Fri 10:00-18:00, Sat-Sun 11:00-18:00, closed Mon, Herbert-von-Karajan-Strasse 10.

▲Musical Instruments Museum (Musikinstrumenten Museum)— This impressive hall is filled with 600 exhibits spanning the 16th century to modern times. Wander among old keyboard instruments and funny-looking tubas. Pick up the included audioguide and free English brochure at the entry. In

addition to the English commentary, the audioguide has clips of various instruments being played (just punch in the number next to the instrument you want to hear). This place is fascinating if you're into pianos.

Cost and Hours: €4, covered by €8 Kulturforum combo-ticket, Tue-Fri 9:00-17:00, Thu until 22:00, Sat-Sun 10:00-17:00, closed Mon, low-profile white building east of the big yellow Phil-harmonic Concert Hall, tel. 030/2548-1178.

Philharmonic Concert Hall—Poke into the lobby of Berlin's yellow Philharmonic building and see if there are tickets avail-able during your stay. The interior is famous for its extraordinary acoustics. Even from the outside, this is a remarkable building, designed by a nautical engineer to look like a ship—notice how different it looks from each angle. Inexpensive and legitimate tickets are often sold on the street before performances. Or you can buy tickets from the box office in person, by phone, or online (ticket office open Mon-Fri 15:00-18:00, Sat-Sun 11:00-14:00, info tel. 030/2548-8132, box office tel. 030/2548-8999—an-swered daily 9:00-18:00, www.berliner-philharmoniker.de). For guest performances, you must buy tickets through the organizer (see website for details).

Sights in Western Berlin

Throughout the Cold War, Western travelers—and most West Ber-liners—got used to thinking of western Berlin's Kurfürstendamm boulevard as the heart of the city. But those days have gone the way of the Wall. With the huge changes the city has undergone since 1989, the real "city center" is now, once again, Berlin's historic center (the Mitte district, around Unter den Linden and Friedrich-strasse). While western Berlin still works well as a home base, it's no longer the obvious place from which to explore Berlin. After the new Hauptbahnhof essentially put Bahnhof Zoo out of busi-ness in 2006, the area was left with an identity crisis. Now, more than 20 years after reunification, the west side is back and has fully embraced its historical role as a chic, classy suburb.

In the Heart of Western Berlin

A few interesting sights sit within walking distance of Bahnhof Zoo and the Savignyplatz hotels.

▲**Kurfürstendamm**—Western Berlin's main drag, Kurfürsten-damm boulevard (nicknamed "Ku'damm"), starts at Kaiser Wil-helm Memorial Church and does a commercial cancan for two miles. In the 1850s, when Berlin became a wealthy and important capital, her "new rich" chose Kurfürstendamm as their street. Bis-marck made it Berlin's Champs-Elysées. In the 1920s, it became a chic and fashionable drag of cafés and boutiques. During the Third Reich, as home to an international community of diplomats and journalists, it enjoyed more freedom than the rest of Berlin. Throughout the Cold War, economic subsidies from the West made sure that capitalism thrived on Ku'damm. And today, while much of the old charm has been hamburgerized, Ku'damm is still a fine place to enjoy elegant shops (around Fasanenstrasse), department stores, and people-watching.

▲**Kaiser Wilhelm Memorial Church (Gedächtniskirche)**—This church was originally dedicated to the first emperor of Germany. Reliefs and mosaics show great events in the life of Germany's favorite *Kaiser*, from his coronation in 1871 to his death in 1888. The church's bombed-out ruins have been left standing as a poignant memorial to the destruction of Berlin in World War II.

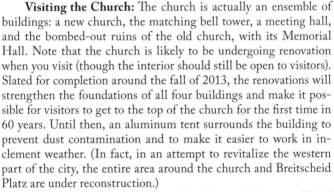

Cost and Hours: Church—free, daily 9:00-19:00; Memorial Hall—free, Mon-Sat 10:00-18:00, shorter hours on Sun. Located on Breitscheidplatz, U2/U9 and S-Bahn: Zoologischer Garten or U1/U9: Kurfürstendamm, www.gedaechtniskirche.com.

Visiting the Church: The church is actually an ensemble of buildings: a new church, the matching bell tower, a meeting hall, and the bombed-out ruins of the old church, with its Memorial Hall. Note that the church is likely to be undergoing renovation when you visit (though the interior should still be open to visitors). Slated for completion around the fall of 2013, the renovations will strengthen the foundations of all four buildings and make it possible for visitors to get to the top of the church for the first time in 60 years. Until then, an aluminum tent surrounds the building to prevent dust contamination and to make it easier to work in inclement weather. (In fact, in an attempt to revitalize the western part of the city, the entire area around the church and Breitscheid Platz are under reconstruction.)

Under a Neo-Romanesque mosaic ceiling, the **Memorial Hall** features a small exhibit of interesting photos about the bombing and before-and-after models of the church. After the war, some Berliners wanted to tear down the ruins and build it anew. Instead, it was decided to keep what was left of the old church as a memorial and stage a competition to design a modern, add-on section. The winning entry—the short, modern church (1961) next to the Memorial Hall—offers a meditative world of 11,000 little blue windows. The blue glass was given to the church by the French as a reconciliation gift. For more information on both churches, pick up the English flier (€0.50).

As you enter the **church,** a peaceful blue oasis in the middle of the busy city, turn immediately right to find a simple charcoal sketch of the Virgin Mary wrapped in a shawl. During the Battle of Stalingrad, German combat surgeon Kurt Reuber rendered the Virgin on the back of a stolen Soviet map to comfort the men in his care. On the right are the words "Light, Life, Love" from the gospel of John; on the left, "Christmas in the cauldron 1942"; and at the bottom, "Fortress Stalingrad." Though Reuber died in captivity a year later, his sketch had been flown out of Stalingrad on the last medical evacuation flight, and postwar Germany embraced it as a symbol of the wish for peace. Copies of the drawing, now known as the *Stalingrad Madonna,* hang in the Berlin Cathedral, in England's Coventry, and in Russia's Volgograd (formerly Stalingrad) as a sign of peaceful understanding between the nations. As another act of reconciliation, every Friday at 13:00 a "Prayers for Peace" service is held simultaneously with the cathedral in Coventry.

Nearby: The lively square between the churches and the Europa Center (a once-impressive, shiny high-rise shopping center built as a showcase of Western capitalism during the Cold War) usually attracts street musicians and performers—especially in the summer. Berliners call the funky fountain "the wet meatball."

The Story of Berlin—Filling most of what seems like a department store right on Ku'damm (at #207), this sprawling history exhibit tells the stormy 800-year story of Berlin in a creative way. While there are almost no real historic artifacts, the exhibit does a good job of cobbling together many dimensions of the life and tumultuous times of this great city. It's particularly strong on the story of the city from World War I through the Cold War. However, for similar information, and more artifacts, the German History Museum on Unter den Linden is a far better use of your time and money.

Cost and Hours: €10, daily 10:00-20:00, last entry 2 hours before closing, tel. 030/8872-0100, www.story-of-berlin.de. Times for the 30-minute bunker tour are posted at the entry.

▲**Käthe Kollwitz Museum**—This local artist (1867-1945), who experienced much of Berlin's stormiest century, conveys some powerful and mostly sad feelings about motherhood, war, and suffering through the stark faces of her art. This small yet fine collection (the only one in town of Kollwitz's work) consists of three floors of charcoal drawings, topped by an attic with a handful of sculptures.

Cost and Hours: €6, €1 pamphlet has necessary English explanations of a few major works, daily 11:00-18:00, a block off Ku'damm at Fasanenstrasse 24, U-Bahn: Uhlandstrasse, tel. 030/882-5210, www.kaethe-kollwitz.de.

▲**Kaufhaus des Westens (KaDeWe)**—The "Department Store of the West" has been a Berlin tradition for more than a century. With a staff of 2,100 to help you sort through its vast selection of 380,000 items, KaDeWe claims to be the biggest department store on the Continent. You can get everything from a haircut and train ticket (third floor) to souvenirs (fourth floor). The theater and concert box office on the sixth floor charges an 18 percent booking fee, but they know all your options (cash only). The sixth floor is a world of gourmet taste treats. The biggest selection of deli and exotic food in Germany offers plenty of classy opportunities to sit down and eat. Ride the glass elevator to the seventh floor's glass-domed Winter Garden, a self-service cafeteria—fun but pricey.

Hours: Mon-Thu 10:00-20:00, Fri 10:00-21:00, Sat 9:30-20:00, closed Sun, S-Bahn: Zoologischer Garten or U-Bahn: Wittenbergplatz, tel. 030/21210, www.kadewe.de.

Nearby: The Wittenbergplatz U-Bahn station (in front of KaDeWe) is a unique opportunity to see an old-time station. Enjoy its interior with classic advertisements still decorating its venerable walls.

Berlin Zoo (Zoologischer Garten Berlin)—More than 1,500 different kinds of animals call Berlin's famous zoo home...or so the zookeepers like to think. The big hit here is the lonely panda bear (straight in from the entrance).

Cost and Hours: €13 for zoo, €13 for world-class aquarium, €20 for both, kids half-price, daily 9:00-18:00, aquarium closes 30 minutes earlier; feeding times—*Fütterungszeiten*—posted just inside entrance, the best feeding show is the sea lions—generally at 15:15; enter near Europa Center in front of Hotel Palace or opposite Bahnhof Zoo on Hardenbergplatz, Budapester Strasse 34, tel. 030/254-010, www.zoo-berlin.de.

Erotic Art Museum—This offers two floors of graphic art (especially East Asian), old-time sex-toy knickknacks, and a special exhibit on the queen of German pornography, the late Beate Uhse. This amazing woman, a former test pilot for the Third Reich and groundbreaking purveyor of condoms and sex ed in the 1950s, was the female Hugh Hefner of Germany and CEO of a huge chain of porn shops. She is famously credited with bringing sex out of the bedroom...and onto the kitchen table ("where it belongs," adds my Berliner friend). FYI: You'll see much more sex for half the price in a private video booth next door.

Cost and Hours: €9, Mon-Sat 9:00-24:00, Sun 11:00-24:00, last entry at 23:00, hard-to-beat gift shop, at corner of Kantstrasse and Joachimstalerstrasse, a block from Bahnhof Zoo, tel. 030/886-0666.

Charlottenburg Palace Area

The Charlottenburg district—with a cluster of museums across the street from a grand palace—is an easy side-trip from downtown. The palace isn't much to see, but if the surrounding museums appeal to you, consider making the trip. To get here, ride U2 to Sophie-Charlotte Platz and walk 10 minutes up the tree-lined boulevard Schlossstrasse (following signs to *Schloss*), or—much faster—catch bus #M45 (direction Spandau) direct from Bahnhof Zoo.

Eating near Charlottenburg Palace: For a Charlottenburg

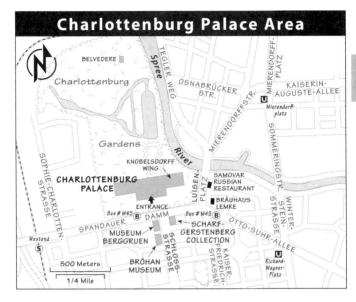

Charlottenburg Palace Area

lunch, the **Bräuhaus Lemke** is a comfortable brewpub restaurant with a copper and woody atmosphere, good local microbeers (*dunkles* means "dark," *helles* is "light"), and traditional German grub (€8-15 meals, daily 11:00-24:00, fun for groups, across from palace at Luisenplatz 1, tel. 030/3087-8979). Or consider lunching like the Russians, who have been part of Charlottenburg ever since Frederick the Great invited them in the 18th century. The small **Samovar** serves traditional Russian specialties in a comfortable, intimate setting (€6-20 meals, €3.40 Russian tea, daily 11:00-22:00, just past Bräuhaus Lemke at Luisenplatz 3, tel. 030/341-4154).

▲**Charlottenburg Palace (Schloss Charlottenburg)**—If you've seen the great palaces of Europe, this Baroque palace, also known as the Altes Schloss, comes in at about number 10 (behind Potsdam, too). It's the largest former residence of the royal Hohenzollern family in Berlin and contains the biggest collection of 17th-century French fresco painting outside France. The **Neue Flügel** (a.k.a. the Knobelsdorff Wing) has a separate entry fee and features a few royal apartments. Go upstairs and take a substantial hike through restored-since-the-war gold-crusted white rooms.

   Cost and Hours: Palace—€12, includes audioguide, Tue-Sun 10:00-18:00, until 17:00 Nov-March, closed Mon, last entry 30 minutes before closing, tel. 030/320-911; Neue Flügel—€6, more during special exhibitions, includes audioguide, Wed-Mon 10:00-17:00, closed Tue, last entry at 16:30, when facing the palace walk toward the right wing, tel. 030/3209-1442, www.spsg.de. The only WC is within the castle, mid-tour.

▲**Museum Berggruen: Picasso and His Time**—This tidy little museum is a pleasant surprise. Climb three floors through a fun and substantial collection of Picassos. Along the way, you'll see plenty of notable works by Henri Matisse and Paul Klee.

Cost and Hours: €8 combo-ticket includes the Scharf-Gerstenberg Collection, covered by Museumspass, open Tue-Sun 10:00-18:00, closed Mon, Schlossstrasse 1, tel. 030/326-95815, www.smb.museum.

▲**Bröhan Museum**—Wander through a dozen beautifully furnished *Jugendstil* and Art Deco living rooms, a curvy organic world of lamps, glass, silver, and posters. English descriptions are posted on the wall of each room on the main floor. While you're there, look for the fine collection of Impressionist paintings by Karl Hagemeister.

Cost and Hours: €6, Museumspass doesn't cover special exhibits, Tue-Sun 10:00-18:00, closed Mon, Schlossstrasse 1A, tel. 030/3269-0600, www.broehan-museum.de.

▲**Scharf-Gersternberg Collection**—This small museum houses a collection of more than 250 works of Surrealist and pre-Surrealist art. The *Surreal Worlds* exhibit shows just how freaky the world looked to artists like Salvador Dalí, Paul Klee, and Francisco de Goya. Be sure to check out Dalí's film of his birth from an egg on the beach.

Cost and Hours: €8 combo-ticket includes Museum Berggruen—described earlier, open Tue-Sun 10:00-18:00, closed Mon, Schlossstrasse 70, tel. 030/3435-7315, www.smb.museum.

Nightlife in Berlin

Berlin is a happening place for nightlife—whether it's clubs, pubs, jazz music, cabaret, hokey-but-fun German variety shows, theater, or concerts.

Sources of Entertainment Info: *Berlin Programm* lists a non-stop parade of concerts, plays, exhibits, and cultural events (€2, in German, www.berlin-programm.de); *Exberliner Magazine* (€3, www.exberliner.com) doesn't have as much hard information, but is colorfully written in English (both sold at kiosks and TIs). For the young and determined sophisticate, *Zitty* and *Tip* are the top guides to alternative culture (in German, sold at kiosks). Also pick up the free schedules *Flyer* and *030* in bars and clubs. Visit KaDeWe's ticket office for your music and theater options (sixth floor, 18 percent fee but access to all tickets). Ask about "competitive improvisation" and variety shows.

Berlin Jazz—To enjoy live music near my recommended Savignyplatz hotels in western Berlin, consider **A Trane Jazz Club** (all jazz, great stage and intimate seating, €7-18 cover depending on act, opens at 21:00, live music nightly 22:00-2:00 in the morning, Bleibtreustrasse 1, tel. 030/313-2550, www.a-trane.de). **B-Flat Acoustic Music and Jazz Club,** in the heart of eastern Berlin, also has live music nightly—and shares a courtyard with a tranquil tea house (shows vary from free to €10-12 cover, open Mon-Thu from 20:00 with shows starting at 21:00, Fri-Sat from 21:00 with shows at 22:00, closed Sun, a block from Rosenthaler Platz U-Bahn stop at Rosenthaler Strasse 13, tel. 030/283-3123, www.b-flat-berlin. de).

Berliner Rock and Roll—Berlin has a vibrant rock and pop scene, with popular venues at the Spandau Citadel and at the outdoor Waldbühne ("Forest Stage"). Check out what's playing on posters in the U-Bahn, in *Zitty,* or at any ticket agency. Great Berlin bands include The Beatsteaks, Jennifer Rostock, and the funky ska band Seeed.

Cabaret—Bar Jeder Vernunft offers modern-day cabaret a short walk from my recommended hotels in western Berlin. This variety show—under a classic old tent perched atop the modern parking lot of the Berliner Festspiele theater—is a hit with German-speakers, but can still be worthwhile for those who don't speak the language (as some of the music shows are in a sort of "Denglish"). Even some Americans perform here periodically. Tickets are generally about €22-25, and shows change regularly (performances start Mon-Sat at 20:00, Sun at 19:00, seating can be a bit cramped, south of Ku'damm at Schaperstrasse 24, U-3 or U-9: Spichernstrasse, tel. 030/883-1582, www.bar-jeder-vernunft.de).

German Variety Show—To spend an evening enjoying Europe's largest revue theater, consider "YMA—Too Beautiful to Be True" at the **FriedrichstadtPalast.** It's a passionate visual spectacle, a weird ballet that pulsates like a visual poem (€17-105, Tue at 18:30, Thu-Sat at 19:30, Sat also at 15:30, Sun at 15:30, no shows Mon or Wed, Friedrichstrasse 107, U6: Oranienburger Tor, tel. 030/2326-2326, www.show-palace.eu). The Friedrichstrasse area around the Palast and to the south has been synonymous with Berliner entertainment for at least 200 years. The East German government built the current Palast in 1984 on the ruins of an older theater, which itself was a horse barn for the Prussian Army. The current exterior is meant to mimic the interior design of the older theater.

Nightclubs and Pubs—Oranienburger Strasse's trendy scene has been eclipsed by the action at Friedrichshain (farther east). To the north, you'll find the hip Prenzlauer Berg neighborhood, packed with everything from smoky pubs to small art bars and dance clubs (best scene is around Helmholtzplatz, U2: Eberswalder Strasse).

Dancing—Cut a rug at **Clärchens Ballhaus,** an old ballroom that's been a Berlin institution since 1913. At some point everyone in Berlin comes through here, as the dance hall attracts an eclectic Berlin-in-a-nutshell crowd of grannies, elegant women in evening dresses, yuppies, scenesters, and hippies. The music (swing, waltz, tango, or cha-cha) changes every day, with live music on Friday and Saturday (from 23:15, €4 cover; dance hall open daily from 10:00—12:00 in winter—until the last person goes home, in the heart of the Auguststrasse gallery district at Auguststrasse 24, S-Bahn: Oranienburger Strasse, tel. 030/282-9295, www.ballhaus.de). Dancing lessons are also available (€8, Mon-Tue at 19:00, Thu at 19:30, 1.5 hours). The "Gypsy" restaurant, which fills a huge courtyard out front, serves decent food and good pizza.

Art Galleries—Berlin, a magnet for new artists, is a great city for gallery visits. Galleries—many of which stay open late—welcome visitors who are "just looking." The most famous gallery district is in eastern Berlin's Mitte neighborhood, along **Auguststrasse** (branches off from Oranienburger Strasse at the ruined Tacheles building). Check out the Berlin outpost of the edgy-yet-accessible art of the New Leipzig movement at **Galerie Eigen+Art** (Tue-Sat 11:00-18:00, closed Sun-Mon, Auguststrasse 26, tel. 030/280-6605, www.eigen-art.com). The other gallery area is in western Berlin, along **Fasanenstrasse.**

Pub Crawls—Various companies offer pub crawls to some of Berlin's fun watering holes. The (unrelated) binge-drinking death of a 16-year-old in Berlin a few years ago reinforced the tours' strict 18-year-old minimum age limit. Pub crawls depart around 20:15, cost €12, generally visit four bars and two clubs, and provide a great way to drink it up with new friends from around the world while getting a peek at Berlin's bar scene...or at least how its bars look when invaded by 50 loud tourists. You could take a pub crawl offered by **Insider Tour** or **Sandeman's New Europe Berlin**, or look around town for fliers from other companies.

Sleeping in Berlin

When in Berlin, I used to sleep in the former West, on or near Savignyplatz—and I still list good options there. But these days, the focus of Berlin is in the East, and I've recommended places in the colorful Prenzlauer Berg district. Berliners say that this sort of homey, homogenous neighborhood is in the heart of the *Kiez* (literally "gravel").

Berlin is packed and hotel prices go up on holidays, including Green Week in mid-January, Easter weekend, the first weekend

Sleep Code

(€1 = about $1.30, country code: 49, area code: 030)
S = Single, **D** = Double/Twin, **T** = Triple, **Q** = Quad, **b** = bathroom, **s** = shower only. Unless otherwise noted, credit cards are accepted, English is spoken, and breakfast is included.

To help you sort easily through these listings, I've divided the accommodations into three categories, based on the price for a standard double room with bath:

$$$ **Higher Priced**—Most rooms €125 or more.
$$ **Moderately Priced**—Most rooms between €85-125.
$ **Lower Priced**—Most rooms €85 or less.

Prices can change without notice; verify the hotel's current rates online or by email.

in May, Ascension weekend in May, German Unity Day (Oct 3), Christmas, and New Year's. Keep in mind that many hotels have limited staff after 20:00, so if you're planning to arrive after that, let the hotel know in advance.

In Eastern Berlin
Prenzlauer Berg

If you want to sleep in the former East Berlin, set your sights on the colorful and fun Prenzlauer Berg district. After decades of neglect, this corner of eastern Berlin has quickly come back to life. Gentrification has brought Prenzlauer Berg great hotels, tasty ethnic and German eateries (see "Eating in Berlin," later), and a happening nightlife scene. Think of all the graffiti as just some people's way of saying they care. The huge and impersonal concrete buildings are enlivened with a street fair of fun little shops and eateries.

This loosely defined area is about 1.5 miles north of Alexanderplatz, roughly between Kollwitzplatz and Helmholtzplatz, and to the west, along Kastanienallee (known affectionately as "Casting Alley" for its generous share of beautiful people). The closest U-Bahn stops are U-2: Senefelderplatz at the south end of the neighborhood, U-8: Rosenthaler Platz in the middle, or U-2: Eberswalder Strasse at the north end. Or, for less walking, take the S-Bahn to Hackescher Markt, then catch tram #M1 north.

$$$ Precise Hotel Myer's Berlin rents 52 simple, small rooms. The gorgeous public spaces include a patio and garden. This peaceful hub—off a quiet garden courtyard and tree-lined street, just a five-minute walk from Kollwitzplatz or the nearest U-Bahn stop (Senefelderplatz)—makes it hard to believe you're in a capi-

BERLIN

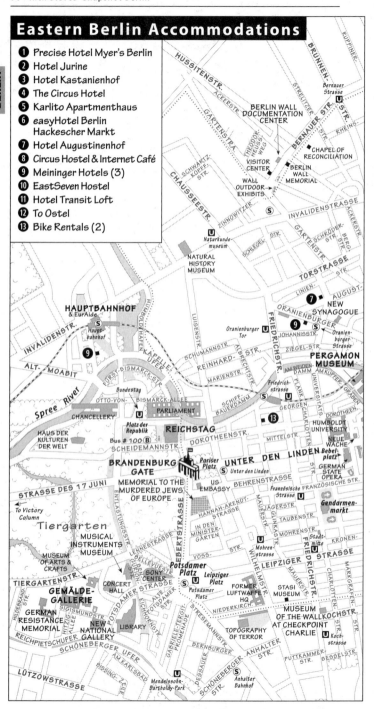

Eastern Berlin Accommodations

1 Precise Hotel Myer's Berlin
2 Hotel Jurine
3 Hotel Kastanienhof
4 The Circus Hotel
5 Karlito Apartmenthaus
6 easyHotel Berlin Hackescher Markt
7 Hotel Augustinenhof
8 Circus Hostel & Internet Café
9 Meininger Hotels (3)
10 EastSeven Hostel
11 Hotel Transit Loft
12 To Ostel
13 Bike Rentals (2)

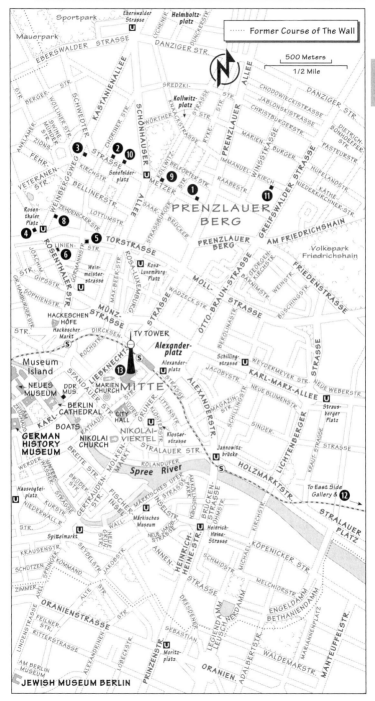

BERLIN

tal city. Their four classes of rooms range from three to five stars, hence the wide price range (Db-€95-200, price also depends on season—check rates online for your dates, air-con in some rooms, elevator, free Internet access and Wi-Fi, Metzer Strasse 26, tel. 030/440-140, fax 030/4401-4104, www.myershotel.de, myers@ precisehotels.com).

$$$ Hotel Jurine (zhoo-REEN—the family name) is a pleasant 53-room business-style hotel whose friendly staff aims to please. In good weather, you can enjoy the breakfast buffet on the lush backyard patio (Sb-€90-110, Db-€130-160, extra bed-€37, rates vary by season, check their website for discounts July-Aug, skip breakfast to save a few euros, elevator, free Wi-Fi, parking garage-€13.50—reserve ahead, Schwedter Strasse 15, 10-minute walk to U2: Senefelderplatz, tel. 030/443-2990, fax 030/4432-9999, www.hotel-jurine.de, mail@hotel-jurine.de).

$$ Hotel Kastanienhof feels less urban-classy and more like a traditional small-town German hotel. It's wonderfully located on the Kastanienallee #M1 tram line, with easy access to the Prenzlauer Berg bustle. Its 38 slightly overpriced rooms come with helpful service (Sb-€79-94, Db-€105-140, extra bed-€29, reception closed 22:00-6:30—call ahead to make arrangements to get key if you'll arrive late, elevator, free cable Internet in rooms, Wi-Fi in lobby, parking-€9/day, 20 yards from #M1 Zionskirche tram stop at Kastanienallee 65, tel. 030/443-050, fax 030/4430-5111, www.kastanienhof.biz, info@kastanienhof.biz).

$$ The Circus Hotel, run by the popular hostel listed later, caters to youth hostelers who've outgrown the backpacker lifestyle. Each of its 60 colorful, trendy rooms has a unique bit of decoration. It overlooks a busy intersection, so there's some nighttime noise—try asking for a quieter back room. Owing to its idealistic youth-hostel roots, it's very service-oriented, with lots of included extras, a very "green" attitude, and occasional special events for guests (Sb-€70, small standard Db-€80, larger Db-€90, junior suite Db-€100, breakfast-€4-8, elevator, free Internet access and Wi-Fi, mellow ground-floor restaurant, Rosenthaler Strasse 1, directly at U8: Rosenthaler Platz, tel. 030/2000-3939, www.circus-berlin.de, info@circus-berlin.de). The Circus also offers a range of spacious, modern **apartments** two blocks away on Choriner Strasse (Db-€130-€250 depending on size and furnishings, 3-night minimum stay preferred).

$ Karlito Apartmenthaus offers 12 well-located, modern, and comfortable apartments on a tranquil side street and above a hip café near Hackescher Markt. All of the sleek, Ikea-esque units have miniature balconies and are fully equipped (Sb-€62-77, Db-€72-85, price depends on season, extra person-€15, up to 2 children under 8 sleep free with 2 paying adults, breakfast in Café

Lois-€5, no minimum stay, elevator, free Wi-Fi, bike rental-€8/ day, Linienstrasse 60—check in at Café Lois around the corner on Gormannstrasse, 350 yards from S-Bahn: Hackescher Markt, even closer to U8: Rosenthaler Platz, mobile 0179-704-9041, www.kar lito-apartments.de, info@karlito-apartments.de).

BERLIN

$ **easyHotel Berlin Hackescher Markt** is part of an unapologetically cheap Europe-wide chain where you pay for exactly what you use—nothing more, nothing less. Based on parent company easyJet's sales model of nickel-and-dime air travel, the hotel has inexpensive base rates (small Db-€25-65, larger Db-€35-65, prices vary by season, it's cheaper to book earlier), then charges you separately for optional extras (breakfast, Wi-Fi, using the TV, and so on). The 125 orange-and-gray rooms are very small, basic, and feel popped out of a plastic mold, but if you skip the extras, the price is right, and the location—at the Hackescher Markt end of Prenzlauer Berg—is wonderful (air-con, elevator, after booking online call to request a quieter back room, Rosen-thaler Strasse 69, tel. 030/4000-6550, www.easyhotel.com).

Near Oranienburger Strasse: $$$ **Hotel Augustinenhof** is a clean hotel with 66 spacious rooms, nice woody floors, and some of the most comfortable beds in Berlin. While not exactly in Prenzlauer Berg, the hotel is on a side street near all of the Oranienburger Strasse action. Rooms in front overlook the courtyard of the old Imperial Post Office, rooms in back are a bit quieter, and all rooms have old, thin windows (official rates: Sb-€119, Db-€151—but you'll likely pay closer to Db-€99, elevator, free Wi-Fi or cable Internet in rooms, Auguststrasse 82, 50 yards from S-Bahn: Oranienburger Strasse, tel. 030/308-860, fax 030/308-86100, www.hotel-augustinenhof.de, augustinen-hof@albrechtshof-hotels.de).

Hostels in Eastern Berlin

Berlin is known among budget travelers for its fun, hip hostels. These range from upscale-feeling hostels with some hotelesque private rooms comfortable enough even for non-hostelers, to more truly backpacker-type places where comfort is secondary to socializing. These are scattered around eastern Berlin, including some (Circus, Meininger, and EastSeven) in the Prenzlauer Berg area just described.

Comfortable Hostels with Hotelesque Rooms

$ **Circus** is a brightly colored, well-run place with 230 beds, a trendy lounge with upscale ambience, and a bar downstairs. It has typical hostel dorms as well as some very hotel-like private rooms; for a step up in quality, see the listing for the Circus Hotel, earlier (€19/bed in 8- to 10-bed dorms, €23/bed in 4- to 5-bed dorms,

S-€43, Sb-€53, D-€56, Db-€70, T-€75, 2-person apartment with kitchen-€85, 4-person apartment-€140, breakfast-€4-8, no curfew, elevator, pay Internet access, free Wi-Fi, bike rental, Weinbergsweg 1A, U8: Rosenthaler Platz, tel. 030/2000-3939, www.circus-berlin.de, info@circus-berlin.de).

$ **Meininger** is a Europe-wide budget-hotel chain with several locations in Berlin. With sleek, nicely decorated rooms, these are a great-value budget option, even for non-hostelers. They have three particularly appealing branches: in Prenzlauer Berg (Schönhauser Allee 19 on Senefelderplatz), at Oranienburger Strasse 67 (next to the Aufsturz pub), and near the Hauptbahnhof, at Ella-Traebe-Strasse 9 (rates vary by availability, but usually €18-19/bed in 6-bed dorms, Sb-€52, Db-€70, Tb-€86; rates at Hauptbahnhof location about €5-10 more; all locations: breakfast-€5.50, elevator, 24-hour reception, pay Internet access, free Wi-Fi in lobby, tel. 030/666-36100, www.meininger-hostels.de).

Backpacker Havens

$ **EastSeven Hostel** rents the best cheap beds in Prenzlauer Berg. It's sleek and modern, with all the hostel services and more: 60 beds, inviting lounge, fully equipped guests' kitchen, lockers, garden, and bike rental. Children are welcome. Easygoing people of any age are comfortable here (€18/bed in 8-bed dorms, €22/bed in 4-bed dorms with private bathroom—or €20/bed in dorm with bathroom down the hall, S-€38, D-€52, T-€66, private rooms have bathrooms down the hall, includes sheets, towel-€1, continental breakfast-€2, free Internet access and Wi-Fi, laundry-€5, no curfew, 100 yards from U2: Senefelderplatz at Schwedter Strasse 7, tel. 030/9362-2240, www.eastseven.de, info@eastseven.de).

$ **Hotel Transit Loft,** actually a hostel, is located in a refurbished factory. Its 62 clean, high-ceilinged, modern rooms and wide-open lobby have an industrial touch. The reception—staffed by friendly, hip Berliners—is open 24 hours, with a bar serving drinks all night long (€21/bed in 4- to 6-bed dorms, Sb-€59, Db-€69, Tb-€89, includes sheets and breakfast, elevator, cheap Internet access, free Wi-Fi, fully wheelchair-accessible, down alley facing inner courtyard at Immanuelkirchstrasse 14A; U2/U5/U8 or S-Bahn: Alexanderplatz, then tram #M4 to Hufelandstrasse and walk 50 yards; tel. 030/4849-3773, fax 030/4405-1074, www.transit-loft.de, loft@hotel-transit.de).

$ **Ostel** is a fun retro-1970s-DDR apartment building that re-creates the lifestyle and interior design of a country relegated to the dustbin of history. All the furniture and room decorations have been meticulously collected and restored to their former socialist glory—only the psychedelic wallpaper is a replica. Guests buy ration vouchers (€7.50/person) for breakfast in the attached restaurant. Kitschy, sure—but also clean and memorable (€15/bed in a 4- or 6-bed "Pioneer Camp" room or in 12-bunk dorm—includes lockers, S-€33, Sb-€40, D-€54, Db-€61, 4-person apartments-€120, includes sheets and towels, 24-hour reception, free Wi-Fi in lobby, bike rental, free parking, free collective use of the people's barbeque, right behind Ostbahnhof station on the corner of Strasse der Pariser Kommune at Wriezener Karree 5, tel. 030/2576-8660, www.ostel.eu, contact@ostel.eu).

In Western Berlin: Near Savignyplatz and Bahnhof Zoo

While Bahnhof Zoo and Ku'damm are no longer the center of the action, this western Berlin neighborhood is still a comfortable and handy home base (thanks to its easy transit connections to the rest of the city). The streets around the tree-lined Savignyplatz (a 10-minute walk behind the station) have a neighborhood charm, with an abundance of simple, small, friendly, good-value places to sleep and eat. The area has an artsy aura going back to the cabaret days in the 1920s, when it was the center of Berlin's gay scene. The hotels and pensions I list here—which are all a 5- to 15-minute walk from Bahnhof Zoo and Savignyplatz (with S- and U-Bahn stations)—are generally located a couple of flights up in big, run-down buildings. Inside, they're clean and spacious enough so that their well-worn character is actually charming. Asking for a quieter room in back gets you away from any street noise. Of the accommodations listed here, Pension Peters offers the best value for budget travelers.

$$ Hecker's Hotel is a modern, four-star business hotel with 69 big, fresh rooms and all the Euro-comforts. Their "superior" rooms cost €10 more than their "comfort" rooms, and—while the same size—have more modern furnishings and air-conditioning. Herr Kiesal promises free breakfasts (otherwise €16/person) for those reserving direct with this book (Sb-€85, Db-usually €95-100—though all rooms €180 during conferences, generally €100 July-Aug, look for deals on their website, non-smoking rooms, elevator, free Wi-Fi, parking-€12-18/day, between Savignyplatz and Ku'damm at Grolmanstrasse 35, tel. 030/88900, fax 030/889-0260, www.heckers-hotel.com, info@heckers-hotel.com).

$$ Hotel Askanischerhof, the oldest B&B in Berlin, is posh as can be, with 16 sprawling, antique-furnished living rooms you can call home. Photos on the walls brag of famous movie-star guests. It oozes Old World service and classic Berlin atmosphere (Sb-€110, Db-€120, Tb-€130, elevator, free Wi-Fi, free parking, Ku'damm 53, tel. 030/881-8033, fax 030/881-7206, www.askanischer-hof.de, info@askanischer-hof.de).

$$ Hotel Astoria is a friendly three-star business-class hotel

Western Berlin

1 Hecker's Hotel
2 Hotel Askanischerhof
3 Hotel Astoria
4 Hotel Carmer 16
5 Hotel-Pension Funk
6 Hotel Bogota
7 Pension Peters
8 Restaurant Marjellchen
9 Rest. Leibniz-Klause
10 Dicke Wirtin Pub
11 To Restaurant Weyers
12 Café Literaturhaus
13 Die Zwölf Apostel Rest,
14 Zillemarkt Restaurant
15 Technical University Mensa
16 Ullrich Supermarkt
17 Schleusenkrug Beer Garden
18 Winter Garden Buffet
19 A Trane Jazz Club
20 Bar Jeder Vernunft
21 Internet Café
22 Fat Tire Bikes

with 32 comfortably furnished rooms and affordable summer and weekend rates (Db-€108-126, often Db-€80 in summer, check their website for deals, non-smoking floors, elevator, free Wi-Fi and Internet access, bike rental, parking-€9/day, around corner from Bahnhof Zoo at Fasanenstrasse 2, tel. 030/312-4067, www.hotelastoria.de, info@hotelastoria.de).

$$ **Hotel Carmer 16,** with 34 bright and airy (if a bit dated) rooms, is both business-like and homey, and has an inviting lounge and charming balconies (Db-€99 for those reserving direct with this book, extra person-€30, some rooms have balconies, family suites, elevator and a few stairs, free Wi-Fi, parking €9.50/day, Carmerstrasse 16, tel. 030/3110-0500, fax 030/3110-0510, www.hotel-carmer16.de, info@hotel-carmer16.de).

$$ **Hotel-Pension Funk,** the former home of a 1920s silent-movie star, is a delightfully quirky time warp. Kind manager Herr Michael Pfundt offers 15 elegant old rooms with rich Art Nouveau furnishings (S-€42, Ss-€60, Sb-€72, D-€72, Ds-€85, Db-€99,

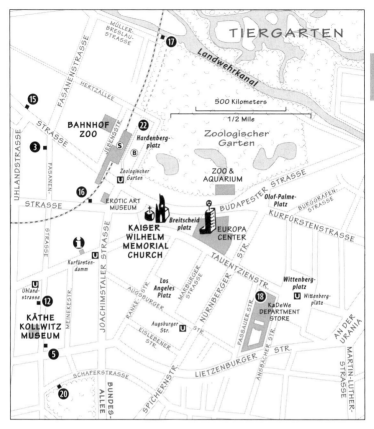

extra person-€25, cash preferred, free Wi-Fi, a long block south of Ku'damm at Fasanenstrasse 69, tel. 030/882-7193, www.hotel-pensionfunk.de, berlin@hotel-pensionfunk.de).

$$ Hotel Bogota is a slumbermill just steps off Ku'damm, renting 115 rooms in a sprawling maze of a building that used to house the Nazi Chamber of Culture. A creaky, well-worn place with big, simple rooms and old furniture, it has the feel of a once-grand hotel (S-€49, Ss-€62, Sb-€98, D-€77, Ds-€84, Db-€89-150, extra bed-€21, check their website for deals and great last-minute prices in summer, children under 14 free, elevator, free Wi-Fi and Internet access, little back garden, 10-minute walk from Savigny-platz at Schlüterstrasse 45, tel. 030/881-5001, fax 030/883-5887, www.hotel-bogota.de, info@hotel-bogota.de).

$ Pension Peters, run by a German-Swedish couple, is sunny and central, with a cheery breakfast room and a super-friendly staff who go out of their way to help their guests. With its sleek Scandinavian decor and 34 renovated rooms, it's a good choice. Some of the ground-floor rooms facing the back courtyard are a bit dark—and cheaper for the inconvenience (Sb-€58, Db-€79, big Db-€85, extra bed-€15, family room-€85, these special prices offered only with this book in 2013-mention when you reserve, up to 2 kids under 13 free with 2 paying adults, cash preferred, free Wi-Fi and Internet access, bike rental, 10 yards off Savignyplatz at Kantstrasse 146, tel. 030/312-2278, www.pension-peters-berlin.de, info@pension-peters-berlin.de, Annika and Christoph with help from his sister, Daisy).

Eating in Berlin

There's a world of restaurants to choose from in this ever-changing city. Your best approach may be to select a neighborhood and browse until you find something that strikes your fancy, rather than seeking out a particular restaurant.

Don't be too determined to eat "Berlin-style." The city is known only for its mildly spicy sausage and for its street food (*Currywurst* and *Döner Kebab*—see the sidebar on the next page).Germans—especially Berliners—consider their food old-school; when they go out to eat, they're not usually looking for the "traditional local fare" many travelers are after. Nouveau German is California cuisine with scant memories of wurst, kraut, and pumpernickel. If the kraut is getting the wurst of you, take a break with some international or ethnic offerings—try one of the many Turkish, Italian, pan-Asian, and Balkan restaurants.

Colorful pubs—called *Kneipen*—offer light, quick, and easy meals and the fizzy local beer, *Berliner Weiss*. Ask for it *mit Schuss* for a shot of fruity syrup in your suds.

In Eastern Berlin
Near Unter den Linden
While this government/commercial area is hardly a hotspot for eateries, I've listed a few places handy for your sightseeing, all a short walk from Unter den Linden.

Cheap Eats: Bier's **Curry und Spiesse,** under the tracks at the Friedrichstrasse S-Bahn stop, is a great, greasy, cheap, and generous place for an old-fashioned German hot dog. This is the local favorite near Unter den Linden for €2 *Currywurst.* Experiment with variations (the *Flieschspiess* is excellent) and sauces—and don't hold the fried *Zwiebeln* (onions). You'll munch standing at a counter, where the people-watching is great (daily 11:00-5:00 in the morning; from inside the station, take the Friedrichstrasse exit and turn left).

Near the Pergamon Museum: Georgenstrasse, a block behind the Pergamon Museum and under the S-Bahn tracks, is lined with fun eateries filling the arcade of the train trestle—close to the

Berliner Street Fare

In Berlin, it's easy to eat cheap, with a glut of *Imbiss* snack stands, bakeries (for sandwiches), and falafel/kebab counters.

Train stations have grocery stores, as well as bright and modern fruit-and-sandwich bars.

Sausage stands are everywhere (I've listed a couple of local favorites). Most specialize in **Currywurst,** created in Berlin after World War II, when a fast-food cook got her hands on some curry and Worcestershire sauce from British troops stationed here. It's basically a grilled *Bockwurst*-type pork sausage smothered with curry sauce. *Currywurst* comes either *mit Darm* (with casing) or *ohne Darm* (without casing). If the casing is left on to grill, it gives the sausage a smokier flavor. (*Berliner Art*—"Berlin-style"—means that the sausage is boiled *ohne Darm*, then grilled.) Either way, the grilled sausage is then chopped into small pieces or cut in half (East Berlin style) and topped with sauce. While some places simply use ketchup and sprinkle on some curry powder, real *Currywurst* joints use tomato paste, Worcestershire sauce, and curry. With your wurst comes either a toothpick or small wooden fork; you'll usually get a plate of fries as well, but rarely a roll. You'll see *Currywurst* on the menu at some sit-down restaurants, but local purists say that misses the whole point: You'll pay triple and get a less authentic dish than you would at a street stand under elevated S-Bahn tracks.

Other good street foods to consider are *Döner Kebab* (Turkish-style skewered meat slow-roasted and served in a sandwich) and *Frikadelle* (like a hamburger patty; often called *Bulette* in Berlin).

sightseeing action but in business mainly for students from nearby Humboldt University. **Deponie3** is a trendy Berlin *Kneipe* usually filled with students. Garden seating in the back is nice if you don't mind the noise of the S-Bahn passing directly above you. The interior is a cozy, wooden wonderland of a bar with several inviting spaces. They serve basic salads, traditional Berlin dishes, and hearty daily specials (€4-8 breakfasts, good €8 brunch Sun 10:00-15:00, €5-11 lunches and dinners, open daily from 9:00, sometimes live music, Georgenstrasse 5, tel. 030/2016-5740). For Italian food, a branch of **Die Zwölf Apostel** is nearby (daily until 24:00, food served until 22:00; described later, under "Near Savignyplatz").

In the Heart of Old Berlin's Nikolai Quarter: The *Nikolaiviertel* marks the original medieval settlement of Cölln, which would eventually become Berlin. The area was destroyed during the war but was rebuilt for Berlin's 750th birthday in 1987. The whole area has a cute, cobbled, and characteristic old town feel...Middle Ages meets Socialist Realism. Today, the district is pretty soulless by day but a popular restaurant zone at night. **Bräuhaus Georgbrau** is a thriving beer hall serving homemade suds on a picturesque courtyard overlooking the Spree River. Eat in the lively and woody but mod-feeling interior, or outdoors with fun riverside seating—thriving with German tourists. It's a good place to try one of the few typical Berlin dishes: *Eisbein* (boiled ham hock) with sauerkraut and mashed peas with bacon (€10 with a beer and schnapps). The statue of St. George once stood in the courtyard of Berlin's old castle—until the Nazis deemed it too decadent and not "German" enough, and removed it (€10-13 plates, three-foot-long sampler board with a dozen small glasses of beer, daily 10:00-24:00, 2 blocks south of Berlin Cathedral and across the river at Spreeufer 4, tel. 030/242-4244).

In City Hall: Consider lunching at one of Berlin's many *Kantine*. Located in government offices and larger corporations, *Kantine* offer fast, filling, and cheap lunches, along with a unique opportunity to see Germans at work (though the food can hardly be considered gourmet). There are thousands of *Kantine* in Berlin, but the best is **Die Kantine im Roten Rathaus,** in the basement of City Hall. For less than €4, you can get filling German dishes like *Leberkäse* (German-style baloney) or stuffed cabbage (Mon-Fri 11:00-15:00, closed Sat-Sun, Rathausstrasse 15).

Near Gendarmenmarkt, South of Unter den Linden

The twin churches of Gendarmenmarkt seem to be surrounded by people in love with food. The lunch and dinner scene is thriving with upscale restaurants serving good cuisine at highly competitive prices to local professionals. If in need of a quick-yet-classy lunch, stroll around the square and along Charlottenstrasse. For a quick bite, head to the cheap *Currywurst* stand behind the German Cathedral.

Lutter & Wegner Restaurant is well-known for its Austrian cuisine (*Schnitzel* and *Sauerbraten*) and popular with businesspeople. It's dressy, with fun sidewalk seating or a dark and elegant interior (€9-18 starters, €16-22 main dishes, daily 11:00-24:00, Charlottenstrasse 56, tel. 030/202-9540). They have a second location, called **Beisl am Tacheles,** near the New Synagogue (Oranienburger Strasse 52, tel. 030/2478-1078).

Augustiner am Gendarmenmarkt, next door to Lutter & Wegner, lines its sidewalk with trademark Bavarian white-and-blue-checkerboard tablecloths; inside, you'll find a classic Bavarian beer-hall atmosphere. Less pretentious than its neighbor, it offers good beer and affordable Bavarian classics in an equally appealing location (€6-12 light meals, €10-15 bigger meals, daily 9:00-24:00, Charlottenstrasse 55, tel. 030/2045-4020).

Galeries Lafayette Food Circus is a French festival of fun eateries in the basement of the landmark department store. You'll find a good deli and prepared-food stands, dishing up cuisine that's good-quality but not cheap (most options €10-15, cheaper €8-10 sandwiches and savory crepes, Mon-Sat 10:00-20:00, closed Sun, Friedrichstrasse 76-78, U-Bahn: Französische Strasse, tel. 030/209-480).

Near Checkpoint Charlie: **Fresco Espresso Bar** is a touristy joint, handy for made-to-order sandwiches. Israeli-born Sagi makes his own bread daily and piles on the fixin's for €4-6. This is a popular stop for walking-tour groups: If you get here when they do, expect a line (Mon-Sat 7:30-19:00, Sun 8:00-19:00, in summer until 20:30, Friedrichstrasse 200, tel. 030/2061-6693).

At and near Hackescher Markt

Hasir Turkish Restaurant is your chance to dine with candles, hardwood floors, and happy Berliners savoring meaty Anatolian specialties. As Berlin is the world's largest Turkish city outside of Asia Minor, it's no wonder you can find some good Turkish restaurants here. But while most locals think of Turkish food as fast and cheap, this is a dining experience. The restaurant, in a courtyard next to the Hackeschen Höfe shopping complex, offers indoor and outdoor tables filled with an enthusiastic local crowd. The service can be a bit questionable, so bring some patience (€6-10 starters, €14-20 main dishes, large and splittable portions, daily 11:30-1:00 in the morning, in late evening the courtyard is dominated by an unpleasantly loud underground disco, a block from the Hackescher Markt S-Bahn station at Oranienburger Strasse 4, tel. 030/2804-1616).

Weihenstephaner Bavarian Restaurant serves upmarket Bavarian traditional food for around €10-15 a plate; offers an atmospheric cellar, an inner courtyard, and a busy people-watching street-side terrace; and, of course, has excellent beer (daily 11:00-23:00, Neue Promenade 5 at Hackescher Markt, tel. 030/8471-0760).

Restaurant Simon dishes up tasty Italian and German specialties—enjoy them either in the restaurant's simple yet atmospheric interior, or opt for streetside seating (€6-12 main dishes, daily 12:00-23:00, Auguststrasse 53, at intersection with Kleine Auguststrasse, tel. 030/2789-0358).

Aufsturz, a lively pub with live music, pours more than 100 different beers and 40 varieties of whiskey, and dishes up "traditional Berliner pub grub"—like nachos—and great potato soup for

Eastern Berlin Eateries & Nightlife

1 Bier's Curry und Spiesse
2 Deponie3 Pub
3 Die Zwölf Apostel
4 Bräuhaus Georgbrau
5 Die Kantine im Roten Rathaus
6 Lutter & Wegner Restaurant; Augustiner am Gendarmenmarkt
7 Beisl am Tacheles
8 Galeries Lafayette Food Circus
9 Fresco Espresso Bar
10 Hasir Turkish Restaurant
11 Weihenstephaner Bavarian Restaurant
12 Restaurant Simon

13 Aufsturz Pub
14 Prater Biergarten
15 Zum Schusterjungen Speisegaststätte
16 La Bodeguita del Medio Cuban Bar Restaurant
17 Konnopke's Imbiss
18 Restaurant "Die Schule"
19 Kauf Dich Glücklich
20 Fleischmöbel Pub
21 Gugelhof Restaurant
22 Luigi Zuckermann Deli & Transit Restaurant
23 Metzer Eck Pub
24 Lemongrass Scent
25 Humboldt-Box Café
26 To Café Sibylle

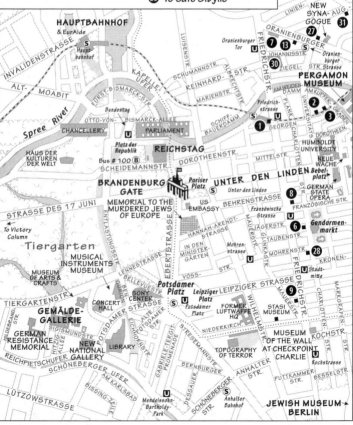

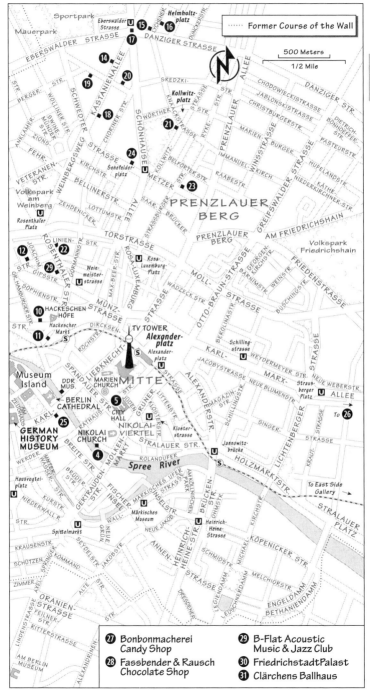

Sportpark

Mauerpark

Helmholtz-platz

Eberswalder Strasse

..... Former Course of the Wall

500 Meters

1/2 Mile

EBERSWALDER STRASSE

DANZIGER STRASSE

CHODOWIECKISTRASSE

DANZIGER STR.

JABLONSKISTRASSE

CHRISTBURGERSTR.

DIETRICH-BONHOEFFER-STR.

PASTEURSTR.

SREDZKI-

Kollwitz-platz

KASTANIENALLEE

SCHÖNHAUSER ALLEE

WÖRTHER STRASSE

KOLLWITZ-

RYKE STR.

PRENZLAUER ALLEE

MARIEN-BURGER

WINSTR.

IMMANUEL-K.IRCH

RAABESTR.

NIEDERKIRCHNER-STR.

KÄTHE-

HUFELANDSTR.

GREIFSWALDER STRASSE

Benefelder-platz

METZER

SAAR-

STRASBURGER

BRÜCKER

BELFORTER STR.

PRENZLAUER BERG

PRENZLAUER BERG

AM FRIEDRICHSHAIN

Volkspark am Weinberg

Volkspark Friedrichshain

Rosenthaler Platz

ZEHDENICKER

LOTTUMSTR.

BELLINERSTR.

KIRCHSTR.

TORSTRASSE

FRIEDENSTRASSE

GEORGEN-KIRCHSTR.

BARNIMSTR.

WEINSTR.

BÜSCHINGSTR.

LINIEN-STR.

ROSENTHALER STR.

GORMANNSTR.

JOACHIMSTR.

GIPSSTR.

SOPHIENSTR.

MAX-BEER-STR.

ROSA-LUXEMBURG-STRASSE

Weinmeister-strasse

Rosa-Luxemburg-Platz

MOLL-STRASSE

OTTO-BRAUN-STRASSE

WADZECK STR.

MÜNZ-STRASSE

HACKESCHEN HÖFE

HACKESCHE

STR.

Hackescher Markt

DIRCKSEN-

BEROLINASTR.

KARL-

Schilling-strasse

ALEXANDERSTR.

WEYDEMEYER STR.

NEUE WEBERSTR.

Strausberger Platz

ALLEE

TV TOWER

Alexander-platz

Alexander-platz

Museum Island

DDR MUS.

MARIEN-CHURCH

SPANDAUER STR.

MITTE

GRUNER-

LITTENSTR.

KLOSTERSTR.

MAGAZIN-STR.

JACOBYSTRASSE

NEUE BLUMENSTR.

SCHILLINGSTR.

SINGER-

STRASSE

LICHTENBERGER

To 26

BERLIN CATHEDRAL

LIEBKNECHT-

CITY HALL

RATHAUS-STR.

MÖLKEN-MARKT

NIKOLAI-VIERTEL

Kloster-strasse

Jannowitz-brücke

GERMAN HISTORY MUSEUM

KARL-

NIKOLAI CHURCH

BREITE STR.

STRALAUER STR.

HOLZMARKTSTR.

KRAUT-

STR.

Hausvogtei-platz

WERDER-

WASSER-

BRÜDER-

GERTRAUDEN-

FISCHER-

INSEL-

STR.

Spree River

ROLANDUFER

MÄRKISCHES UFER

ANKLAMER

PARK

To East Side Gallery

STRALAUER PLATZ

NIEDERWALL-

KURSTR.

WALL-

STR.

NEUE GRÜN-

Märkisches Museum

NEUE JAKOBSTR.

BRÜCKEN-STR.

Heinrich-Heine-Strasse

KÖPENICKER STR.

Spittelmarkt

SEYDELSTR.

JAKOBSTR.

ANNEN-

HEINRICH-HEINE-STR.

SCHMIDSTR.

MICHAEL-KIRCHSTR.

MELCHIORSTR.

ENGELDAMM

KRAUSENSTR.

ALTE

SCHÜTZENSTR.

AXEL-SPRINGER-

KOMMAND.

ZIMMER-

ORANIEN-STRASSE

LINDENSTRASSE

FEILNER-STR.

RITTERSTRASSE

STR.

ALEXANDRINEN-

LEGIENDAMM

LEUSCHNERDAMM

DRESDENER-

BETHANIENDAMM

AM BERLIN MUSEUM

27 Bonbonmacherei Candy Shop

28 Fassbender & Rausch Chocolate Shop

29 B-Flat Acoustic Music & Jazz Club

30 FriedrichstadtPalast

31 Clärchens Ballhaus

under €5. The traditional "Berlin board" for €17 can easily feed three voracious carnivores (daily 12:00-24:00, a block beyond New Synagogue at Oranienburger Strasse 67, tel. 030/2804-7407).

In Prenzlauer Berg

Prenzlauer Berg is packed with fine restaurants—German, ethnic, and everything in between. Even if you're not staying in this area, it's worth venturing here for dinner. Before making a choice, I'd spend at least half an hour strolling and browsing through this bohemian wonderland of creative eateries. Because Prenzlauer Berg sprawls over a wide area, I've organized my listings by neighborhood.

Near Eberswalder Strasse

The area surrounding the elevated Eberswalder Strasse U-Bahn station (on the U2 line, at the confluence of Kastanienallee, Danziger Strasse, Ebwerswalder Strasse, and Schönhauser Allee) is the epicenter of Prenzlauer Berg—a young, hip, and edgy place to eat and drink. While a bit farther north than other areas I recommend (and a 10- to 15-minute walk from most of my recommended hotels), it's worth the trip to immerse yourself in quintessential Prenzlauer Berg.

Prater Biergarten offers two great eating opportunities: a rustic indoor restaurant and a mellow, shaded, super-cheap, and family-friendly outdoor beer garden (with a playground)—each proudly pouring Prater's own microbrew. In the beer garden—Berlin's oldest—you step up to the counter and order (simple €3-5 plates and an intriguing selection of beer munchies, daily in good weather 12:00-24:00). The restaurant serves serious traditional *Biergarten* cuisine and good salads (€7-17 plates, Mon-Sat 18:00-24:00, Sun 12:00-24:00, cash only, Kastanienallee 7, tel. 030/448-5688).

Zum Schusterjungen Speisegaststätte ("The Cobbler's Apprentice") is a classic old-school, German-with-attitude eatery that retains its circa-1986 DDR decor. Famous for its filling €7-10 meals (including various types of schnitzel and Berlin classics such as pork knuckle), it's a no-frills place with quality ingredients and a strong local following. It serves the eating needs of those Berliners lamenting the disappearance of solid traditional German cooking amid the flood of ethnic eateries (small 40-seat dining hall plus outdoor tables, daily 12:00-24:00, corner of Lychener Strasse and Danziger Strasse 9, tel. 030/442-7654).

La Bodeguita del Medio Cuban Bar Restaurant is purely fun-loving Cuba—graffiti-caked walls, Che Guevara posters, animated staff, and an ambience that makes you want to dance. Come early to eat or late to drink. This restaurant has been here since 1994—and in fast-changing Prenzlauer Berg, that's an eternity.

The German-Cuban couple who run it take pride in their food, and the main dishes are big enough to split. You can even puff a Cuban cigar at the sidewalk tables (€4-10 tapas, €6 Cuban ribs and salad, Tue-Sun 18:00-24:00, closed Mon, a block from U2: Eberswalder Strasse at Lychener Strasse 6, tel. 030/4050-0601).

Konnopke's Imbiss, a super-cheap German-style sausage stand, has been a Berlin institution for more than 70 years—it was family-owned even during DDR times. Berliners say Konnopke's

cooks up some of the city's best *Currywurst* (less than €2). Located beneath the U2 viaduct, the stand was demolished in summer of 2010 during roadwork. Berliners rioted, and Konnopke's was rebuilt in a slick glass-and-steel hut (Mon-Fri 10:00-20:00, Sat 12:00-20:00, closed Sun; Kastanienallee dead-ends at the elevated train tracks, and under them you'll find Konnopke's at Schönhauser Allee 44A). Don't confuse this with the nearby Currystation—look for the real Konnopke's.

Restaurant "Die Schule" is a modern place with a no-frills style where you can sample traditional German dishes tapas-style. Assemble a collection of little €2.50 plates of old-fashioned German food you might not try otherwise (good indoor and outdoor seating, €24 full 3-course dinner, daily 11:00-22:00, Kastanienallee 82, tel. 030/780-089-550).

After-Dinner Dessert and Drinks: There are oodles of characteristic funky pubs and nightspots in the area around Helmholtzplatz (and elsewhere in Prenzlauer Berg). Oderberger Strasse is a fun zone to explore; I've listed two places on this street that I particularly like. **Kauf Dich Glücklich** makes a great capper to a Prenzlauer Berg dinner. It serves an enticing array of sweet Belgian waffles and ice cream in a candy-sprinkled, bohemian lounge on a great Prenzlauer Berg street (daily 11:00-24:00, indoor and outdoor seating—or get your dessert to go, wait possible on busy nights, Oderberger Strasse 44, tel. 030/4435-2182). **Fleischmöbel** ("Meat Furniture") is a fun place to drink with locals, despite the lack of beer on tap. Here you'll find strong cocktails, cool classic rock, and a big blackboard. It's a bit hipster-pretentious, but offers a good glimpse into the Prenzlauer Berg lifestyle. Its two smallish rooms unashamedly offer a bit of 1960s retro in an increasingly trendy part of town; on warm evenings, tables fill the sidewalk out front (daily 12:00 until "whenever," Oderberger Strasse 2).

BERLIN

Near Kollwitzplatz

This square, home of the DDR student resistance in 1980s, is now trendy and upscale, popular with hip parents who take their hip kids to the leafy playground park at its center. It's an especially good area to prowl among upmarket restaurants—walk the square and choose. Just about every option offers sidewalk seats in the summer (great on a balmy evening). It's a long block up Kollwitz-strasse from U2: Senefelderplatz.

Gugelhof, right on Kollwitzplatz, is an institution famous for its Alsatian German cuisine. You'll enjoy French quality with German proportions. It's highly regarded, with a boisterous and enthusiastic local crowd filling its minimalist yet classy interior. In good weather, outdoor seating sprawls along its sidewalk. Their fixed-price meals are fun, and they welcome swapping (€20-30 three-course meal, €5-10 starters, €12-20 main dishes, Mon-Fri 16:00-24:00, Sat-Sun 10:00-24:00, reservations required during peak times, where Knaackstrasse meets Kollwitzplatz, tel. 030/442-9229).

Near Rosenthaler Platz, Closer to Hackescher Markt

Surrounding the U8: Rosenthaler Platz station, a short stroll or tram ride from the Hackescher Markt S-Bahn station, and an easy walk from the Oranienburger Strasse action, this busy neighborhood has a few enticing options.

Luigi Zuckermann is a trendy young deli with Israeli/New York style. It's a great spot to pick up a custom-made deli sandwich (choose your ingredients at the deli counter), hummus plate, salad, fresh-squeezed juice, or other quick, healthy lunch. Linger in the interior, grab one of the few sidewalk tables, or take your food to munch on the go (€5-8 meals, daily 8:00-24:00, Rosenthaler Strasse 67, tel. 030/2804-0644).

Transit is a stylish, innovative, affordable Thai/Indonesian/pan-Asian small-plates restaurant at the bustling Hackescher Markt end of Prenzlauer Berg. Sit at one of the long shared tables and dig into a creative menu of €3 small plates and €7 big plates. Two people can make a filling meal out of three or four dishes (daily 11:00-late, Rosenthaler Strasse 68, tel. 030/2478-1645).

Near Senefelderplatz (near Recommended Hotels on Metzer Strasse and Schwedter Strasse)

While neither of these places—in a sedate corner of Prenzlauer Berg near the Senefelderplatz U-Bahn stop—is worth going out of your way for, they're handy for those staying at one of my recommended accommodations nearby.

Metzer Eck is a time-warp *Kneipe* with a family tradition dating to 1913 and a cozy charm. It serves cheap, basic, typical Berlin food with five beers on tap, including the Czech Budvar (€5-8 meals, Mon-Fri 16:00-24:00, Sat 18:00-24:00, closed Sun, Metzer Strasse 33, on the corner of Metzer Strasse and Strassburger Strasse, tel. 030/442-7656).

BERLIN

Lemongrass Scent, with a gaggle of inviting sidewalk tables, offers tasty and affordable "Asian street kitchen" food near several recommended hotels (two-course weekday lunch special for less than €5, €3-4 starters, €5-8 main dishes, Mon-Fri 11:30-24:00, Sat-Sun 12:00-24:00, Schwedter Strasse 12, tel. 030/4057-6985).

In Western Berlin
Near Savignyplatz
Many good restaurants are on or within 100 yards of Savignyplatz, near my recommended western Berlin hotels. Savignyplatz is lined with attractive, relaxed, mostly Mediterranean-style places. Take a walk and survey these; continue your stroll along Bleibtreustrasse to discover many trendier, more creative little eateries.

Restaurant Marjellchen is a trip to East Prussia. Dine in a soft, jazzy elegance in one of two six-table rooms. While it doesn't have to be expensive (€10-18 main courses, €27 two-course meals), plan to go the whole nine yards here, as this can be a great Prussian experience with caring service. The menu is inviting, and the place family-run—all the recipes were brought to Berlin by the owner's mother after she was expelled from East Prussia. Reservations are smart (daily 17:00-23:30, Mommsenstrasse 9, tel. 030/883-2676).

Restaurant Leibniz-Klause is a good place for a dressy German meal. You'll enjoy upscale presentation on white tablecloths, hunter-sized portions, service that's both friendly and professional, and no pretense. Their *Berliner Riesen-Eisbein* ("super-pork-leg on the bone"), with sauerkraut and horseradish, will stir even the tiniest amount of Teutonic blood in your veins (€15-22 plates, good indoor and outdoor seating, daily 12:00-late, Leibnizstrasse near corner with Mommsenstrasse, tel. 030/323-7068).

Dicke Wirtin is a pub with traditional old-Berlin *Kneipe* atmosphere, six good beers on tap, and solid home cooking at reasonable prices—such as their famously cheap *Gulaschsuppe* (€4). Their interior is fun and pubby, with soccer on the TV; their streetside tables are also inviting. Pickled eggs are on the bar—ask about how these can help you avoid a hangover (€5 daily specials, Bavarian Andechs beer on tap, open daily from 12:00, dinner served from 18:00, just off Savignyplatz at Carmerstrasse 9, tel. 030/312-4952).

Weyers offers modern German cuisine in a simple, elegant setting, with dining tables in the summer spilling out into the idyllic neighborhood park in front (€5-10 starters, €10-16 main plates, daily 8:00-24:00, facing Ludwigkirchplatz at corner of Pariser Strasse and Pfalzburger Strasse, tel. 030/881-9378).

Café Literaturhaus is a neighborhood favorite for a light meal, sandwich, or dessert. It has the ambience of an Old World villa with a big garden perfect for their evening poetry readings (€5-15 meals, daily 9:30-24:00, Fasanenstrasse 23, tel. 030/882-5414).

Die Zwölf Apostel ("The Twelve Apostles") is popular for good Italian food. Choose between indoors with candlelit ambience, outdoors on a sun-dappled patio, or overlooking the people-parade on its pedestrian street. A local crowd packs this restaurant for €12 pizzas and €15-20 meals (long hours daily, cash only, immediately across from Savignyplatz S-Bahn entrance, Bleibtreustrasse 49, tel. 030/312-1433).

Zillemarkt Restaurant, which feels like an old-time Berlin *Biergarten,* serves traditional Berlin specialties in the garden or in the rustic candlelit interior. Their *Berliner Allerlei* is a fun way to sample a bit of nearly everything (cabbage, pork, sausage, potatoes and more for a minimum of two people...but it can feed up to five). They have their own microbrew (€10 meals, daily 10:00-24:00, near the S-Bahn tracks at Bleibtreustrasse 48A, tel. 030/881-7040).

Technical University Mensa puts you in a thriving, modern student scene. It feels like a student union building (because it is), with shops, a travel agency, a lounge, kids making out, and lots of international students to chat with. The main cafeteria *(Mensa)* is upstairs—bustling with students and lots of eating options. Streetside is a cafeteria with a more limited selection. Even with the non-student surcharge, eating here is very cheap (€3-5 meals, Mon-Fri 11:00-14:30, closed Sat-Sun, general public entirely welcome but pays the highest of the three prices, coffee bar downstairs with Internet access, just north of Uhlandstrasse at Hardenbergstrasse 34).

Supermarket: The neighborhood grocery store is **Ullrich** (Mon-Sat 9:00-22:00, Sun 11:00-22:00, Kantstrasse 7, under the tracks near Bahnhof Zoo). There's plenty of fast food near Bahnhof Zoo and on Ku'damm.

Near Bahnhof Zoo

Schleusenkrug beer garden is hidden in the park overlooking a canal between the Bahnhof Zoo and Tiergarten stations. Choose from an ever-changing self-service menu of huge salads, pasta, and some German dishes (€7-12 plates, daily 10:00-24:00, food served until 22:00; standing in front of Bahnhof Zoo, turn left and walk 5 minutes, following the path into the park between the zoo and train tracks; tel. 030/313-9909).

Self-Service Cafeterias: The top floor of the famous department store, **KaDeWe,** holds the Winter Garden Buffet view cafeteria, and its sixth-floor deli/food department is a picnicker's nirvana. Its arterials are clogged with more than 1,000 kinds of sausage and 1,500 types of cheese (Mon-Thu 10:00-20:00, Fri 10:00-21:00, Sat 9:30-20:00, closed Sun, U-Bahn: Wittenbergplatz).

Berlin Connections

By Train

Berlin used to have several major train stations. But now that the Hauptbahnhof has emerged as the single, massive central station, all the others have wilted into glorified subway stations. Virtually all long-distance trains pass through the Hauptbahnhof—ignore the other stations.

EurAide is an agent of DeutscheBahn (German Railway) that sells reservations for high-speed and overnight trains, with staff that can answer your travel questions in English (located in the Hauptbahnhof).

From Berlin by Train to: Potsdam (2/hour, 30 minutes on RE1 train; or take S-Bahn from other points in Berlin, S-7 direct, S-1 with a change at Wannsee, 6/hour, 30-50 minutes), **Oranienburg** and Sachsenhausen Concentration Camp Memorial (hourly, 20 minutes; or take the S-1 line from Friedrichstrasse or other stops in town, 3/hour, 45-50 minutes), **Warnemünde** cruiseship port (sporadic but roughly hourly, 3-4 hours, most include a transfer in Rostock), **Wittenberg** (a.k.a. *Lutherstadt Wittenberg,* hourly on ICE, 42 minutes; also every 2 hours on slower regional train, 1.25 hours), **Dresden** (every 2 hours, more with a transfer in Leipzig, 2.25 hours), **Leipzig** (hourly direct, 1.25-1.5 hours), **Erfurt** (hourly, 2.5-3 hours, transfer in Leipzig or Naumburg/Saale), **Eisenach** and Wartburg Castle (hourly, 3-3.5 hours, transfer in Leipzig or Naumburg/Saale), **Hamburg** (1-2/hour direct, 1.75-2 hours), **Frankfurt** (hourly, 4 hours), **Bacharach** (hourly, 6.5-7.5 hours, 1-3 changes), **Würzburg** (hourly, 4 hours, change in Göttingen or Fulda), **Rothenburg** (hourly, 5-6 hours, often via Göttingen or Fulda, then Würzburg, then Steinach), **Nürnberg** (hourly, 4.5 hours), **Munich** (1-2/hour, 6-6.75 hours, every 2 hours direct, otherwise change in Göttingen), **Köln** (hourly, 4.25 hours), **Amsterdam** (6/day direct to Amsterdam Zuid, 6.5 hours; plus 1 night train/day to Amsterdam Centraal, 9.5 hours), **Budapest** (3/day including one overnight, 11.75-14.25 hours, these go via Czech Republic and Slovakia; if your railpass doesn't cover these countries, save money by going via Vienna—but this route takes longer), **Copenhagen** (8/day, 6.75-8 hours, reservation required, change in Hamburg, 1/day direct departs at 11:25; also consider the direct overnight train-plus-ferry route to Malmö Central Station, Sweden, which is just 20 minutes from Copenhagen—covered by a railpass that includes Germany or Sweden), **London** (8/ day, 10-12.75 hours, 2-3 changes—you're better off flying cheap on easyJet or Air Berlin, even if you have a railpass), **Paris** (11/ day, 8-9.5 hours, change in Köln—via Belgium—or in Mannheim, 1 direct 13.25-hour night train), **Zürich** (1-2 hour, 8.5-9 hours, transfer in Basel; 1 direct 11-hour night train), **Prague** (6/day direct, 4.75-5.25 hours, 4 overnight trains, 11-13 hours), **Warsaw** (7/day, 5.5-6.5 hours, reservations required on all Warsaw-bound trains), **Kraków** (1/day direct, 10 hours; 2 more with transfer in Warsaw, 8.5 hours), **Vienna** (8/day, most with 1-2 changes, 2/day plus 1/night are direct, 9.5-12 hours; some via Czech Republic, but trains with a change in Nürnberg, Munich, or Würzburg avoid that country—useful if it's not covered by your railpass). It's wise but not required to reserve in advance for trains to or from Amsterdam or Prague. Train info: Tel. 0180-599-6633, www.bahn.com. Before buying a ticket for any long train ride from Berlin (over 7 hours), consider taking a cheap flight instead (buy it well in advance to get a super fare).

Night trains run from Berlin to these cities: Munich, Paris, Amsterdam, Vienna, Budapest, Malmö (Sweden, near Copenhagen), Basel, and Zürich. There are no night trains from Berlin to anywhere in Italy or Spain. A *Liegeplatz*, a.k.a. *couchette* berth (€13-36), is a great deal; inquire at EurAide at the Hauptbahnhof for details. Beds generally cost the same whether you have a first- or second-class ticket or railpass. Trains are often full, so reserve your *couchette* a few days in advance from any travel agency or major train station in Europe.

By Plane

Berlin has finally whittled down its three airports to a single main hub, the new **Willy Brandt Berlin-Brandenburg International** (opens in March of 2013, airport code: BER, tel. 01805-000-186), designed to handle all air traffic for the area. (For British Air, tel. 01805-266-522; Delta, tel. 01803-337-880; SAS, tel. 01805-117-002; Lufthansa, tel. 01803-803-803.)

Located about 13 miles from central Berlin, next to the formerly busy Schönefeld Airport, it's connected to the city center by fast and frequent Airport Express regional **trains** (ignore the S-Bahn, as there are no direct S-Bahn trains to the city center; likewise, buses to the U-Bahn lines make little sense for anyone heading straight into central Berlin). The airport station (Flughafen Berlin Brandenburg Bahnhof) sits directly under the terminal, a five-minute walk from the airlines' check-in desks. To reach my recommended hotels in eastern Berlin, take the RE7 or RB14 to Alexanderplatz (2/hour, 25 minutes, direction: Dessau or Nauen); for my hotels in western Berlin, take either of those trains to Zoologischer Garten (40 minutes). Two additional trains per hour connect the airport to the main train station, via Potsdamer Platz (RE9, 30 minutes). Any train into the city center costs €3 (railpasses valid—but don't use up a travel day just for this trip). Buy your ticket at a machine and validate it before boarding by stamping it in one of the nearby boxes. A **taxi** to the city center costs about €35 (same rates 24/7).

If you happen to be arriving before the new airport is fully operational, you may find yourself at **Tegel Airport**, four miles from the center (airport code: TXL). Bus #TXL goes between the airport, the Hauptbahnhof (stops by Washingtonplatz entrance), and Alexanderplatz in eastern Berlin. For western Berlin, take bus #X9 to Bahnhof Zoo, or slower bus #109 to Ku'damm and Bahnhof Zoo (€2.30). Bus #128 goes to northern Berlin. A taxi from Tegel Airport costs €15 to Bahnhof Zoo, or €25 to Alexanderplatz (taxis from Tegel levy a €0.50 surcharge).

Berlin is the continental European hub for budget airlines such as easyJet (lots of flights to Spain, Italy, Eastern Europe, the Baltics, and more—book long in advance to get incredible €30-and-less fares, www.easyjet.com). Ryanair (www.ryanair.com), Air Berlin (www.airberlin.com), and German Wings (www.germanwings.com) make the London-Berlin trip (and other routes) dirt-cheap, so consider this option before booking an overnight train. Consequently, British visitors to the city are now outnumbered only by Americans.

By Cruise Ship

The closest cruise-ship terminal to Berlin is 150 miles north, at Warnemünde on the Baltic Sea. Train connections run between the cruise center (Warnemünde station) and Berlin's Hauptbahnhof. Although trains run about every two hours, the trip is hardly worth it—the schedule is sporadic (very roughly hourly), the ride into Berlin takes three to four hours, and by the time you disembark, you won't have time to see much of anything before catching a return train. (The charming old Hanseatic town of Rostock, an easy S-Bahn ride from Warnemünde, could be more satisfying on a short visit.)

If you decide to go for it, board the local S-Bahn at the dock (direction Rostock Hauptbahnhof) and change at the Rostock train station for Berlin. A more convenient, 2.75-hour, direct connection between Warnemünde and Berlin leaves Friday and Saturday mornings at around 9:00 (on other days, this connection departs just before 7:00— too early for most arriving cruise ships). To return to your ship, take the train to Rostock and transfer to the S-Bahn (direction Warnemünde). There's no need to book tickets in advance; it's easy to buy them at the station with cash or credit card.

A better option is a private excursion to Berlin. One of many excursion companies is **ship2shore,** which offers Berlin day trips starting at €99 per person (based on a minimum of 12 people). Their guides are great (tel. 030/243-58058, www.ship2shore.de, info@ship2shore.de). The **Original Berlin Walks** walking-tour company also runs excursions from Warnemünde into Berlin (€760 for up to 3 people in a minibus, €60/additional person up to a maximum of 7—team up with others on your cruise to reduce the per-person cost).

NEAR BERLIN

Potsdam • Sachsenhausen Concentration Camp Memorial

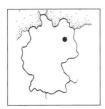

While you could spend days in Berlin and not run out of things to do, a few worthwhile side-trips are just outside the city center (within an hour of downtown Berlin). Frederick the Great's opulent palace playground at Potsdam is a hit with those who enjoy ornate interiors and pretty parks. At the opposite end of the city—and the sightseeing spectrum—Sachsenhausen Concentration Camp Memorial provides a somber look at the Nazis' mass production of death during the Holocaust. A third side-trip possibility—the small town of Wittenberg, with excellent Martin Luther-related sights—is within a 45-minute train ride of Berlin.

Planning Your Time

Either Potsdam or Sachsenhausen can take anywhere from a half-day to a full day of your time, depending on your interests. Think twice before visiting Potsdam on a Monday (when Sanssouci Palace is closed) or a Tuesday (when the New Palace is closed); make your pilgrimage to Sachsenhausen any day but Monday (when the grounds are open but interior exhibits are closed).

Potsdam: It takes about an hour one-way from downtown Berlin to the palaces at Potsdam (including the train to Potsdam, then a bus to the palace of your choice). Visiting either Sanssouci or the New Palace takes about an hour to an hour and a half, plus a potential wait for your Sanssouci entry time (aim to arrive at Sanssouci by 10:00 to avoid waiting in the ticket line) and about a half-hour on foot to connect them. Give yourself five hours round-trip to do the whole shebang (the two palaces are

Near Berlin

To Rostock & Warnemünde

SACHSENHAUSEN CONCENTRATION CAMP

Oranienburg ● ↖Bus #804 & #821 or Walk

Note:
Map shows main rail lines.
Oranienburg/Sachsenhausen can also be reached from Berlin via S-Bahn (S-1) line.
Potsdam can be reached via S-7.

3 Miles
5 Kilometers

To Szczecin (Poland)

TEGEL AIRPORT

COURSE OF FORMER WALL

CITY LIMITS

To Frankfurt & Hamburg

Tegelersee   Bus #X9 & #109

SPANDAU

HAUPTBAHNHOF

Bus #TXL

CHARLOTTEN-BURG

ZOO STN.

OST-BAHNHOF

Berlin Center

Spree R.

To Warsaw (Poland)

Wannsee   *Grünewald*

Müggelsee

NEW PALACE

SANSSOUCI PALACE

Bus #695 or Walk

● **Potsdam**

Templinersee

CITY LIMITS

SCHÖNEFELD AIRPORT & FUTURE SITE OF WILLY BRANDT INT'L AIRPORT (2013)

To Wittenberg, Erfurt, Leipzig, Dresden & Nürnberg

quite different but complementary, and connected by a pleasant stroll through the park). On a quicker visit, you can make a bee-line from the train station to your choice of palaces (Sanssouci is closer and more intimate, but may require a wait; New Palace is grander but at the far end of the park). It's tempting to stretch your Potsdam visit into a full day so you can linger in the park and tour other royal buildings, poke around the inviting town center of Potsdam, or visit nearby attractions (such as Cecilien-hof, the site of the post-WWII Potsdam Conference).

If you're an avid cyclist, it's particularly enjoyable to combine a visit to Potsdam with a bike ride along skinny lakes and through green parklands back into the city (rent a bike in Berlin and bring it on the train).

Sachsenhausen: Two hours at the camp is enough for a quick walk through the grounds, but three hours is a minimum if you want to read the many worthwhile exhibits. Factoring in transit time, leave yourself at least six hours round-trip from central Berlin.

Both: For an exhausting day of contrasts, you could get an early start to visit Sachsenhausen (opens at 8:30), munch a picnic lunch on the train down to Potsdam (connected by the S-1 line in about 1.5 hours, with a change at Wannsee; several basic lunch options in Potsdam train station), and tour Frederick the Great's palaces before collapsing on an evening train back to Berlin.

Potsdam

Featuring a lush park strewn with the escapist whimsies of Frederick the Great, the sleepy town of Potsdam has long been Berlin's holiday retreat. And until the City Palace in downtown Berlin is rebuilt, it's your best opportunity to get a taste of Prussia's Hohenzollern royalty. While Potsdam's palaces are impressive, they don't quite crack Europe's top 10—perhaps because the audioguides don't inject the Hohenzollerns' personalities into the place (or maybe the Hohenzollerns were really that boring). But Potsdam is convenient to reach from downtown Berlin, and it makes for a great break from the city's heavy history. It's also ideal on a sunny day, thanks to its strolling- and picnic-friendly park.

Getting to Potsdam

You have two easy train options for zipping from Berlin to Potsdam's Hauptbahnhof (main train station; round-trip covered by €6.80 Berlin transit day pass with zones ABC). Direct **Regional Express/RE1 trains** depart twice hourly from Berlin's Bahnhof Zoo (20 minutes to Potsdam), Hauptbahnhof (30 minutes), and Friedrichstrasse (35 minutes; any train to Brandenburg or Magdeburg stops in Potsdam). Note: Some RE1 trains continue past the Potsdam Hauptbahnhof to a stop called Park Sanssouci, a good choice closer to the palaces (check the schedule).

The **S-Bahn** is slightly slower, but more frequent and handier from some areas of Berlin. The S-7 line goes directly to Potsdam from Alexanderplatz, Hackescher Markt, Friedrichstrasse, Hauptbahnhof, Bahnhof Zoo, and Savignyplatz (6/hour, 30-45 minutes depending on starting point). The S-1 line, which requires a transfer at Wannsee, leaves from Potsdamer Platz, Brandenburger Tor, Friedrichstrasse, Oranienburger Strasse, and other city-center stations; after the line ends at Wannsee, cross the platform to an S-7 train, and ride it three more stops to Potsdam (6/hour, about 45-50 minutes total from downtown Berlin).

Orientation to Potsdam

Potsdam is about 15 miles southwest of Berlin. The city center is enjoyable to explore, but the big draws here are Frederick the Great's palaces, which surround the gigantic, sprawling Sanssouci Park at the northwest edge of town.

Tourist Information

A handy TI is inside Potsdam's train station (April-Oct Mon-Sat 9:30-20:00, Sun 10:00-16:00; Nov-March Mon-Sat 9:30-18:00, Sun 10:00-16:00; tel. 0331/2755-8830, www.potsdamtourismus. de). Another TI branch, closer to the town center at Luisenplatz, is less convenient for most visitors (April-Oct Mon-Fri 9:30-18:00, Sat-Sun 9:30-16:00; Nov-March Mon-Fri 10:00-18:00, Sat-Sun 9:30-14:00; Brandenburger Strasse 3, tel. 0331/505-8838). Get a map and ask about bus tours if you're interested (see "Tours in Potsdam," later).

The **palace information office** is very helpful, with friendly English-speaking staff. It's across the street from the windmill near the Sanssouci entrance (daily April-Oct 8:30-18:00, Nov-March 8:30-17:00, tel. 0331/969-4200—then press 1, www.spsg. de; clean WC in same building, €0.30).

To supplement the English tour handouts and audioguides at the palaces, consider picking up the blue "official guide" booklets (available individually for each of the sights, €4 apiece at palace information office and gift shops).

Arrival in Potsdam

From Potsdam's **Hauptbahnhof** (main train station), you have several options for reaching the palaces. It's a long (but scenic) 45-minute **walk** (get directions and pick up a map at the TI), or— easier—you can take a bus or tram. To find the bus/tram stops, exit the station toward *Landtag/Friedrich-Engels-Strasse*; this takes you out the main door, where you'll find a row of stops. Various **buses** leave the station about every 10 minutes and connect to either palace (single ride-€1.80, all-day pass-€3.90, buy tickets at machine on board the bus, also covered by any Berlin pass with zones ABC). The convenient but packed bus #695 cruises through the appealing town center of Potsdam, stopping first at Sanssouci, then at the New Palace (3/hour, 15-20 minutes, leaves from lane 4). Bus #606 only goes to Sanssouci, and bus #605 stops only at the New Palace (3/hour apiece, 10-15 minutes, both leave from lane 5). If you're up for a hike, another option is to take **tram** #91 to Luisenplatz (3/hour, 11 minutes, leaves from lane 1), then walk 20 minutes uphill through the park, which lets you enjoy a classic view of Sanssouci Palace.

If you arrive at Potsdam's **Park Sanssouci Station,** just walk straight out and head up the boulevard called Am Neuen Palais, with the big park on your right-hand side. In about 10 minutes, you'll reach the New Palace.

Tours in Potsdam

Local Tours—The Potsdam TI offers a bus tour of Potsdam sights, plus the interior of Sanssouci Palace. This normally wouldn't be worth the time...except that it's the only way to get into Sanssouci with a live, English-speaking guide (often with some German, too; €27 covers tour, palace, and park in 3.5 hours; April-Oct Tue-Sun at 11:00, no tours Mon or Nov-March; departs from Luisenplatz TI at 11:00 or from train station TI at 11:10; reserve by phone, in summer reserve at least 2 days in advance, tel. 0331/275-8899).

Various bus tours (including hop-on, hop-off options) conveniently connect this town's spread-out sights. Pick up brochures at the TI.

Tours from Berlin—Original Berlin Walks, Vive Berlin, and other companies offer inexpensive all-day tours from Berlin through Potsdam (1-3/weekly, small groups, English-language only, admissions and public transportation not included, doesn't actually go into Sanssouci Palace). **Original Berlin Walks'** tour leaves Berlin at 9:50 every Sunday from April through October (also on Thu June-Sept; €15, no reservations necessary, meet at taxi stand at Bahnhof Zoo, tel. 030/301-9194, www.berlinwalks.de). The guide takes you to Cecilienhof Palace (site of postwar Potsdam conference attended by Churchill, Stalin, and Truman), through pleasant green landscapes to the historic heart of Potsdam for lunch, and finishes outside Sanssouci Palace. The youthful guides of **Vive Berlin** lead private, six-hour tours to Potsdam (reservations required several days in advance, tel. 0157/845-46696, www.viveberlintours.de).

Sights in Potsdam

Frederick the Great's Palaces

Frederick the Great was a dynamic 18th-century ruler who put Prussia on the map with his merciless military prowess. Yet he also had tender affection for the finer things in life: art, architecture, gardens, literature, and other distinguished pursuits. During his reign, Freder-

ick built an impressive ensemble of palaces and other grand buildings around Sanssouci Park, with the two top palaces located at either end. Frederick's super-Rococo Sanssouci Palace is dazzling, while his equally extravagant New Palace was built to wow guests and disprove rumors that Prussia was running out of money after the costly Seven Years' War.

Getting Between the Palaces: It's about a 30-minute walk between Sanssouci and the New Palace. To save time, you can hop on bus #695, which takes you between the palaces in either direction (covered by the cheaper €1.30 *Kurzstrecke* ticket, as well as by a Berlin transit pass with zones ABC). If you do walk, you'll find the park wilder, more forested, and less carefully manicured than other palace complexes, such as Versailles and Vienna's Schönbrunn.

▲▲**Sanssouci Palace**—*Sans souci* means "without a care," and this was the carefree summer home of Frederick the Great (built 1745-

1747). Of all the palatial buildings scattered around Potsdam, this was his actual residence. While the palace is small and the audioguide does little to capture the personality of its former resident, it's worth seeing for its opulence.

Cost and Hours: €12, €8 Nov-March, includes audioguide, April-Oct Tue-Sun 10:00-18:00, Nov-March Tue-Sun 10:00-17:00, closed Mon year-round, last entry 30 minutes before closing; in winter (Nov-March), entrance is with a live guided German tour only (departs about every 20 minutes)—about once an hour, they let English-speakers with audioguides tag along; tel. 0331/969-4200, www.spsg.de.

Crowd-Beating Tips: At this popular sight, your ticket comes with an appointed entry time. (Tickets are sold for the same day only.) For the most stress-free visit, come early: In the summer, if you arrive by 10:00 (when the ticket office opens), you'll get right in. If you arrive after 11:00, plan to stand in line to buy your ticket. You'll probably have to wait for your entry time, too—usually an hour or two later (pass this time visiting the Ladies' Wing and Palace Kitchen or exploring the sprawling gardens; if you have a very long wait, zip over to visit the New Palace, then come back to Sanssouci).

Visiting the Palace: Your ticket covers three parts—The Ladies' Wing (to the left as you face the palace from the front/garden side); the Palace Kitchen (to the right); and the living quarters and festival halls (the main, central part). You can visit the first two sights anytime, but you must report to the main part of the palace at the time noted on your ticket (you'll receive your audioguide there).

The **Ladies' Wing (Damenflügel),** worth a visit only if you have time to kill (and maybe not even then), contains apartments for ladies-in-waiting and servants. Borrow the dull English descriptions and walk past rooms cluttered with cutesy decor. The servants' quarters upstairs have been turned into a painting gallery.

At the **Palace Kitchen (Schlossküche),** see well-preserved mid-19th-century cooking equipment (with posted English information). Hike down the tight spiral staircase to the wine cellar, which features an exhibit about the grapes that were grown on the terraced vineyards out front.

The **Main Palace** was where Frederick the Great spent his summers. The dry audioguide narrates your stroll through the classic Rococo interior, where golden grapevines climb the walls and frame the windows. First explore the Royal Apartments, containing one of Frederick's three libraries (he found it easier to buy extra copies of books rather than move them around), the "study bedroom" where he lived and worked, and the chair where he died. The domed, central Marble Hall resembles the Pantheon in Rome (on a smaller scale), with an oblong oculus, inlaid marble floors, and Corinthian columns made of Carrara marble.

Finally you'll visit the guest rooms, most of which exit straight out onto the delightful terrace. Each room is decorated differently: Chinese, Italian, all yellow, and so on; the niche at the back was for a bed. As you exit (in the servants' quarters), keep an eye out for the giant portrait of Frederick by Andy Warhol.

▲▲**New Palace (Neues Palais)**—This gigantic showpiece palace (with more than 200 rooms) is, in some ways, more impressive than the intimate Sanssouci. While Frederick the Great lived primarily

at Sanssouci, he built the New Palace later (1763-1769) to host guests and dazzle visiting dignitaries. And unlike at Sanssouci, there's rarely a long wait to buy tickets or enter the palace.

Cost and Hours: €6, includes audioguide, April-Oct Wed-Mon 10:00-18:00, Nov-March Wed-Mon 10:00-17:00, closed Tue year-round. To see the king's ho-hum apartments—eight small rooms that are a watered-down version of what you'll see at Sanssouci—you must take a required 45-minute tour in German (€5, offered May-Oct daily at 10:00, 11:00, 14:00, and 16:00). During the off-season (Nov-March), the king's apartments are closed, and you can visit the rest of the New Palace by tagging along with a German tour (with an English audioguide; may have to wait up to 30 minutes for next tour). Tel. 0331/969-4200, www.spsg.de.

Visiting the Palace: The tour includes a pair of loaner slippers (to protect the floors) and a one-hour English audioguide that takes you through the ornate halls. From the Grotto Hall, decorated with seashells, you can peer into the lavish Marble Hall, used for fancy gatherings. Continue on through the eight suites of the Lower Princes' Apartments, which accommodated guests and royal family members. In the 19th and early 20th century, German emperors Frederick III (different from the earlier Frederick who built the place) and Wilhelm II (the last Kaiser) resided here. The Gentlemen's Bedchamber holds the red-canopy bed where Kaiser Frederick III died in 1888. The Ladies' Bedchamber is a reminder that noblemen and their wives slept separately.

Upstairs, the Upper Princes' Quarters include a small blue-tiled bathroom that was later installed for Kaiser Wilhelm II. You'll also find Wilhelm's bedroom, as well as a small painting gallery with portraits of Frederick the Great and Russia's Catherine the Great (who was actually a German princess). From up here, you also get a look into the sumptuous, 52-foot-high Marble Hall, with its ceiling painting of the Greek myth of Ganymede and the floors inlaid with Silesian marble. Through the windows, enjoy the views out into the gardens, which recede into the horizon.

Other Palaces—The two main palaces (Sanssouci and the New Palace) are just the beginning. The sprawling Sanssouci Park con-

tains a variety of other palaces and royal buildings, many of which you can enter. Popular options include the Italian-style **Orangerie** (the last and largest palace in the park, with five royal rooms that must be toured with a German guide, plus a view tower); the **New Chambers** (a royal guest house); the **Chinese House;** and other viewpoints, including the **Klausberg Belvedere** and the **Norman Tower.**

Cost and Hours: Each has its own entry fee and hours, some are open weekends only (get a complete list from the Potsdam TI or the palace information office). If you have plenty of time and really want to see it all, you can buy a combo-ticket that covers all of the palaces at Potsdam (€19 for everything, €15 for all but Sanssouci, sold at palace ticket offices); www.spsg.de.

Bornstedt Royal Estate (Krongut Bornstedt)—Designed to

look like an Italian village, this warehouse-like complex once provided the royal palaces with food and other supplies. Today the estate houses the Bornstedt Buffalo brewery and distillery, which delivers fine brews and (sometimes) schnapps, as it has since 1689. The brewpub's restaurant is a good place for lunch, serving local specialties (€10-16 plates). The kid-friendly grounds also house a wood-fired bakery with fresh bread and pastries. You can watch hatmakers, candlemakers, coopers, potters, and glassmakers produce (and sell) their wares using traditional techniques.

NEAR BERLIN

Cost and Hours: Free except during special events, daily 10:00-19:00, restaurant serves food until 22:00, Ribbeckstrasse 6, tel. 0331/550-650, www.krongut-bornstedt.de.

Getting There: From Sanssouci, walk toward the windmill and follow the street An der Orangerie about 500 yards.

More Sights in Potsdam

Potsdam Town—The easy-to-stroll town center has pedestrianized shopping streets lined with boutiques and eateries. For a small town, this was a cosmopolitan place: Frederick the Great imported some very talented people. For example, Dutch merchants and architects built the Dutch Quarter (Holländisches Viertel, at the intersection of Leiblstrasse and Benkertstrasse) with gabled red-brick buildings that feel like a little corner of Amsterdam. The city also has a good film museum and a museum of Prussian history (both near Breite Strasse). Even if you're just racing through Potsdam on your way to the palaces, you can still catch a glimpse of the town center by riding bus #695 (described earlier, under "Arrival in Potsdam"). Skip Potsdam's much-promoted Wannsee boat rides, which are exceedingly dull.

Cecilienhof—This former residence of Crown Prince William was the site of the historic Potsdam Conference in the summer of 1945. During these meetings, Harry Truman, Winston Churchill, and Joseph Stalin negotiated how best to punish Germany for dragging Europe through another devastating war. It was here that the postwar map of Europe was officially drawn, setting the stage for a protracted Cold War that would drag on for four and half decades. Designed to appear smaller and more modest than it actually is, Cecilienhof pales in comparison to the grand palaces concentrated around Sanssouci Park; it's only worth visiting if you're a WWII or Cold War history buff (or would like to visit the nearby Meierei brewpub).

Cost and Hours: €6, April-Oct Tue-Sun 10:00-18:00,

Nov-March Tue-Sun 10:00-17:00, closed Mon year-round, tel. 0331/969-4224, www.spsg.de.

Eating: Try the brewery called **Meierei** ("Creamery") at Cecilienhof. Its nice beer garden offers spectacular views of the lake, solid German food, and great homemade beer. When you walk down the hill into the restaurant, note the big open field to the right—it used to be part of the Berlin Wall (€6-15 meals, daily 11:00-22:00, follow *Meierei* signs to Im Neuen Garten 10, tel. 0331/704-3211).

Getting There: First, go to the Reiterweg stop, at the northern end of Potsdam (from Sanssouci Palace, take bus #695; from the train station, ride tram #92 or #96). At Reiterweg, transfer to bus #603 (toward Höhenstrasse), and get off at the Schloss Cecilienhof stop.

Babelsberg—Movie buffs might already know that the nearby suburb of Babelsberg (just east of Potsdam) hosts the biggest film studio in Germany, where classics such as *The Blue Angel* and *Metropolis*, as well as recent hits *The Reader* and *Inglourious Basterds*, were filmed (for information about visiting, see www.filmpark-babelsberg.de).

Sachsenhausen Concentration Camp Memorial

About 20 miles north of downtown Berlin, the small town of Oranienburg was the site of one of the most notorious Nazi concentration camps (which collectively claimed the lives of millions of innocent people). Sachsenhausen's proximity to the capital gave it special status as the  place to train camp guards and test new procedures. It was also the site of the Third Reich's massive counterfeiting operation, depicted in the Oscar-winning 2007 movie *The Counterfeiters*. Today Sachsenhausen, worth ▲▲, is open to visitors as a memorial and a museum (Gedenkstätte und Museum Sachsenhausen), honoring the victims and survivors, and teaching visitors about the atrocities that took place here.

Getting There

Take a train to the town of Oranienburg (20-50 minutes); from there, it's a 20-minute walk or a quick trip by bus or taxi to the camp. The whole journey takes just over an hour each way.

From downtown Berlin, a regional train speeds from Hauptbahnhof to Oranienburg (hourly, 20 minutes). Or you can take the S-Bahn (S-1) line from various stops downtown, including Potsdamer Platz, Brandenburger Tor, Friedrichstrasse, and Oranienburger Strasse (3/hour, 45-50 minutes depending on starting point). Note that the slower S-Bahn may not necessarily take longer if you factor in the time it takes to get to the Hauptbahnhof, find the correct platform, and wait for the train. The S-1 line also connects southward to Potsdam (with a change in Wannsee)—making it possible to connect Sachsenhausen and Potsdam's palaces in one extremely busy day.

Once at the Oranienburg train station, it's usually best to **walk** to the memorial (since the bus runs infrequently). Turn right out of the train station and head up Stralsunder Strasse for about two blocks. Turn right under the railroad trestle onto Bernauer Strasse, following signs for *Gedenkstätte Sachsenhausen*. At the traffic light, turn left onto André-Pican-Strasse, which becomes Strasse der Einheit. After two blocks, turn right on Strasse der Nationen, where you'll pass a memorial stone commemorating the death march. This leads right to the camp, where you can enter the grounds through the gaps in the wall.

To avoid the walk, take a taxi or catch **bus** #804 from in front of the Oranienburg station (hourly, every 2 hours on weekends, lane 4; bus #821 also possible but only 4/day; both covered by Berlin transit pass with zones ABC).

Orientation to Sachsenhausen

Cost and Hours: Free, mid-March-mid-Oct Tue-Sun 8:30-18:00, mid-Oct-mid-March Tue-Sun 8:30-16:30; avoid visiting on Mon, when the grounds and visitors center are open but the exhibits inside the buildings are closed; Strasse der Nationen 22.

Information: The visitors center has WCs, a bookshop, and a helpful information desk. If visiting on your own, pick up the good €0.50 map of the camp. Also consider the €3 audioguide, with up to five hours of commentary (includes map). Tel. 03301/200-200, www.gedenkstaette-sachsenhausen.de.

Tours from Berlin: While you can visit Sachsenhausen on your own, a tour helps you understand the camp's complicated and important story. Virtually all walking-tour companies in Berlin offer side-trips to Sachsenhausen. You'll meet in the city,

NEAR BERLIN

Sachsenhausen

BURIAL GROUND

MUSEUM

GUARD TOWER E

WC

BRICK BARRACKS

SOVIET SPECIAL CAMP

100 Meters

100 Yards

MEMORIAL

PERIMETER FENCE

EXECUTION TRENCH

BURIAL GROUND

CREMATORIUM

STATION Z

INDUSTRIAL YARD

WC   WC

LAUNDRY BUILDING

KITCHEN BUILDING
EXHIBITS & FILM

CAMP PRISON

"BOOT TESTING RACK"

Appelplatz

RECONSTRUCTED BARRACKS

FORMER BARRACKS

MAIN GUARD TOWER A
"ARBEIT MACHT FREI" GATE

NEW MUSEUM

INFIRMARY

MORGUE

MASS GRAVES

WC

ENTRANCE

R&R BUILDING

SS COMMANDANT'S HOUSE

Bus #804
(To/From Oranienburg Train Station) B

WC

P

CAMP MODEL

CAMP STREET

PERIMETER FENCE

VISITORS CENTER

STRASSE DER NATIONEN

T-BUILDING

To Oranienburg Train Station

STANDING BUILDINGS

BUILDING FOUNDATIONS

then ride together by train to Oranienburg, and walk to the camp. (Bring along or buy lunch en route, as there's no place to eat at the camp.) The round-trip takes about six hours, much of which is spent in transit—but the time that you spend at the camp is made very meaningful by your guide's commentary.

Check the walking-tour companies' websites, or compare brochures to find an itinerary that fits your schedule. Here are a few options: **Original Berlin Walks** (€15, April-Oct Tue-Fri and Sun at 10:00, runs less frequently off-season), **Vive Berlin** (free because they believe a visit here should be accessible to anyone, tipping the guide is encouraged; Tue, Fri and Sun at 10:00), and **Insider Tour** (€15, Tue-Sun at 10:00).

Eating: You can't buy food at the camp. If you need lunch, bring it with you from Berlin, or buy it at the Oranienburg train station.

Background

Completed in July of 1936, Sachsenhausen was the first concentration camp built under SS chief Heinrich Himmler. It was custom-designed in the panopticon ("all-seeing") model popular in British prisons. The grounds were triangular so they could be observed from a single point, the main guard tower. The design was intended to be a model for other camps, but they soon discovered a critical flaw that prevented its widespread adoption: It was very difficult to expand without interfering with sight lines.

Sachsenhausen was not, strictly speaking, a "death camp" for the mass production of murder (like Birkenau); it was a labor camp, intended to wring hard work out of the prisoners. Many toiled in a brickworks, producing materials that were to be used in architect Albert Speer's grandiose plans for erecting new buildings all over Berlin.

Between 1936 and 1945, about 200,000 prisoners did time at Sachsenhausen; about 50,000 died here, while numerous others were transported elsewhere to be killed (in 1942, many of Sachsenhausen's Jews were taken to Auschwitz). Though it was designed to hold 10,000 prisoners, by the end of its functional life the camp had up to 38,000 people. In the spring of 1945, knowing that the Red Army was approaching, guards took 35,000 able-bodied prisoners on a death march, leading them into the forest for seven days and nights with no rations. Rather than "wasting" bullets to kill them, SS troops hoped that the prisoners would expire from exhaustion. On the eighth day, after 6,000 had already died, the guards abandoned the group in the wilderness, leaving them free. When Soviet troops liberated Sachsenhausen on April 22, 1945, they discovered an additional 3,000 prisoners who had been too weak to walk and were left there to die (all but 300 ended up surviving).

Just three months after the war, Sachsenhausen was converted into a Soviet Special Camp No. 7 for the USSR's own prisoners. It was a notorious "silent camp," where prisoners would disappear with no information. The prisoners were Nazis as well as anti-Stalin Russians. By the time the camp closed in 1950, 12,000 more prisoners had died here.

In 1961, Sachsenhausen became the first concentration camp turned into a memorial.

NEAR BERLIN

The East German government did it largely for propaganda purposes: to deflect attention from the controversial construction of the Berlin Wall and to exalt the USSR as the valiant anti-fascist liberators of the camp and all of Germany (rather than to commemorate the victims).

Since the end of communism, the country has redeveloped Sachsenhausen into a true memorial, with updated museum exhibits (scattered throughout the grounds in various buildings) and an emphasis on preservation—documenting and sharing the story of what happened here.

Self-Guided Tour

There's a lot to experience, but this outline covers the basics.

Entrance

First get your bearings in the **visitors center,** where you can peruse the bookshop, buy a map of the grounds, and rent an audioguide.

In the courtyard next to the visitors center, a **model** of the camp illustrates its unique triangular layout, containing the prisoners' barracks. This allowed guards stationed in tower A (at the main gate) to see everything going on inside those three walls. Along the left side of the triangle is the crematorium, called Station Z. (Nazis perversely joked that inmates entered the camp at A and exited at Z.) The smaller buildings outside the main triangle served as workshops, factories, and extra barracks that were added when the camp ran out of room.

Walk up the dusty lane called Camp Street. On the right is the SS officers' R&R building, nicknamed the **"Green Monster,"** where prisoners were forced to dress up and wait on SS officers. Officials mostly chose Jehovah's Witnesses because they had a strong pacifist code and could be trusted not to attempt to harm their captors.

Turn left through the fence into the courtyard in front of **guard tower A.** The clock on the tower is frozen at 11:07—the exact time that the Red Army liberated the camp (and a reminder that the Soviets—who were initially responsible for turning the camp into this memorial—were the "good guys"). The building on the right—misnamed the **"New Museum"**—has an interesting DDR-era stained-glass window inside, as well as temporary exhibits and information on Oranienburg Concentration Camp (which preceded Sachsenhausen). To the left as you face the guard tower is the **SS commandant's house,** which is being turned into a museum about the administration of the camp.

Go through the gate cruelly marked *Arbeit Macht Frei*— "Work will set you free."

Main Grounds

Entering the triangular field, you can see that almost none of the original buildings still stand. Following the war, the Germans dismantled all of the barracks here in order to use them for building materials. Tracing the perimeter, notice the electric fence and barbed wire. A few feet in front of the

NEAR BERLIN

wall is a gravel track called the **"neutral zone"**—any prisoner setting foot here would be shot. This became a common way for prisoners to attempt suicide. Guards quickly caught on: If they sensed a suicide attempt, they'd shoot to maim instead of kill. It was typical upside-down Nazi logic: Those who wanted to live would die, and those who wanted to die would live.

The daily **roll call** took place in the Appelplatz, the area in front of the guard tower. After a 4:15 wake-up call, prisoners would scramble to eat, bathe, and dress in time for the 5:00 roll call. Dressed in their standard-issue uniforms—thin, striped pajamas and wooden clogs—prisoners would line up while guards, in long coats with angry dogs, barked orders in German and accounted for each person, including those who had died in the barracks overnight. It could take hours, in any weather. One misbehaving prisoner would bring about punishment for all others. One day, after a prisoner escaped, SS officer Rudolf Höss (who later went on to run Auschwitz-Birkenau) forced the entire population of the camp to stand here for 15 hours in a foot of snow and subzero temperatures. A thousand people died.

To the far right, the wooden **barracks** (containing good museum displays and English descriptions) are reconstructed from original timbers. Barrack 38 focuses on the Jewish experience at Sachsenhausen, as well as the general mistreatment of German Jews under the Nazis (including anti-Semitic propaganda). Barrack 39 explains everyday life, with stories following 20 individual internees. You'll see how prisoners lived: long rows of bunks, benches for taking paltry meals, latrines crammed wall-to-wall with toilets, and communal fountains for washing. Inmates would jockey for access to these facilities. The strongest, meanest, most aggressive prisoners—often here because they had been convicted of a violent crime—would be named *Kapo,* the head of the barrack. This was another example of depraved Nazi logic: The worst prisoners (rather than the best) were "promoted." Like many others, this camp had a prostitution ring—the Nazis brought in female inmates from the women's-only Ravensbrück concentration camp and forced them to "reward good prisoners" at Sachsenhausen.

Next to the barracks is the **camp prison,** where political prisoners or out-of-line inmates were sent. It was run not by the SS, but by the Gestapo (secret police), who would torture captives to extract information. Other prisoners didn't know exactly what went on here, but they could hear howls from inside and knew it was no place they wanted to be. This was also where the Nazis held special hostages, including three Allied airmen who had participated in a bold escape from a Nazi prisoner-of-war camp (the basis for *The Great Escape;* they later managed to escape from Sachsenhausen as well, before being recaptured) and Joseph Stalin's son, Yakov

Dzhugashvili, who had been captured during the fighting at Stalingrad. (The Nazis offered to exchange the young man for five German officers. Stalin refused, and soon after, Yakov died here under mysterious circumstances.) The cells contain exhibits about the prisoners and the methods used by their captors. Outside, you'll find three posts (out of an original 15) with iron pegs near the top. Guards would execute people by tying their hands behind their backs, then hanging them on these pegs by their wrists until they died—a medieval method called *strappado.*

Walk around the semicircle toward the buildings in the middle of the camp. On the gravel **"boot-testing track,"** prisoners were forced to put on boots two sizes too small and walk in a circle all day, supposedly to "test" the shoes for fighting at Stalingrad. The patches of gravel show where each of the barrack buildings once stood. A marker represents the location of the gallows, where prisoners would be publicly executed as a deterrent to others.

Two buildings stand in the middle of the triangle. The one on the left is the **laundry building,** with special exhibits on topics such as Operation Bernhard, Sachsenhausen's counterfeiting ring. Nazi authorities created the world's largest counterfeiting operation by forcing inmates who were skilled forgers to create fake bills that would flood the US and British economies and devalue their currencies. The 2007 movie *The Counterfeiters* depicts the moral dilemma the prisoners faced: Do we create perfect fakes, which will ultimately work against our own cause? Or do we risk execution by intentionally doing bad work to sabotage the operation?

On the right is the **kitchen building,** with exhibits that trace

chronologically the history of the camp. You'll learn how Sachsenhausen was actually built by prisoners, and see original artifacts including the gallows, a bunk from the barracks, uniforms, and so on. There are also photos, quotes, and a 22-minute film. The basement walls feature some bizarre cartoons of vegetables preparing themselves to be eaten (these were drawn later by Soviets).

Memorial and Crematorium

Head back to the far end of the camp, dominated by the towering, 130-foot-tall, 1961 pro-communist DDR **memorial** to the victims of Sachsenhausen. The 18 triangles at the top are red, the color designated for political prisoners (rather than honoring the other Nazi victims who died here). At the base of the monument, two prisoners are being liberated by a noble Soviet soldier. The prisoners are unrealistically robust, healthy, and optimistic (they will survive and become part of the proud So-

viet proletariat!). The podium in front was used by the East German army for speeches and rallies—exploiting Sachsenhausen as a backdrop for their propaganda.

Go through the gap in the fence to find the execution trench, used for mass shootings. Because this system proved too inefficient, the Nazis built Station Z, the **crematorium,** where they could execute and dispose of prisoners more systematically. Prior to the camp's liberation by Soviet troops, Nazi guards destroyed the crematorium to remove evidence of their crimes; the ruins are inside the white building. The ramp took

NEAR BERLIN

prisoners down into the "infirmary," while the three steps led up to the dressing room. This is where the Nazis tested Zyklon-B (used five times here, this was the chemical responsible for killing hundreds of thousands at Auschwitz). Most of the building's victims died in the room with the double row of bricks (for soundproofing; the Nazis also blasted classical music to mask noise). Victims would report here for a "dental check," to find out if they had gold or silver teeth that could be taken. They would then stand against the wall to have their height measured—and a guard would shoot them through a small hole in the wall with a single bullet to the back of the skull. (The Nazis found it was easier for guards to carry out their duties if they didn't have to see their victims face-to-face.)

Bodies were taken to be incinerated in the ovens (which still stand). Notice the statue of the emaciated prisoner—a much more accurate depiction than the one at the DDR monument. Outside, a burial ground is filled with ashes from the crematorium.

The Rest of the Camp

Return to the main part of the camp to visit the remaining sights. You can head left, up to the tip of the triangle (behind the big monument) to find the museum about the postwar era, when Sachsenhausen served as a **Soviet Special Camp**—the often-forgotten second act. Nearby is a burial ground for victims of that camp. At this corner of the triangle, the gate in the fence—called **tower E**—holds a small exhibit about the relationship between the camp and the town of Oranienburg.

Or you can turn right and walk along the wall toward the front corner. The long, green barracks were the **infirmary,** used for medical experiments on inmates (and explained by the exhibits inside). This was also where Soviet soldiers found the 3,000 remaining survivors when they liberated the camp. The small building in back was the morgue—Nazis used the long ramp for wheelbarrows bringing in the day's bodies. Behind that is a field with six stones, each marking 50 bodies for the 300 prisoners who died after the camp was freed.

While all of this is difficult to take in, as with all concentration camp memorials, the intention of Sachsenhausen is to share its story and lessons—and prevent this type of tragedy from ever happening again.

DRESDEN

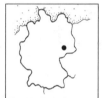

Dresden surprises visitors, with fanciful Baroque architecture in a delightful-to-stroll cityscape, a dynamic history that mingles tragedy with inspiration, and some of the best museum-going in Germany. Today's Dresden is a young and vibrant city, crawling with proud locals, cheery tourists, and happy-go-lucky students who barely remember communism. This intriguing and fun city winds up on far fewer American itineraries than it deserves to. Don't make that mistake.

At the peak of its power in the 18th century, this capital of Saxony ruled most of present-day Poland and eastern Germany from the banks of the Elbe River. Dresden's answer to Louis XIV was Augustus the Strong. As both prince elector of Saxony and king of Poland, he imported artists from all over Europe, peppering his city with fine Baroque buildings and filling his treasury with lavish jewels and artwork. Dresden's grand architecture and dedication to the arts—along with the gently rolling hills surrounding the city—earned it the nickname "Florence on the Elbe."

Sadly, these days Dresden is better known for its destruction in World War II. American and British pilots firebombed the city on the night of February 13, 1945. More than 25,000 people were killed, and 75 percent of the historical center was destroyed. American Kurt Vonnegut, who was a POW in Dresden during the firebombing, later memorialized the event in his novel *Slaughterhouse-Five*. As you walk through Dresden, you may see some circa-1946 photos on display.

During the Cold War, Dresden was in what was facetiously called the "Valley of the Clueless"—the part of East Germany where you couldn't get Western television. Under the communists, Dresden patched up some of its damaged buildings, left many others in ruins, and replaced even more with huge, modern, ugly sprawl. After the Berlin Wall fell and Germany was reunited, new funding became available for Dresden. The city built apartment complexes and shopping centers and rebuilt the Royal Palace and the Frauenkirche. Even though the city plan still feels bombed-out (as in Polish cities such as Warsaw)—with big gaps, wide boulevards, and old streetscapes gone—the transformation has been astonishing, and all the most important historic buildings have been reconstructed.

While bombs devastated the Old Town, they missed most of the New Town, across the river. While well-worn, it retains its prewar character and has emerged as the city's fun and lively people zone—especially the Outer New Town, north of Bautzner Strasse. Most tourists never cross the bridge away from the famous Old Town museums...but a visit to Dresden isn't complete without a wander through the New Town.

Planning Your Time

Dresden, conveniently located about halfway between Prague and Berlin, is well worth even a quick stop. If you're short on time, Dresden's top sights can be seen in a midday break from your Berlin-Prague train ride (each one is less than a 2.5-hour ride away). Catch the early train, throw your bag in a locker at the main train station, follow my self-guided walk, and visit some museums before taking an evening train out. If possible, reserve far ahead to visit one of Dresden's top sights, the Historic Green Vault.

If you have more time, Dresden merits spending at least one night. The city is a handy home base for a quick bike ride to the "Blue Wonder" bridge, a paddleboat cruise along the Elbe, getting back to nature at Saxon Switzerland National Park, or an architectural side-trip to the town of Görlitz (see next chapter).

Orientation to Dresden

Dresden is big, with half a million residents. Its city center hugs a curve on the Elbe River. Despite the city's size, most of its sights are within easy strolling distance along the south bank of the Elbe in the Old Town (Altstadt). South of the Old Town (a 5-minute tram ride or 15-minute walk away) is the main train station (Hauptbahnhof). North of the Old Town, across the river, you'll find the residential-feeling New Town (Neustadt). While the New Town boasts virtually no sights, it's lively, colorful, and fun to explore—especially after dark, when the funky, cutting-edge

DRESDEN

Dresden

1 Hotel Kipping
2 Ibis Hotels Bastei, Königstein & Lilienstein
3 Hotel Bayerischer Hof Dresden
4 Hotel Martha Dresden
5 AHA Hotel
6 Hostel Louise 20
7 Hostel Mondpalast Dresden
8 Wenzel Prager Bierstuben
9 Good Friends Restaurant
10 To Brauhaus am Waldschlösschen
11 To Ball und Brauhaus Watzke
12 Watzke Brauereiausschank am Goldenen Reiter
13 Feldschlösschen Stammhaus
14 Kunsthofpassage
15 Lebowski-Bar
16 Kneipe Raskolnikoff
17 To Carte Blanche & Zora Bars
18 Bike Rental
19 Nightwalk Dresden Meeting Point & Launderette
20 Supermarkets (2)

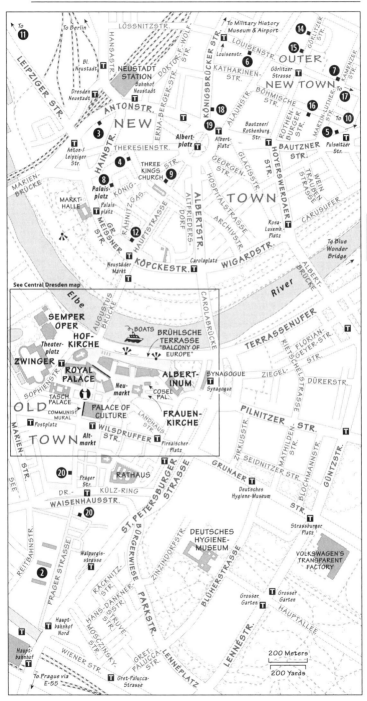

Outer New Town (Äussere Neustadt) sets the tempo for Dresden's emerging nightlife scene.

Tourist Information

Dresden has a tiny TI kiosk in the main hall of the main train station (Hauptbahnhof, daily 9:00-19:00) and a larger office at Schössergasse 23, near the south side of the Royal Palace (May-Dec Mon-Fri 10:00-19:00, Sat 10:00-18:00, Sun 10:00-15:00; Jan-April Mon-Sat 10:00-18:00, Sun 10:00-14:00—or sometimes later, at intersection of Schössergasse and Sporergasse, TIs share phone number—tel. 0351/5016-0160, www.dresden.de/tourismus).

Both TIs stock a handy, free one-page city map with a listing of key sights, hours, and prices on the back, and offer a room-booking service (€3/person). To find out about live entertainment and cultural events, skim the monthly *Theater Konzert Kunst* (free, in German only). Dresden's city website, www.dresden.de, has good information, including a free downloadable city guide and map.

Discount Deals: The two-day **Dresden-City-Card** includes entry to the state-run Zwinger, Royal Palace, and Albertinum museums (but not the Historic Green Vault), use of the city's transit system, and small discounts for many other museums. Think of it as a combi-ticket for the three state-run museums, which pays for itself if you visit two of them and ride the trams a few times (€25, €46 family ticket covers 2 adults and up to 4 children). The one-day version (€9.90, €12.50 family) includes public transit, but offers only discounts at sights—not free admission. It can still pay off, especially for families. The **Dresden-Regio-Card** also covers outlying areas for three or five days. Cards are sold at both TIs, state museums, the airport, and by mail order at www.dresden.de/dresdencard.

Arrival in Dresden

Dresden has two major train stations: Dresden Hauptbahnhof and Dresden-Neustadt. Most trains stop at both stations (coming from Berlin, first at Neustadt, then at Hauptbahnhof; from Prague, it's the other way around). If you're coming for the day and want the easiest access to sights, use the Hauptbahnhof. S-Bahn trains, as well as tram #3, connect the two stations (€2 public transport ticket valid).

By Train at the Hauptbahnhof: Dresden's main train station owes its chic look to Norman Foster (of Reichstag Dome fame). In the bright, white arrivals hall, you'll find the TI kiosk, Internet access (in the Point Shop To Go, described later under "Helpful Hints"), and a *Reisezentrum* (Mon-Fri 5:45-21:00, Sat-Sun 7:00-21:00). In the north entryway *(Ausgang 2)* is a WC (€0.70) and lockers (€3-4).

To reach the beginning of my self-guided walk quickly by **tram**, exit the station following the *Ausgang 1* signs, carefully cross the tram tracks, and hop on tram #8 to Theaterplatz in the Old Town (five stops).

If you'd rather **walk,** the 20-minute stroll to the Old Town gives you an insightful glimpse of the communist era as you head down Prager Strasse. From the station, exit toward *Ausgang 2/ City/Prager Strasse,* and continue straight along Prager Strasse, then Seestrasse and Schlossstrasse until you emerge at the river.

By Train at Neustadt: The Neustadt train station serves the New Town north of the river, near some recommended hotels. It has lockers (€2-3), WCs (€0.70), and a *Reisezentrum* (Mon-Fri 8:00-19:00, Sat 8:00-16:30, Sun 10:00-19:00). To reach the Old Town from Neustadt Station, take tram #11 (direction Zschertnitz) four stops to Postplatz.

Helpful Hints

Sightseeing Strategies: Note that many of Dresden's top museums are closed either Monday or Tuesday.

The Historic Green Vault treasuries requires a reservation well in advance; if you don't get one, try to line up early to buy a same-day ticket, sold at 10:00. Once you have your appointed Historic Green Vault visit time, plan the rest of your day around it (it's conveniently located right in the center of the Old Town).

The Hofkirche hosts free pipe-organ concerts twice a week (Wed and Sat at 11:30, sometimes more—check schedule at door).

Internet Access: In the Hauptbahnhof, find the Sidewalk Express computers in the **Point Shop To Go** (€2/hour, one-hour minimum, limited functionality—no Skype, Mon-Thu 5:30-23:00, Fri-Sun 6:00-24:00). **Mondial** in the Outer New Town offers more service (€2/hour, Mon-Fri 10:00-24:00, Sat-Sun 11:00-24:00, Louisenstrasse 42, at corner of Görlitzer Strasse).

Laundry: Eco-Express SB-Waschsalon is a self-service launderette, just off Albertplatz in the New Town (Mon-Sat 6:00-23:00, closed Sun, English instructions, Königsbrücker Strasse 2).

Bike Rental: Roll on Dresden rents bikes and will gladly deliver and pick up the bike at your hotel for €0.25 per kilometer extra (€8/day, Mon-Fri 10:00-13:00 & 16:00-19:00, Sat 10:00-13:00, Sun usually 10:00-13:00 summer only, drop off until 20:30; in New Town, near Albertplatz tram stop at Königsbrücker Strasse 4a, mobile 0152-2267-3460, www.rollon dresden.de, info@rollondresden.de). Reservations can be made by email.

Supermarkets: Flanking the Prager Strasse tram stop are big shopping centers with basement supermarkets. In the huge Altmarkt Galerie mall to the north is a discount Aldi (Mon-Sat 9:30-21:00, closed Sun) and a mid-priced REWE (Mon-Sat 9:00-21:00, closed Sun). The Karstadt department store to the south has a more upscale supermarket (Mon-Sat 9:30-21:00, closed Sun).

Local Guides: Liane Löwe enjoys sharing the story of her hometown (€80/2-hour tour, lianeloewe@gmx.de).

Getting Around Dresden

Dresden's efficient **trams** work well for visitors, and there are a few useful buses (which use the same stops as trams in the city center). Buy tickets at the machines on the platforms or in the trams (€2 for a single *Einzelfahrkarte* ticket for rides up to 1 hour; €5 for a 4-pack of *Kurzstrecke* tickets for rides up to 4 stops in length; machines accept coins only). A day ticket *(Tageskarte)* is valid for one calendar day (€5, €7.50 family). Validate your ticket by date-stamping it in the little boxes on train platforms and on board buses and trams (for the day ticket, stamp it only the first time you ride). Free use of public transit is included with the Dresden-City-Card (described earlier). For transit information, see www.vvo-online.de.

Taxis are reasonable, plentiful, and generally honest (tel. 0351/211-211).

Self-Guided Walk

▲▲▲Do-It-Yourself Dresden Baroque Blitz Tour

Dresden's major sights are conveniently clustered along a delightfully strollable promenade next to the Elbe River. Lace these sights together by taking this walk. You'll get to know the four eras that have most shaped the city: Dresden's Golden Age in the mid-18th century under Augustus the Strong; the city's destruction by firebombs in World War II; the communist regime (1945-1989); and the current "reconstruction after reunification" era.

This walk takes about an hour, not counting museum stops. It includes the three major sights (Zwinger, Royal Palace with Historic Green Vault treasuries, and Frauenkirche), each of which is described later in the chapter. Incorporating these visits into the walk will fill your day.

• Begin at Theaterplatz *(a convenient drop-off point for tram #8 from the Hauptbahnhof).*

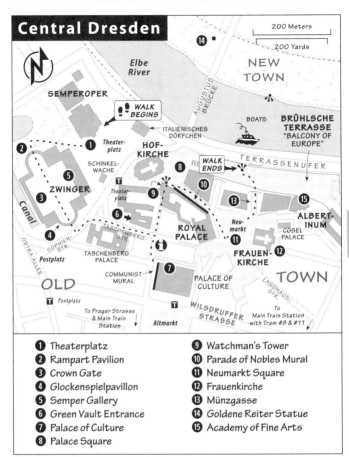

Central Dresden

200 Meters
200 Yards

Elbe River

NEW TOWN

SEMPEROPER

WALK BEGINS

ITALIENISCHES DÖRFCHEN

HOF-KIRCHE

Theater-platz

AUGUSTUS BRÜCKE

BOATS

BRÜHLSCHE TERRASSE "BALCONY OF EUROPE"

TERRASSENUFER

WALK ENDS

SCHINKEL-WACHE

ZWINGER

Theater-platz

Canal

OSTRA ALLEE

COSEL PALACE

ALBERT-INUM

ROYAL PALACE

Neu-markt

FRAUEN-KIRCHE

TASCHENBERG-STR.

SOPHIEN-STR.

Postplatz

TASCHENBERG PALACE

COMMUNIST MURAL

PALACE OF CULTURE

TOWN

LANDHAUS-STR.

OLD

Postplatz

To Prager Strasse & Main Train Station

Altmarkt

WILSDRUFFER STRASSE

To Main Train Station with Tram #8 & #11

DRESDEN

1 Theaterplatz
2 Rampart Pavilion
3 Crown Gate
4 Glockenspielpavillon
5 Semper Gallery
6 Green Vault Entrance
7 Palace of Culture
8 Palace Square

9 Watchman's Tower
10 Parade of Nobles Mural
11 Neumarkt Square
12 Frauenkirche
13 Münzgasse
14 Goldene Reiter Statue
15 Academy of Fine Arts

Theaterplatz

Face the equestrian statue (King John, an unimportant mid-19th-

century ruler) in the middle of the square. In front of you, behind the statue, is the Saxon State Opera House—nicknamed the **Semperoper** after its architect, Gottfried Semper (visits only with a tour).

As you face the Opera House, the smaller building on your left is the Neoclassical guardhouse called the Schinkel-wache (housing the opera box office). The big building behind it is the vast Zwinger palace complex (your next stop). Across the square from the Opera House is the Hofkirche, with its distinctive green-copper steeple, and to its right is the sprawling Royal Palace (with shiny new clock; both described later). All the buildings you see here—Dresden's Baroque treasures—are thoroughly reconstructed. The originals were destroyed in a single night by American and British bombs, with only walls and sometimes just foundations left standing. For more than 60 years, Dresden has been rebuilding.

Note the building along the river with a facade that looks a bit like a Florentine villa. It's a remnant from the time of Augustus the Strong, whose son set about building the Hofkirche to gain the pope's favor. Since Protestant locals refused to build the church, he had to import Catholic workers from Italy. Knowing that the workers wouldn't exactly be welcomed here, Frederick Augustus II built them their own lodgings, in the Italian Renaissance style. Today the Italienisches Dörfchen (Italian Hamlet) is overlooked by most visitors. Inside the main building is, no surprise, an Italian restaurant.

• Walk up the path between the Semperoper and the Zwinger. Notice the small statue of composer Carl Maria von Weber to your left. Weber's Der Freischütz was the last opera performed in the building before its destruction in 1945—and the first opera performed when the building reopened in 1985.

In the little corner by the café, go up the stairs and turn left up the path. As you turn the corner onto the upper balcony, you'll pass above a small courtyard (on the left) with a soothing, cooling fountain. Then head out to the railing and absorb the breathtaking view of the grand courtyard. As you stand on the balcony, imagine yourself as one of Dresden's 18th-century burghers, watching one of Augustus' wild parties in the courtyard below.

Walk down the stairs onto the Zwinger courtyard (either at the far end of the balcony, or via the pleasant fountain courtyard). Once you're down in the main courtyard, stand in the middle to survey all four wings.

The Zwinger

This palace complex is a Baroque masterpiece—once the pride and joy of the Wettin dynasty, and today filled with fine museums. The Wettins ruled Saxony for more than 800 years, right up until the end of the First World War (just like the Romanovs in Russia and the Habsburgs in Austria). Saxony wasn't ruled by a king, but by a prince elector—one

of a handful of nobles who elected the Holy Roman Emperor. The prince elector of Saxony was one of Germany's most powerful people. In the 18th century, the larger-than-life Augustus the Strong—who was both prince elector of Saxony and king of Poland—kicked off Saxony's Golden Age.

The word "Zwinger" refers to the no-man's-land in between the outer and inner city walls. As the city expanded, the complex of buildings you see today was built here. By Augustus' time, the Zwinger was used for Saxon royal celebrations. Imagine an over-the-top royal wedding in this complex. The courtyard served as an open-air palace, complete with orange trees in huge Chinese porcelain pots.

Let's get oriented. Face the northwest wing (where you entered). You're looking at the **Rampart Pavilion** (Wallpavillon), the first wing of the palace—an orangerie capped with a sun pavilion built for Augustus' fruit trees and parties. Up top is Atlas (who happens to have Augustus' features) with the Earth on his back—a fitting symbol for Augustus the Strong. Stairs lead to a fine view from the terrace above. This wing of the Zwinger houses the fun **Mathematics-Physics Salon** (described later, under "Sights in Dresden").

Turn to the left, facing the **Crown Gate** (Kronentor). The gate's golden crown is topped by four golden eagles supporting a smaller crown—symbolizing Polish royalty (since Augustus was also king of Poland).

Turn again to the left to see the **Glockenspielpavillon.** The glockenspiel near the top of the gate has 40 bells made of Meissen porcelain (bells chime every 15 minutes and play a sweet 3-minute melody at 10:15, 14:15, and 17:15). This wing of the Zwinger also houses Augustus the Strong's **Porcelain Collection** (see listing, later).

Turn once more to the left (with the Crown Gate behind you) to see the **Semper Gallery.** This Zwinger wing was added to the original courtyard a hundred years later by Gottfried Semper (of Opera House fame). It houses Dresden's best painting collection, the **Old Masters Gallery,** as well as the **Royal Armory** (both described later).

Throughout the city, you'll see the local sandstone looking really sooty. It's not from pollution, but natural oxidation that turns the stone black in about 30 years. Once restored, the statues are given a silicon treatment that lets the stone breathe but keeps it from going black. Among Dresdeners, this is a controversial approach. Many think that the resulting combination of black and white stone is odd, arguing that it departs from what Dresden "should" look like.

Take time to enjoy some of the Zwinger's excellent museums. Anticipating WWII bombs, Dresdeners preserved their town's art treasures by storing them in underground mines and cellars in the countryside. This saved these great works from Allied bombs...but not from the Russians. Nearly all of the city's artwork ended up in Moscow until after Stalin's death in 1953, when it was returned by the communist regime to win over their East German subjects. Today, Russians invade only as tourists.

When you're finished with the museums, exit the Zwinger through the Glockenspielpavillon (south gate). Halfway through the corridor, look for the **timelines** telling the history of the Zwinger in German: to the right, its construction, and to the left, its destruction and reconstruction. Notice the Soviet spin: On February 13, 1945, gangs of Anglo-American bombers obliterated (*vernichteten*) the city. On May 8, 1945, the Soviet army liberated (*befreite*) Dresden from "fascist tyranny" (*faschistischen Tyrannei*), and from 1945 to 1964, the Zwinger was rebuilt with the "power of the workers and peasants" (*Arbeiter- und Bauern-Macht*).

• *As you exit the corridor, cross the street and the tram tracks and jog left, walking down the perpendicular street called Taschenberg, with the yellow Taschenberg Palace on your right (ruined until 1990, today the city's finest five-star hotel). The yellow-windowed sky bridge ahead connects the Taschenberg, which was the crown prince's palace, with the prince electors'* **Royal Palace.** *The gate on your left is one of several entrances to the* **Green Vault** *treasuries (described later, under "Sights in Dresden"; entrance is before crossing under the sky bridge, through fancy gate). But if your Historic Green Vault reservation is for later today, you can continue this walk for now.*

Exiting the Royal Palace, go under the sky bridge. Ahead of you and to the right, the blocky modern building is the...

Palace of Culture (Kulturpalast)

Built by the communist government in 1969, today this hall is still used for concerts. Notice the mural depicting communist themes: workers, strong women, care for the elderly, teachers and students, and—of course—the red star and the seal of former East Germany. The bronze doors on the street side give a Marxist interpretation of the history of Dresden. Little of this propaganda, which once inundated the lives of locals, survives in post-communist Germany. The palace is currently closed for restoration work.

• *Now turn left (with the Palace of Culture behind you). Walk along the palace wall toward the two small copper domes, through a tunnel with (mostly Russian) musicians, until you emerge into* **Palace Square.** *Ahead*

Augustus the Strong
(1670-1733)

Friedrich Augustus I of the Wettin family exemplified royal excess, and made Dresden one of Europe's most important cities of culture. Legends paint Augustus as a macho, womanizing, powerful, ambitious, properly Baroque man—a real Saxon superstar. A hundred years after his death, historians dubbed Augustus "the Strong." Today, tour guides love to impart silly legends about Augustus, who supposedly fathered 365 children and could break a horseshoe in half with his bare hands.

As prince elector of Saxony, Augustus wheeled and dealed—and pragmatically converted from his Saxon Protestantism to a more Polish-friendly Catholicism—to become King Augustus II of Poland. Like most Wettins, Augustus the Strong was unlucky at war, but a clever diplomat and a lover of the arts.

The Polish people blame Augustus and his successors—who were far more concerned with wealth and opulence than with sensible governance—for Poland's precipitous decline after its own medieval Golden Age. According to Poles, the Saxon kings did nothing but "eat, drink, and loosen their belts" (it rhymes in Polish).

Whether you consider them the heroes of history, or the villains, Augustus and the rest of the Wettins—and the nobles who paid them taxes—are to thank for Dresden's rich architectural and artistic heritage.

of you and to the left is the **Katholische Hofkirche** *(described later, under "Sights in Dresden"). Now turn around and face the gate you just came through. You're looking at the palace complex entry (with the* **Watchman's Tower** *above on the right—see listing, later). To the left, next to one of the palace's entrances, you'll see a long, yellow mural called the...*

Parade of Nobles (Fürstenzug)

This mural is painted on 24,000 tiles of Meissen porcelain. Longer than a football field, it illustrates 700 years of Saxon royalty. It was built to commemorate Saxon history and heritage after Saxony

became a part of Germany in 1871. The artist carefully studied armor and clothing through the ages, allowing you to accurately trace the evolution of weaponry and fashions for seven centuries. (This is great for couples—try this for a switch: As you stroll, men watch the fashions, women the weaponry.)

The very last figure (or the first one you see, coming from this direction) is the artist himself, Wilhelm Walther. In front of him are commoners (miners, farmers, carpenters, teachers, students, artists), and then the royals, with 35 names and dates marking more than 700 years of Wettin rule. Stop at 1694. That's August II (Augustus the Strong), the most important of the Saxon kings. His horse stomps on the rose (symbol of Martin Luther, the Protestant movement, and the Lutheran church today) to gain the Polish crown. The first Saxon royal is Konrad der Grosse ("the Great"). And waaay up at the very front of the parade, an announcer with a band and 12th-century cheerleaders excitedly herald the arrival of this wondrous procession. The porcelain tiles are originals (from 1907)—they survived the Dresden bombing. They were fired three times at 2,400 degrees Fahrenheit when created...and then fired again during the 1945 firestorm, at only 1,800 degrees.

• *When you're finished looking at the mural, dogleg right and walk into the big square. Find a statue of Martin Luther.*

Neumarkt

This "New Market Square" was once a central square ringed by rich merchants' homes. After many years of construction, it is once again alive with people and cafés. The statue of Martin Luther shows him holding not just any Bible, but the German version of the Word of God that he personally translated so that regular people could wrestle with it directly—basically what the Protestant Reformation was all about. (Luther came from this part of Germany and spent most of his life in nearby Erfurt and Wittenberg.) Toppled in 1945, Luther has been cleaned up and is back on his feet again.

• *The big church looming over the square is the...*

Frauenkirche
(Church of Our Lady)

This church is the symbol and soul of the city. When completed in 1743, this was Germany's tallest Protestant church (310 feet high). Its unique central-stone-cupola design gave it the nickname "the stone bell." While it's a great church, this building garners the world's attention primarily because of its tragic history and phoenix-like resurrection: On the night of February 13, 1945, the firebombs came. When the smoke cleared the next morning, the Frauenkirche was smoldering but still standing. It burned for two days before finally collapsing. After the war, the Frauenkirche was left a pile of rubble and turned into a peace monument. Only after reunification was the decision made to rebuild it completely and painstakingly. It reopened to the public in 2005 (see listing later, under "Sights in Dresden").

A big hunk of the bombed **rubble** stands in the square (near door E, river side of church) as a memorial. Notice the small metal relief of the dome that shows where this piece came from.

• *From here, stroll downhill through a busy little restaurant-lined street, Münzgasse, and up the stairs to Dresden's grand river-view balcony. Find a bulge in the promenade 30 yards to the left. Belly up to that banister.*

Brühlsche Terrasse

This delightful promenade overlooking the river was once a defensive rampart— look along the side of the terrace facing the Elbe River to see openings for cannons. Later, it was given as a reward to a Saxon minister named Brühl, who had distinguished himself as a tax

collector, raising revenue for Frederick Augustus II's state treasury. In the early 1800s, it was turned into a public park, with a leafy canopy of linden trees, and was given the odd nickname "The Balcony of Europe."

Dresden claims to have the world's largest and oldest fleet of historic paddleboat steamers: nine riverboats from the 19th century. The hills in the distance (to the left) are home to Saxon vineyards, producing some of Germany's northernmost wine. Because only a small amount of the land is suitable for vineyards, the area's respected, expensive wine (mostly white) is consumed almost entirely by Saxons.

Below you to the left is the **Augustus Bridge** (Augustusbrücke), connecting Dresden's old and new towns. During massive floods in August of 2002, the water reached two-thirds of the way up the arches. At the far end of the Augustus

Bridge, you may be able to faintly see the golden equestrian statue,

a symbol of Dresden. It's Augustus the Strong, the **Goldene Reiter** (Golden Rider), facing east to his kingdom of Poland.

The area across the bridge is the **New Town** (Neustadt). While three-quarters of Dresden's Old Town was decimated by Allied firebombs, much of the New Town survived. The 18th-century apartment buildings here still stand—although a few blocky Soviet constructions sit along Hauptstrasse, just on the New Town side of the Augustus Bridge. Today, the New Town is a trendy district well worth exploring. The **Three Kings Church** (Dreikönigskirche, steeple visible above the Goldene Reiter) marks a neighborhood with some recommended restaurants.

To the far left, the interesting **mosque-shaped building** in the distance (marked *Yenidze*), originally a tobacco factory designed to advertise Turkish cigarettes, is now an office building with restaurants and nightclubs. A few steps to your left is the recommended **Radeberger Spezialausschank Café**—a good place for a drink or meal with a river view.

Behind you on the right, you'll see the glass domes of the **Academy of Fine Arts,** capped by a trumpeting gold angel. (Locals call the big dome on the right "the lemon juicer.") Around the far side of this building is another great museum, the **Albertinum,** which houses sculpture and modern art collections (see listing later).

• *Your tour is over. Stairs at the end of the promenade lead back to Palace Square; just beyond the Hofkirche is Theaterplatz, where you began.*

Sights in Dresden

The Zwinger, the Royal Palace, and the Albertinum

Dresden's three most established museums are in the center of the Old Town: the Zwinger, the Royal Palace, and the Albertinum. Each of them houses a number of collections, all covered by a single ticket (except for the Historic Green Vault in the Royal Palace, which must be reserved in advance). Tickets are valid all day, so you can come and go as you please. The Dresden-City-Card includes admission or discounts to all three museums, and use of public transport as well.

The Zwinger Museums

Four museums are located off the Zwinger palace courtyard: the Old Masters Gallery, Royal Armory, Mathematics-Physics Salon, and Porcelain Collection.

Cost and Hours: €10 ticket covers entrance to all of the museums; museums share the same hours: Tue-Sun 10:00-18:00, closed Mon; tel. 0351/4914-2000, www.skd.museum.

▲▲Old Masters Gallery (Gemäldegalerie Alte Meister)—
Dresden's best-known museum, in the Zwinger's Semper Gallery, features works by Raphael, Titian, Rembrandt, Peter Paul Rubens, Jan Vermeer, and more. While
it hangs 750 paintings at a time, it feels
particularly enjoyable for its "quality, not
quantity" approach to showing off great
art. Locals remember the Old Masters
Gallery as the first big public building
reopened after the war, in 1956.

Information: The dry €3 audioguide covers 55 paintings. Consider the
good €15 English *Old Masters Picture
Gallery* guidebook.

Visiting the Museum: The ground floor features temporary
exhibits. To see the permanent collection, make your way up the
stairs. You'll first pass through a small room (101) with portraits of
the Wettin kings who patronized the arts and founded this collection, plus two cityscapes of Dresden painted by **Bernardo Bellotto**
(sometimes called Canaletto) during the city's Golden Age. (Nine
more city views are in the Royal Armory—see below.) Next, you
enter a world of **Rubens** and Belgian Baroque (rooms 104 and 105).
This high-powered Catholic art is followed by the humbler, quieter
Protestant art of the Dutch Masters, including a fine collection of
Rembrandts (don't miss his jaunty self-portrait in room 106—with
Saskia on his lap and a glass of ale held aloft) and, in room 108, a
pristine **Vermeer** *(Girl at a Window Reading a Letter).*

Take a detour into the side room (107) to find the German
late-Gothic/early-Renaissance rooms, with exquisite canvases
by **Hans Holbein the Younger, Lucas Cranach,** and **Albrecht
Dürer.** Farther on, in room 118, the Venetian masters include a
sumptuous *Sleeping Venus* by **Giorgione** (1510). He died while still
working on this, so Titian stepped in to finish it. Giorgione's idealized Venus sleeps soundly, at peace with the plush nature.

The collection's highlight: **Raphael**'s masterful *Sistine Madonna*. The portrait features the Madonna and Child, two early
Christian martyrs (Saints Sixtus and Barbara), and wispy angel
faces in the clouds. Mary is in motion, offering the Savior to a
needy world. Note the look of worry and despair on Mary's face,
making this piece different from most *Madonna* paintings, which
show her smiling and filled with joy. That's because this *Madonna*
was originally part of a larger altarpiece, and Mary's mournful gaze
was directed at another painting—one of the Crucifixion. These
days, the gaze of most visitors is directed at the pair of whimsical
angels in the foreground—which Raphael added after the painting
was completed, just to fill the empty space. These lovable tykes—of

DRESDEN

T-shirt and poster fame—are bored...just hanging out, oblivious to the exciting arrival of the Messiah just behind them. They connect the heavenly world of the painting with you and me.

▲▲**Royal Armory (Rüstkammer)**—The Armory is across the entry passage from the Old Masters Gallery and is packed with swords and suits of armor. The tiny children's armor is especially interesting. In the gallery at the back are nine views of Dresden by **Bernardo Bellotto**, part of the same series that includes the two in room 101 of the Old Masters Gallery. These paintings of mid-18th-century Dresden—showing the Hofkirche (still under construction) and the newly completed Frauenkirche—offer a great study of the city.

You may see Bellotto called "Canaletto." Bellotto's uncle and teacher was Antonio Canal, famous for his paintings of Venice. The uncle is the original Canaletto, but Bellotto used that name, too, to link himself with his uncle's style.

Mathematics-Physics Salon (Mathematisch-Physikalischer Salon)—After extensive renovation, this fun collection should re-open in early 2013. It features globes, lenses, and clocks from the 16th to the 19th centuries (northwest end of Zwinger courtyard).

▲**Porcelain Collection (Porzellansammlung)**—In the early 18th century, porcelain was considered "white gold"—an incredibly valuable material that could only be produced in faraway China and transported to Europe at great expense. Augustus the Strong commissioned an alchemist named Johann Friedrich Böttger to derive a method for creating his own porcelain. Böttger was reluctant—he'd already failed at creating actual gold—but Augustus persuaded him by locking him up until he complied. Eventually Böttger succeeded, and the Saxon prince electors became pioneers in European porcelain production. Every self-respecting European king had a porcelain works, and the Wettins had the most famous: Meissen. They inspired other royal courts to get into the art form. They also collected other types—from France to Japan and China. Augustus the Strong was obsessed with the precious stuff...he liked to say he had "porcelain sickness." Here you can enjoy some of his symptoms, under chandeliers in elegant galleries with a view over the Zwinger courtyard. Peruse the menagerie of delicate white-porcelain animals, the long halls of vases, the small collection of Asian porcelain, and the large collection of locally produced goods. There are two wings to either side of the archway—make sure to visit both (fine English descriptions, southeast end of Zwinger courtyard).

Royal Palace (Residenzschloss)

This Renaissance palace was once the residence of the Saxon prince elector. Formerly one of the finest Renaissance buildings in Germa-

ny, it's been rebuilt since its destruction in World War II. The grand state rooms of Augustus the Strong are closed for the foreseeable future. Until they reopen, the prince's treasures are the big draw here: The New Green Vault is quite remarkable, while the Historic Green Vault (reservation required) is one of the more impressive treasury collections in Europe.

Cost and Hours: €10 includes New Green Vault, Turkish Vault, Watchman's Tower, and special exhibitions; Historic Green Vault requires a separate ticket (€10 on the same day, €2 surcharge to book in advance); hours for the entire complex: Wed-Mon 10:00-18:00, Historic Green Vault until 19:00, closed Tue. The Watchman's Tower is closed Nov-March. The palace has four entrances, each leading to a glass-domed inner courtyard, where you'll find the ticket windows and restrooms. Tel. 0351/4914-2000, www.skd.museum.

▲▲**Historic Green Vault (Historisches Grünes Gewölbe)**— The famed, glittering Baroque treasury collection was begun by Augustus the Strong in the early 1700s. It evolved into the royal family's extravagant treasure trove of ivory, silver, and gold knick-knacks, displayed in rooms as opulent as the collection itself.

Reservations: To protect these priceless items and the extravagant rooms in which they're displayed, the number of visitors each day is carefully controlled. It makes sense to book your required reservation well in advance—at least a week ahead in May, June, or September, and two or three weeks ahead on Saturdays in those months. At other times, you should be able to book just a few days out. You'll be given a 15-minute entry window for your visit (once inside, you can stay as long as you like). You can book online and print your own ticket (www.skd.museum); or you can book by email (besucherservice@skd.museum) and either pick up your ticket at the ticket office or receive an eticket via email. If your preferred dates are listed as sold out, keep checking back, since tour groups often cancel on short notice. If you don't have a reservation, try to nab one of the 200 same-day tickets put on sale at 10:00. The line forms about 9:30, but your chances for an afternoon slot are still decent if you get there at 10:00. The number of spots still available—*Freie Plätze*—is indicated at the ticket desk.

Visiting the Historic Green Vault: Your visit is designed to wow you in a typically Baroque style—starting easy and crescendoing to a climax, taking a quick break, and finishing again with a flurry. You'll enter through a "dust sluice," which protects the vault's delicate collection by cleaning any irritants off visitors—

DRESDEN

a good feeling. Following the included (but torturously dry) audioguide, you'll spend about an hour progressing through nine rooms.

The **Amber Cabinet** serves as a reminder of just how many different things you can do with fossilized tree sap (in a surprising range of colors), and the **Ivory Room** does the same for elephant tusks, with some strikingly delicate hand-carved sculptures. The **White Silver Room,** painted its original vermillion color, holds a chalice carved from a rhino horn, and the **Silver-Gilt Room** displays tableware and gold-ruby glass.

The wide variety of items in the largest room—the aptly named **Hall of Precious Objects**—includes mother-of-pearl sculptures, along with a model of the Hill of Calvary atop a pile of pearls and polished seashells. The oak cupboards that line the **Heraldry Room** are emblazoned with copper-and-gold coats-of-arms boasting of the various territories in Augustus the Strong's domain.

The vault's high-water mark is the grandly decorated **Jewel Room.** The incredible pieces in here (especially the Obeliscus Augustalis) are fine examples of *Gesamtkunstwerk*—a symphony of artistic creations, though obnoxiously gaudy by today's tastes. The *Moor with Emerald Tier*—a "Moor" (actually a Native American) clad in jewels and gold—was designed to carry a chunk of rock embedded with large gems. Nearby, an overly decorated obelisk trumpets the greatness of Augustus the Strong.

The exhibit concludes in the relatively subdued **Bronze Room,** with its eight-foot-tall equestrian statue of Augustus the Strong (designed to compete with similar depictions of his rival, Louis XIV), as well as a statue of Apollo surrounded by six women. Your audioguide also describes treasures in the "pre-vault" (where you pick up and drop off the audioguide). In this room, don't miss photos of vaults before the war and Luther's signature ring.

▲**New Green Vault (Neues Grünes Gewölbe)**—This collection shows off more of the treasure in a modern setting. Don't miss the 6.2-carat one-of-a-kind green diamond that "mysteriously" appeared here from India. The included audioguide describes the best 65 objects in 1.5 hours.

▲**Turkish Vault (Türkisches Cammer)**—In the 16th through 19th centuries, Western European elites were crazy about all things Turkish, and Augustus the Strong was no exception. Augustus collected Ottoman art with a passion, even dressing up as a sultan in his own court. This fascinating collection of Ottoman art is the result of centuries of collecting, diplomatic gifts, trades, and shopping trips to Constantinople. Although the collection consists largely of ornamental swords and longbows (one dating back to 1586), the real reason to visit is to see the 20-yard-long, three-poled ornamented silk tent—the only complete three-masted Ottoman tent on display in Europe.

Watchman's Tower (Hausmannsturm)—This palace tower is completely rebuilt (and feels entirely modern). You can climb past an underwhelming coin collection, see the rebuilt medieval clock mechanism from behind, peruse an extensive series of dome-damage photos, and earn a good city view after a long climb. In bad weather, the view terrace is closed, and you'll peer through small windows—a big disappointment. If climbing the Frauenkirche dome (which affords the best view in town but costs €8), skip this.

▲▲The Albertinum

At the end of the Brühlsche Terrasse, this museum's excellent collections feature artwork from the Romantic period (late 18th and early 19th centuries) to the present. The included audioguide does a beautiful job of explaining the artwork. Recently  redone, the museum's ticket windows are in the building's old courtyard, which has been roofed over into a cavernous, minimalist, white atrium.

Cost and Hours: €8, Tue-Sun 10:00-18:00, closed Mon, entrance on the Brühlsche Terrasse and on Georg-Treu-Platz, tel. 0351/4914-2000, www.skd.museum.

Visiting the Museum: Most visitors come to see the New Masters Gallery (German 19th- and 20th-century art) on the museum's top floor. Moving down from there, contemporary and turn-of-the-20th-century art is on the first floor, and sculpture on the ground floor.

New Masters Gallery (Galerie Neue Meister): On the top floor, take a counterclockwise walk around this chronologically organized collection, showcasing mostly German (and some French) paintings from the Romantic era to 20th-century Modernism. In Caspar David Friedrich's landscapes, notice that people are small and blend into the background, reminding us that German Romanticism is all about the exploration of man's place as a part of nature—not as its dominating force. Friedrich's Norwegian counterpart and friend, Johan Christian Dahl—who moved to Dresden later in life—captures his adopted hometown in his lovely *View of Dresden at Full Moon*, which seems not so different from today's reconstructed city.

Take a breather with Ludwig Richter's bucolic scenes of the

Italian countryside, then move into the top-notch Modernist wing, with works by Paul Gauguin (Polynesian women), Vincent van Gogh *(Still Life with Quinces)*, Max Liebermann (insightful portraits), Oskar Kokoschka (vibrantly colored, almost garish portraits), Claude Monet, Edouard Manet, and more. Some of the lesser-known works are also worth a good look, such as Max Slevogt's evocative paintings of North Africa. Look also for Edgar Degas' sculpture *Little Dancer Aged Fourteen* (one of 29 bronze casts from the wax original).

Don't miss Otto Dix's haunting, frank images—particularly his stirring triptych *War*, rooted in his firsthand experience fighting in the trenches of France and Flanders during World War I. This vision, modeled after a medieval altarpiece, has a circular composition that's kept moving by the grotesque pointing skeleton. In this fetid wasteland, corpses are decomposing, and helmets and gas masks make even the intact bodies seem inhuman. Dix painted this in the 1930s, when Adolf Hitler was building a case for war (ostensibly to reclaim territory Germany lost after World War I). The Führer didn't care for Dix's pacifist message, dismissing the artist from his teaching job at Dresden's art academy and adding Dix's works to his collection of "degenerate art."

The collection wraps up with works by Paul Klee, Pablo Picasso, some harrowing Expressionistic works, and Gerhard Richter's recent acrylics under glass.

Mosaiksaal, Klingersaal, and Contemporary Art: On the first floor up, the Mosaiksaal features sculpture from the Classicist era on up to Ernst Rietschel's mid-19th-century depictions of historically important Germans.

The Klingersaal shows slinky fin de siècle paintings and sculptures. Look for Gustav Klimt's atmospheric *Buchenwald*, a tranquil beech forest that shimmers with color, achieving startling depth. In Ferdinand Hodler's portrait of *Madame de R.*, the subject regards us with a steely gaze.

Running along the other side of this floor is a hall of contemporary, mostly 20th-century German art. Along the short sides of the building, connecting the Klingersaal and Mosaiksaal to the contemporary exhibits, are *Schaudepots*—viewable display storerooms jammed full of sculptures that didn't find a permanent home in the public exhibits. These give a glimpse into the vastness of the Albertinum's collection. (There are two more *Schaudepots* on the ground floor, one in the kids' activity room.)

Sculpture Collection (Skulpturensammlung): Gathered in one huge *Skulpturhalle* on the ground floor, this easy-on-the-eyes collection covers 5,000 years of Western sculpture, with a special focus on the last 200 years. There are several plaster casts by Auguste Rodin, including a *Thinker*. At the contemporary end of the spectrum is Tony Cragg's *Ever After* (2010), a 10-foot-tall wooden sculpture that appears to be melting; look closely to see profiles of human faces emerge on the left side.

Major Churches
▲▲▲Frauenkirche (Church of Our Lady)
This landmark church was originally built by local donations—Protestant-pride. Destroyed by the Allied firebombing in World War II, the church sat in ruins for decades. Finally, in 1992, reconstruction of the church began, following carefully considered guidelines: Rebuild true to the original design; use as much of the original material as possible; avoid using any concrete or rebar; maximize modern technology; and make

it a lively venue for 21st-century-style worship. The church was fitted together like a giant jigsaw puzzle, with about a third made of the darker original stones—all placed lovingly in their original spots. The reconstruction cost more than €100 million, 90 percent of which came from donors around the world.

Cost and Hours: Free but donation requested, 45-minute audioguide-€2.50, Mon-Fri 10:00-12:00 & 13:00-18:00, open between services and concerts on Sat-Sun, enter through door D, www.frauenkirche-dresden.de.

Climbing the Dome: Get a great view over the city by hiking to the top of the dome. After an elevator takes you a third of the way, you still have a long climb up many stairs (€8—consider it a donation to the church, Mon-Sat 10:00-18:00, Sun 12:30-18:00, enter through door G, follow signs to *Kuppelaufstieg*).

Gift Shop: Located between the church and the Albertinum, the church's shop has all of your tasteful-refrigerator-magnet needs covered. Interesting books, videos, and jewelry help fund the work and upkeep of the church (Mon-Sat 10:00-18:00, Sun 11:00-17:00, Georg-Treu-Platz 3, tel. 0351/656-0683).

Visiting the Church: The Frauenkirche is as worthwhile for its glorious **interior** as for its tragic, then uplifting, recent history. Stepping inside, you're struck by the shape—not so wide (150 feet) but very tall (inner dome 120 feet, under a 225-foot main dome).

The color scheme is pastel, in an effort to underline the joy of faith and enhance the festive ambience of the services and ceremonies held here. The curves help create a feeling of community. The seven entrances are perfectly equal (as people are, in the eyes of God). When the congregation exits, the seven exits point to all quarters—a reminder to "go ye," the Great Commission to spread the Word everywhere.

The Baroque sandstone **altar** shows Jesus praying in the Garden of Gethsemane the night before his crucifixion. Soldiers, led by Judas, are on their way, but Christ is firmly in the presence of God and his angels. Eighty percent of today's altar is from original material—in the form of 2,000 individual fragments that were salvaged and pieced back together by restorers.

The **Cross of Nails** at the high altar is from Coventry, England—Dresden's sister city. Two fire-blackened nails found in the smoldering rubble of Coventry's bombed church are used as a symbol of peace and reconciliation. Coventry was bombed as thoroughly as Dresden (so thoroughly, it gave the giddy Luftwaffe a new word for "bomb to smithereens"—to "coventrate"). From the destroyed town of Coventry was born the Community of the Cross of Nails, a worldwide network promoting peace and reconciliation through international understanding.

Near the exit stands the church's **twisted old cross,** which fell 300 feet and burned in the rubble. Lost until restorers uncovered it

from the pile of stones in 1993, it stands exactly on the place it was found, still relatively intact. A copy—a gift from the British people in 2000 on the 55th anniversary of the bombing—crowns the new church. It was crafted by an English coppersmith whose father had dropped bombs on the church on that fateful night. Visitors are invited to light a candle before this cross and enter a wish for peace in the guest book.

Go downstairs to the **cellar** to see a modern-feeling, very stark chapel under vaulted ceilings. Look for the old grave markers, from when the crypt was here in prewar times. In each stairwell, plaques list the names of the donors who helped resurrect this church from the rubble. In a separate room (first up, then down some stairs) is a modest exhibit about the history of the building.

▲Katholiche Hofkirche (Catholic Church of the Royal Court)

Why does Dresden, a stronghold of local boy Martin Luther's Protestant Reformation, boast such a beautiful Catholic cathedral? When Augustus the Strong died, his son wanted to continue as king of Poland, like his father. The pope would allow it only if Augustus Junior built a Catholic church in Dresden. Now, thanks to Junior's historical kissing-up, the mere 5 percent of locals who are Catholic get to enjoy this fine church. The elevated passageway connecting the church with the palace allowed the royal family to avoid walking in the street with commoners.

Cost and Hours: Free, Mon-Thu 9:00-17:00, Fri 13:00-17:00, Sat 10:00-18:00, Sun 12:00-16:00, enter through side door facing palace, tel. 0351/484-4712, www.kathedrale-dresden.de.

Visiting the Church: Inside the cathedral, on the right side of the main nave, is the fine Baroque **pulpit,** carved from linden wood and hidden in the countryside during World War II.

The glorious 3,000-pipe **organ** filling the back of the nave is played for the public for free on Wednesdays and Saturdays at 11:30 (and occasionally at other times as well).

The **Memorial Chapel** (as you face the rear of the church, it's on the left) is dedicated to those who died in the WWII firebombing and to all victims of violence. Its evocative *pietà* altarpiece was constructed in 1976 of Meissen porcelain. Mary offers the faithful the crown of thorns made from Dresden's rubble, as if to remind us that Jesus—on her lap, head hanging lifeless on the left—died to save humankind. Jesus' open heart shows us his love, offers us atonement for our sins, and proves that reconciliation is more powerful than hatred. The altar (freestanding, in front) shows five flaming heads. It seems to symbolize how Dresdeners suffered...in the presence of their suffering savior. The dates on the high altar (30-1-33 and 13-2-45) mark the dark period between Hitler's rise to power and the night Dresden was destroyed.

The basement houses the **royal crypt,** including the heart of the still-virile Augustus the Strong—which, according to legend, still beats when a pretty woman comes near (crypt open only for one 45-minute German tour each day).

DRESDEN

More Sights in Dresden

▲**Semperoper**—This elegant opera house watches over Theaterplatz in the heart of town. Three opera houses have stood in this spot: The first was destroyed by a fire in 1869, the second by firebombs in 1945. The rebuilt Semperoper continues to be a world-class venue.

Tours: The opulent interior can only be visited with a tour. German-language tours (with an English handout) go regularly throughout the day. There is one daily English tour at 15:00. It's wise to reserve in advance by phone, email, or online (€8, €2 extra to take photos, 1 hour, tour schedule depends on rehearsal schedule, enter on right side, tel. 0351/320-7360, www.semperoper-erleben.de).

Performances: Tickets, which go on sale a year in advance, are hard to come by. You can book in advance online or by phone and pick up tickets at the box office in Schinkelwache across the square (Mon-Fri 10:00-18:00, Sat-Sun 10:00-17:00, tel. 0351/491-1705, www.semperoper.de).

Prager Strasse—This street, connecting the Hauptbahnhof train station and the historic center, was in ruins until the 1960s, when communist planners redeveloped it as a pedestrian mall. The design is typical of Soviet-bloc architecture—there are similar streets in Moscow—and it reflects communist ideals: big, blocky, functional buildings without extraneous ornamentation. As you stroll down Prager Strasse, imagine these buildings without much color or advertising (which were unnecessary back in the no-choices days of communism). Today, the street is filled with corporate logos, shoppers with lots of choices, and a fun summertime food circus. The street has developed into exactly what the communists envisioned for it, but never quite achieved: a pedestrian-friendly shopping area where people could stroll and relax, combined with residential space above. These days, it almost feels more '70s than communist.

Deutsches Hygiene-Museum—This family-oriented, newly renovated museum is devoted to the wonders of the human body (don't take the word "hygiene," its historical title, too literally). Visitors with strong stomachs get a kick out of this highly interactive museum, but those easily grossed out should stay away—or at least plan meal times accordingly.

The building, which is huge, was completed in 1930 in a severe functional style. (A few years later, it briefly became a center for Nazi eugenics and "racial studies.") The permanent exhibit on the upper floor is divided into six themed sections (Life and Death; Eating and Drinking; Sexuality; Memory, Thinking, and Learning; Movement; and Beauty, Skin, and Hair). A highlight is the "transparent woman" *(Gläserne Frau)*, a life-size plastic model with bones, veins, and interior organs visible. Check out the little wooden anatomical figures with removable parts (complete with strategically placed fig leaves), X-ray machines from the 1930s, and graphic wax models of venereal diseases. The museum offers some English explanations and an included audioguide, but most of the exhibits speak (or shriek) for themselves.

Your ticket also gets you into Dresden's **children's museum,** in the basement, which stays with the general theme by focusing on the five senses.

Cost and Hours: €7, €11 family ticket, 16 and under free, Tue-Sun 10:00-18:00, closed Mon; Lingnerplatz 1, take tram #1, #2, #4, or #12 to the Deutsches Hygiene-Museum stop or tram #10 to Grosser Garten, then walk one long block; tel. 0351/484-6400, www.dhmd.de.

Volkswagen's Transparent Factory (Gläserne Manufaktur)—You don't need to be automotively inclined to enjoy a pil-

grimage to the recently built VW assembly plant on the southeastern edge of town. Two floors of this fascinating, transparent building are open to visitors interested in the assembly of the high-end VW Phaeton sedan, one of the carmaker's *luxusschlitten* (luxury sleds). If you buy a Phaeton here, you can set yourself on the platform (BYO folding chair) and follow it through every moment of the 36-hour "birth" process. The parts are delivered to the logistics plant on the edge of town, then transported to this manufacturing plant by "cargo trams" (instead of trucks, to keep traffic congestion down).

Visitors have two options: just gaze at the slowly moving assembly line from the building's atrium for free, or pay to take a 70-minute tour (which lets you see the process at close range). German-language tours run every 30-60 minutes; English tours

DRESDEN

run three times a day. Tours are limited to 15 participants and can fill up, so you're encouraged to call ahead and book a spot. However, you can also just show up and take your chances (going on a German tour is a good option if an English one isn't available).

Informative touch-screen terminals in the atrium describe the plant's operations in English, and a mini-movie theater shows classic old VW commercials. The café is expensive.

Cost and Hours: Atrium—free, Sun-Mon 11:00-19:00, Tue and Fri-Sat 9:00-19:00, Wed-Thu 9:00-22:30. Guided tour—€5; English tours generally Mon-Fri at 12:00, 15:00, and 17:00 except no 17:00 tour Jan-Feb, Sat at 12:00 and 15:00, no Sun tours; German tours at least hourly Mon 11:00-18:00, Tue-Sat 9:00-18:00, Wed-Thu until 21:00, Sun 11:00-17:00. Open hours and tour times can vary due to special events; check the website or call ahead to confirm (tel. 0351/420-4411, www.glaesernemanufaktur.de).

Getting There: Take tram #1, #2, or #4 (from the Old Town) or tram #10 (from the Hauptbahnhof) to the Strassburger Platz stop. You'll see the plant on one corner of the intersection; enter off Lennestrasse.

▲**New Town (Neustadt)**—A big sign across the river from the old center declares, "Dresden continues here"—directed at tourists who visit the city without ever crossing the river into the New Town. Don't be one of them: While there are no famous sights in this district, it's the only part of Dresden that looks as it did before World War II. Today, it's thriving with cafés, shops, clubs, and—most importantly—actual Dresdeners. (For hotel and restaurant recommendations in the neighborhood, see "Sleeping in Dresden" and "Eating in Dresden," later.)

Military History Museum (Militärhistorisches Museum der Bundeswehr)—This recently renovated museum covers more than 800 years of German military history and focuses on the causes and consequences of war and violence. At over 180,000 square feet, it's the largest museum in Germany. The museum is housed in Dresden's Neoclassical former arsenal building, forcefully severed by a Daniel Libeskind-designed wedge of glass and steel (signaling the break from Germany's militaristic past and its hope for a transparent government and peaceful future).

Cost and Hours: €5, includes audioguide, Mon 10:00-21:00, Tue and Thu-Sun 10:00-18:00, closed Wed, Olbrichtplatz 2, take tram #7 or #8 to Stauffenbergallee stop (beyond the New Town). Tel. 0351/823-2803, www.mhmbundeswehr.de.

Near Dresden

Dresden is the starting point for two pleasant excursions—a peaceful half-day's walk or bike ride up the Elbe River, and a day of hiking in dramatic "Saxon Switzerland."

Elbe River Valley to the Blue Wonder Bridge

The Elbe River Valley makes for a wonderful excursion from Dresden. For a great slice-of-life glimpse at Germans at play, walk or bike along the 3.5-mile path that hugs the banks of the Elbe River all the way from central Dresden to the Blue Wonder bridge. If the weather's warm, pack a swimsuit.

The path starts underneath and to the right of the Brühlsche Terrasse, and makes its scenic way—past several tempting beer gardens—to the **Blue Wonder** (a.k.a. Loschwitz Bridge), a cantilever truss bridge that connects the Dresden suburbs of Loschwitz and Blasewitz. When the bridge was completed in 1893, Blasewitz and Loschwitz were the most expensive pieces of real estate in Europe—note the ultra-posh villas near the bridge. The bridge is indeed a wonder in that it survived World War II completely untouched, and it is, in fact, blue—but its name is a pun on the German expression, "to witness a blue wonder" *(ein Blaues Wunder erleben)*—to experience a nasty surprise. The real surprise is how relaxing the whole trip is, as the closer you get to the bridge the more opportunities you'll find for swimming and boating (several places rent kayaks, Jet Skis, and so on).

Underneath the bridge, a delightful beer garden awaits: **Schiller Garten,** a vast, 300-year-old complex of gastronomic delights and cold suds. The garden area serves good grilled food, has a self-service buffet (in the building marked *Lichtspiel*), and pours an unfiltered *Zwickel* beer brewed specially for this garden by Feldschlösschen (Dresden's best brewery). The garden includes a playground and a digital departure board for the nearby Schillerplatz tram stop (€3-6 dishes and snacks, daily 11:00-24:00). If you're looking for something fancier, try the sit-down restaurant in the half-timbered house (€9-17 main dishes, daily 11:00-22:00). Both the garden and restaurant have been supplied by their own butcher and pastry kitchen since 1764 (tel. 0351/811-990, www.schiller garten.de).

Getting to the Blue Wonder: If you have enough time and nice weather, you could slow down and do this outing on **foot** (about one hour each way) or by **bike** (about 30 minutes each way; for bike rental, see "Helpful Hints," earlier).

You can also make the trip by **boat**: The Saxon Steamboat Company (Sächische Dampfschiffahrt) runs steam-powered paddle boats along the Elbe (€6.10 one-way, about hourly in summer, 40 minutes, board at Brühlsche Terrasse, get off at Blasewitz dock; to return to Dresden, board at Loschwitz; check schedule in advance—low water levels on the Elbe can limit traffic, www.saechsische-dampfschiffahrt.de).

Finally, **trams** #6 (from the New Town) and #12 (from the Old Town) take you to Schillerplatz, about 50 yards from the Blue Wonder, in about 30 minutes. The tram ride is particularly interesting, as it travels along a path of destruction through communist prefabricated housing, then to post-unification strip-mall urban sprawl, before taking you to a delightful collection of villas and large single-family 19th-century dwellings. On tram #6, keep your eyes peeled at the Trinitatis Platz stop for a beautiful bombed church, which sits amid a sea of dreary prefab architecture. You can take your bike on the tram for €1.40 (choose the *Einzelfahrt-Ermässigt* button for your bike fare).

Saxon Switzerland National Park

Consider a break from big-city sightseeing to spend a half-day taking a *wunderbar* hike through this scenic national park.

Twenty miles southeast of Dresden (an easy 45-minute S-Bahn ride away), the Elbe River cuts a scenic swath through the beech forests and steep cliffs of Saxon Switzerland (Sächsische Schweiz) National Park. You'll share the trails with serious rock climbers and equally serious Saxon grandmothers. Allow five hours (including lunch) to enjoy this day trip.

Take S-Bahn line 1 from either the Hauptbahnhof or Neustadt station (direction Bad Schandau) and get off at the Kurort Rathen stop (2/hour, 35 minutes; €5.60 one-way, or buy regional day passes, also good for Dresden city transport: €12.50, €16/family, €24/group of up to 5 adults). Follow the road downhill five minutes through town to the dock, and take the ferry across the Elbe (€1.50 round-trip, pay on board, crossing takes 2 minutes, runs continuously). When the ferry docks on the far (north) side of the river, turn your back on the river and walk 100 yards through town, with the little creek on your right. Turn left after the **Sonniges Eck Restaurant** (tasty lunch option, check out photos of huge 2002 flood in their front dining room) and walk up the lane. The trail begins with stairs on your left just past Hotel Amselgrundschlösschen (follow *Bastei* signs).

A 45-minute walk uphill through the woods leads you to the **Bastei Bridge** and stunning views of gray sandstone sentries rising several hundred feet above forest ridges. Elbe Valley sandstone was used to build Dresden's finest buildings (including the

Frauenkirche and Zwinger), as well as Berlin's famous Brandenburg Gate. The multiple-arch bridge looks straight out of Oz—built in 1851 specifically for Romantic Age tourists, and scenic enough to be the subject of the first landscape photos ever taken in Germany. Take the time to explore the short 50-yard spur trails that reward you with classic views down on the Elbe 900 feet below. Watch the slow-motion paddleboat steamers leave V-shaped wakes as they chug upstream toward the Czech Republic, just around the next river bend. If you're not afraid of heights, explore the maze of catwalks through the scant remains of the **Felsenberg Neurathen,** a 13th-century Saxon fort perched precariously on the bald stony spires (€1.50, entrance 50 yards before Bastei Bridge).

Just a five-minute uphill hike beyond the bridge is the **Berg Hotel Panorama Bastei,** with a fine restaurant, a snack bar, and memorable views. Return to the Elbe ferry down the same trail.

Nightlife in Dresden

Outer New Town (Äussere Neustadt)

To really connect with Dresden as it unfolds, you need to go to the Outer New Town (a 10-minute walk from Neustadt train station). This area was not bombed in World War II, and after 1989 it sprouted the first entrepreneurial cafés and bistros. Now it's a popular neighborhood for young people and progressive families, reminiscent of parts of New York City or San Francisco. This is a fun place to eat dinner, then join the action, which picks up after 22:00. Eateries range from the merely creative to the truly unconventional. The clientele is young, hip, pierced, and tattooed. You'll find mini-*Biergartens* (but not your grandfather's oompah bands) and see young adults hanging out on the curb, nursing beer bottles. The neighborhood feels more exuberant than rough.

Rather than seek out particular places in this continuously evolving scene, I'd just get to the epicenter—at the corner of Görlitzer Strasse and Louisenstrasse—and wander. From the Old Town, take tram #7 or #8 to Louisenstrasse, or tram #6 or #11 to Bautzner/Rothenburger Strasse. Night trams bring you back to the center even in the wee hours.

Here are a few places and bars worth checking out:

Kunsthofpassage is a series of fanciful, imaginatively decorated courtyards surrounded by boutiques. On one wall the downspouts have been reworked into a fountain made of musical-instrument shapes. The opposite wall sports large metal shavings. This is a delightful fantasy world, tucked improbably between lively urban streets (just as interesting by day; enter at Görlitzer Strasse 21, 23, or 25, or at Alaunstrasse 70; www.kunsthof-dresden.de).

Lebowski-Bar, with a tight interior and screens showing the Coen brothers' masterpiece on a continuous loop, is an inviting spot for fans of The Dude to sip a White Russian (Görlitzer Strasse 5).

The Russian-flavored **Kneipe Raskolnikoff** has a reed fence and a stand of bamboo, giving the bar a Moscow/Maui ambience (Böhmische Strasse 34, a half-block off Lutherplatz).

Carte Blanche Transvestite Bar is a hoot for some (€29 burlesque show, Wed-Sun from about 20:00, no shows Mon-Tue, Priessnitzstrasse 10, tel. 0351/204-720, www.carte-blanche-dresden.de). Across the courtyard (the whole complex used to be a creamery) is the **Zora Cocktail Bar,** an inviting place to enjoy a drink before or after the show.

For a fun tour around the Neustadt neighborhood, call **Nightwalk Dresden.** Their nightly tour is much more than just a pub crawl; it's a journey through the unique culture of a virtually undiscovered part of the city—that just happens to include some free drinks. This is a fine option for travelers looking for company or who hesitate to visit a new area after dark. Tours visit some great pubs and run in English and German simultaneously (€13, daily at 21:00, 3 hours; starts in Neustadt on the north end of Albertplatz, by the artesian well—see website for map; tel. 0172/781-5007, www.nightwalk-dresden.de).

For more sedate evening entertainment, just stroll along the New Town riverbank after dark and enjoy the floodlit views of the Old Town—a scene famous among Germans as the *Dresden-Blick* (Dresden view).

Sleeping in Dresden

Hotels in Dresden tend to be large. Characteristic, family-run places are rare. (Many smaller buildings were destroyed during World War II, and communists didn't do "quaint" very well.) The rates listed are for peak season: For hotels, that's May, June, September, and October. Prices soften at midsummer and drop in winter. Peak season for hostels is July and August (especially weekends). Only the Martha Dresden and the Bayerischer Hof include breakfast in their prices.

In or near the Old Town

$$$ **Aparthotels an der Frauenkirche** rents 133 new units in five beautifully restored houses (many with views) in the heart of the Old Town. Designed for longer stays but also welcoming one- or two-nighters, these modern, comfortable apart-

Sleep Code

(€1 = about $1.30, country code: 49, area code: 0351)
S = Single, **D** = Double/Twin, **T** = Triple, **Q** = Quad, **b** = bathroom, **s** = shower only. All of these places speak English and accept credit cards. Unless otherwise noted, breakfast is *not* included.

To help you sort easily through these listings, I've divided the accommodations into three categories, based on the price for a standard double room with bath:

$$$ **Higher Priced**—Most rooms €120 or more.
$$ **Moderately Priced**—Most rooms between €80-120.
$ **Lower Priced**—Most rooms €80 or less.

Prices can change without notice; verify the hotel's current rates online or by email.

ments come with kitchens and the lived-in works. Two buildings ("Neumarkt" and "Altes Dresden") overlook the pleasant Neumarkt square in front of the Frauenkirche, another is on the touristy Münzgasse restaurant street, a fourth is on Schössergasse, and the fifth is a bit closer to the Hauptbahnhof on Altmarkt square (rates for up to 2 people: studio-€95-155, 2-room apartment-€125-195, 3-room apartment-€135-180, extra person-€25, rates depend on unit size and amenities, cheaper for longer stays and off-season—roughly Nov and Jan-March, breakfast-€12 at nearby café, free Wi-Fi, parking at nearby garage-€15, Münzgasse building has smoking rooms—otherwise non-smoking, reception for Neumarkt and Altmarkt units is in gift shop at An der Frauenkirche 20, reception for Münzgasse apartments is at Münzgasse 10, reception for Schössergasse at Schössergasse 16, tel. 0351/438-1111, fax 0351/438-1122, www.aparthotels-frauen kirche.de, info@aparthotels-frauenkirche.de, Drescher family).

$$ Hotel Kipping, with 20 tidy rooms 100 yards behind the Hauptbahnhof, is professionally run by the friendly and proper Kipping brothers (Rainer and Peter). The building was one of few in this area to survive the firebombing—in fact, people took shelter here during the attack (Sb-€65-105, Db-€80-120; suite: Sb-€115-130, Db-€130-145; extra bed-€25; higher prices are for weekends, May-June, and Sept-Oct; elevator, free Internet access and Wi-Fi, free parking, air-con on upper floors; exit the station following signs for *Bayerische Strasse* near track 6, it's at Winckelmannstrasse 6, from here tram #8 whisks you to the Old Town; tel. 0351/478-500, fax 0351/478-5090, www.hotel-kipping.de, reception@hotel-kipping.de). Their restaurant serves international cuisine and Saxon specialties (€9-12 main courses, Mon-Sat 18:00-22:00, closed Sun).

$ **Hotels Bastei, Königstein,** and **Lilienstein** are cookie-cutter members of the Ibis chain, goose-stepping single-file up Prager Strasse (listed in order from the station to the center). Each place is practically identical, and all together they have 918 rooms. Nobody will pretend they have charm, but they're a good value in a convenient location between the Hauptbahnhof and the Old Town. They're historic, too—a chance to experience communist designers' revolutionary, if warped, vision of urban life (Sb-€59-99, Db-€59-109, extra bed-€25, kids 12 and under free, prices vary with demand—book online for best deal, breakfast-€10, elevator, free Internet access, pay Wi-Fi, parking-€3.50-€6, reservations for all: tel. 0351/4856-2000; individual receptions: tel. 0351/4856-5445, tel. 0351/4856-6445, and tel. 0351/4856-7445, respectively; www.ibis-dresden.de).

$ **Ibis Budget Dresden City,** with 203 simple rooms, is conveniently situated right by the Postplatz tram stop, steps from the major sights (Sb-€41, Db-€51, breakfast-€7.50, air-con, free Wi-Fi, parking-€8/day; Wilsdruffer Strasse 25, tel. 0351/8339-3820, fax 0351/8339-3825, www.ibisbudget.com, h7514-fo@accor.com).

In the New Town

The first two hotels are comfy splurges in the tidy residential neighborhood between the Neustadt train station and the Augustus Bridge. The third hotel, plus the two cheap and funky hostels, are buried in the trendy, happening Outer New Town zone (see "Nightlife in Dresden," earlier).

$$$ **Hotel Bayerischer Hof Dresden,** 100 yards toward the river from the Neustadt train station, offers 50 spacious rooms and elegant, inviting public spaces in a grand old building. Ask for a room facing the quiet courtyard (Sb-€95, Db-€132, Db suite-€159, extra bed-€40, breakfast included, non-smoking rooms, elevator, free Internet access, pay Wi-Fi, free parking, Antonstrasse 33-35, yellow building across from station, tel. 0351/829-370, fax 0351/801-4860, www.bayerischer-hof-dresden.de, info@bayerischer-hof-dresden.de).

$$ **Hotel Martha Dresden,** with 50 rooms near the recommended restaurants on Königstrasse, is bright and cheery. The two old buildings that make up the hotel have been smartly renovated and connected in back with a glassed-in winter garden and an out-

door breakfast terrace. It's a 10-minute walk to the historical center and a five-minute walk to Neustadt Station (four S with private bath down hall-€55, Sb-€79-86, Db-€113, "superior" Db-€121, extra bed-€27, includes breakfast, elevator, free Internet access and Wi-Fi; leaving Neustadt Station, turn right on Hainstrasse, left on Theresenstrasse, then right on Nieritzstrasse to #11; tel. 0351/81760, fax 0351/8176-222, www.hotel-martha-dresden.de, rezeption@hotel-martha-dresden.de).

$$ AHA Hotel has an unassuming facade on a big, noisy street, but inside you'll find a homey and welcoming ambience. The 30 neat and spacious rooms all come with kitchenettes; most have balconies. It's a bit farther from the center, but its friendliness, coziness, and good value make it a winner (Sb-€58-63, Db-€73-83, extra bed-€25, breakfast-€7.50, more expensive rooms on quieter back side worth requesting, non-smoking rooms, elevator, free Internet access and Wi-Fi; Bautzner Strasse 53, 10 minutes by foot east of Albertplatz or take tram #11 from Hauptbahnhof or Neustadt Station to Pulsnitzer Strasse stop; tel. 0351/800-850, fax 0351/8008-5114, www.ahahotel-dresden.de, kontakt@ahahotel-dresden.de).

$ Hostel Louise 20 rents 78 beds in the middle of the Outer New Town action. Though located in this wild-and-edgy nightlife district, it feels safe, solid, clean, and comfy. The recently furnished rooms, guests' kitchen, cozy common room, and friendly staff make it a good place for cheap beds (S-€30-35, D-€38-46, small dorm-€14-18/bed, sheets-€2.50, breakfast-€5.50, free Wi-Fi in common areas, pay Internet access, launderette down street, might be booked on summer weekends, in the courtyard at Louisenstrasse 20, tel. 0351/889-4894, fax 0351/889-4893, www.louise20.de, info@louise20.de).

$ Hostel Mondpalast Dresden is young and hip, with 94 beds above a trendy bar in the heart of the Outer New Town. Its super-groovy vibe makes it one of the coolest hostels in Europe—it's good for backpackers with little money and an appetite for late-night fun (S-€34, Sb-€44, D-€44, Db-€52, dorm bed-€14-18, prices rise by about €5/room Fri-Sat, sheets-€2, breakfast-€6.50, free Wi-Fi, pay Internet access, lockers, kitchen, bike rental-€7/day, launderette across street, near Kamenzer Strasse at Louisenstrasse 77, take tram #11 from Hauptbahnhof or Neustadt Station to Pulsnitzer Strasse stop, tel. 0351/563-4050, fax 0351/563-4055, www.mondpalast.de, info@mondpalast.de).

Eating in Dresden

Nearly every restaurant seems bright, shiny, and modern. Old Town restaurants tend to be nice but touristy, and a bit expensive, with main courses ranging from €9 to €17. For cheaper prices and authentic local character, leave the famous center, cross the river, and wander through the New Town.

A special local dessert sold all over town is *Dresdner Eierschecke,* an eggy cheesecake with vanilla pudding, raisins, and almond shavings.

In the Old Town

Altmarkt Keller (a.k.a. Sächsisch-Böhmisches Bierhaus), a few blocks from the river on Altmarkt square, is a festive beer cellar that serves nicely presented Saxon and Bohemian food (from separate menus) and has good Czech beer on tap. The lively crowd, cheesy brass-band music (live Fri-Sat 19:00-22:00), and jolly murals add to the fun. While the on-square seating is fine, most choose the vast-but-stout air-conditioned cellar. The giant mural inside the entryway portrays the friendship between Dresden and Prague, proclaiming that "the sunshine of life is drinking and being merry" (€9-16 main courses, daily 11:00-24:00, Altmarkt 4, to the right of McDonald's, tel. 0351/481-8130).

Grand Café Restaurant Cosel Palais, which serves Saxon and French cuisine in the shadow of the Frauenkirche, is one of the few places near the church that offers a good value. Indoors is a Baroque, chandeliered dining experience; outdoors there's unusually fine courtyard seating—great for an elegant meal or tea and pastries (€12-14 main courses, cheaper daily specials, daily 10:00-24:00, An der Frauenkirche 12, tel. 0351/496-2444).

Dresden 1900, a streetcar-themed eatery with friendly and efficient waitstaff in conductor uniforms, is right behind the Frauenkirche, and also offers a decent value for a place in the midst of the action. Sure, it's touristy and tacky, but if you're lucky you can get a seat in the 1899-era streetcar. They have a nice breakfast buffet for €10, air-conditioning in summer, and outdoor tables with a great church view (€10-16 main courses, Mon-Sat 8:00-24:00, Sun 9:00-24:00, An der Frauenkirche 20, tel. 0351/4820-5858).

Medieval Theme Restaurants: All the rage among Dresdeners (and German tourists in Dresden) is *Erlebnisgastronomie* ("Experience Gastronomy"). Elaborately decorated theme restaurants have sprouted next to the biggest-name sights around town, with over-the-top theme-park decor and historically costumed waitstaff. These can offer a fun change of pace and aren't the bad value you might expect. The best is **Sophienkeller,** which does its best to take you to the 18th century and the world of Augustus the Strong.

Old Town Hotels & Restaurants

200 Meters
200 Yards

Elbe River

NEW TOWN

SEMPER-OPER

AM ZWINGER-TEICH

Theater-platz

ITALIENISCHES DÖRFCHEN

BOATS

HOF-KIRCHE

BRÜHLSCHE TERRASSE "BALCONY OF EUROPE"

SCHINKEL-WACHE

TERRASSENUFER

ZWINGER

Theater-platz

SYNAGOGUE

Canal

ROYAL PALACE

Neu-markt

COSEL PALACE

ALBERT-INUM

SOPHIEN-STR.

TASCHENBERG

❻

Synagogue

TASCHENBERG PALACE

❶

FRAUEN-KIRCHE

❺

❶

❹

Postplatz

COMMUNIST MURAL

PALACE OF CULTURE

O L D

T O W N

Postplatz

❷

LANDHAUS-STR.

To Main Train Station via Trams #8, 9 & 11

Altmarkt

WILSDRUFFER STRASSE

Pirnaischer Platz

❸

KREUZ-KIRCHE

To Main Train Station via Trams #3 & 7

ST. PETERSBURGER STRASSE

MARIEN-STR.

WALLSTRASSE

To Prager Strasse & Main Train Station

CAROLABRÜCKE

AUGUSTUS-BRÜCKE

OSTRA-ALLEE

❶ Aparthotels an der Frauenkirche Reception Offices (3)
❷ Ibis Budget Dresden City
❸ Altmarkt Keller Restaurant
❹ Grand Café Restaurant Cosel Palais

❺ Dresden 1900 Restaurant
❻ Sophienkeller Restaurant
❼ Radeberger Spezialausschank Café
❽ Augustus Garten Restaurant

DRESDEN

The king himself, along with his countess, musicians, and magicians, stroll and entertain, while court maidens serve traditional Saxon food from ye olde menu. Read their colorful brochure to better understand the place. It's big (470 seats), and it even has a rotating carousel table with suspended swing-chairs that you sit in while you eat. Before choosing a seat, survey the two big and distinct zones—one bright and wide open, the other more intimate and cellar-like (€9-17 main courses, daily 11:00-24:00, in cellar under the five-star Kempinski Taschenberg Palace Hotel at Taschenberg 3, enter across street from Zwinger, tel. 0351/497-260).

With a River View: Radeberger Spezialausschank Café is dramatically situated on the Brühlsche Terrasse promenade, with a rampart-hanging view terrace and three levels taking you down to the river. For river views from the "Balcony of Europe," this is your spot. The tasty-yet-simple menu includes Saxon standards as well as wurst and kraut. This is the only place in town that serves Radeberger's unfiltered beer, and the cool river-level bar comes with big copper brewery vats (€10-16 main courses, €8-10 wurst plates, daily 11:00-24:00, reservations smart for view terrace, Terrassenufer 1, tel. 0351/484-8660).

In the New Town

Venture to these eateries—across Augustus Bridge from the Old Town—for lower prices and a more local scene. I've listed them nearest to farthest from the Old Town.

Just Across Augustus Bridge

Augustus Garten is a lazy, crude-yet-inviting beer garden with super-cheap self-service food (pork knuckle, wurst, kraut, cheap beer, and lots of mustard). You'll eat among big bellies—and few tourists—with a good view back over the river to the Old Town. While enjoyable in balmy weather, this place is dead when it's cool out and closed when it's cold (€5-10 main courses, €3.20 half-liter beers, €2 refundable deposit on beer glasses, daily 11:00-24:00, Wiesentorstrasse 2, tel. 0351/404-5531). As you walk across the bridge from the Old Town, it's on your immediate right.

On Königstrasse

For trendy elegance without tourists, have dinner on Königstrasse. After crossing the Augustus Bridge, hike five minutes up Haupt-strasse, the communist-built main drag of the New Town, then turn left to find this charming Baroque street. As this is a fast-changing area, you might survey the other options on and near Königstrasse (be sure to tuck into a few courtyards) before settling down.

Wenzel Prager Bierstuben serves country Bohemian cuisine in a woodsy bar that spills out into an airy, glassed-in gallery—made doubly big by its vast mirror. Stepping inside, you'll be immediately won over by the interior. There's also peaceful streetside seating. The menu is fun and Bohemian, with three varieties of the great Czech Staropramen beer on tap (€9-10 main-dish-with-small-beer specials on Tue-Thu, €9-14 main courses, daily 11:00-24:00, Königstrasse 1, tel. 0351/804-2010).

Good Friends is a favorite for Thai and Vietnamese food (€8-13 main courses, €6 lunches on weekdays, daily 11:30-15:00 & 17:30-22:30, Sat-Sun from 12:00, An der Dreikönigskirche 8, tel. 0351/646-5814). Walk down Königstrasse to the towering Three Kings Church. It's under the steeple.

Beer Halls

All of Dresden's famous beer halls were destroyed in the war, and the communists refused to rebuild them. But after unification, ambitious Dresdeners began re-creating this tradition. Beer halls usually serve their own brew and meaty German cuisine. Germans love to eat and talk, so beer halls are great places to meet locals and get a taste of life outside of tourist areas. All of these places are far from the city center but easily reached by public transportation.

Brauhaus am Waldschlösschen is fun and lively, with nightly music that really gets going after 21:00. It's worth the extra effort it takes to reach this place. The self-service beer garden on the terrace overlooks the Elbe River Valley, with Dresden's Old Town in the distance (half-chicken-€4, pork knuckle with kraut-€7.50, Mon-Thu €9 daily specials include a large beer). Indoors and under a shady awning, the restaurant serves traditional Saxon cuisine with some fine salads (€9-13 main courses, daily 11:00-24:00, Am Brauhaus 8b, tram #11 to Waldschlösschen—it's in squarish building above tram stop, tel. 0351/652-3900).

Ball und Brauhaus Watzke, the oldest of the beer halls, started life as a ballroom (it still holds public balls once a month). It sits pleasantly on the banks of the Elbe, with nice views of the Old Town. Watzke serves traditional beer-hall food in huge portions and features €10 main-course-with-beer specials on some weekdays (€8-12 main courses, daily 11:00-24:00, Kötzschenbroderstrasse 1, tram #4 or #9 to Altpieschen, tel. 0351/852-920). The brewery also operates the **Watzke Brauereiausschank am Goldenen Reiter** pub in the New Town, just over the Augustus Bridge. It has the same beer and menu, with a good view of the Frauenkirche and an open atmosphere—but lacks the ambience of the original (daily 11:00-24:00, Hauptstrasse 1, in front of Golden Rider statue, tel. 0351/810-6820).

Feldschlösschen Stammhaus was the original brewery and hops warehouse for Feldschlösschen beer, but the company moved to another part of Dresden in the 1970s. Although significantly farther afield than the other beer halls, Stammhaus is worth the trek—it's a cozy, energy-filled spot in a sea of East German prefab apartments. Traditional fare dominates the menu, but Stammhaus sneaks in large portions of fresh vegetables and fresh homemade bread (€8-12 main courses, €5-8 lunch and dinner specials with a beer, daily 11:00-24:00, Budapester Strasse 32, bus #62 from Prager Strasse tram platforms to Agentur für Arbeit stop—yes, there is a beer hall next to the unemployment office, tel. 0351/471-8855). Sadly, they don't brew *Hefeweizen* here.

Dresden Connections

From Dresden by Train to: Görlitz (hourly, 1.25-1.75 hours), **Bautzen** (about hourly, 40-60 minutes; Bautzen-bound trains continue on to Görlitz), **Zittau** (better from Neustadt, hourly, 1.75-2.25 hours), **Leipzig** (1-2/hour direct, 1.25-1.5 hours), **Berlin** (every 2 hours, more with transfer in Leipzig, 2.25 hours), **Erfurt** (nearly hourly direct, 2.5 hours; more possible with change in Leipzig, 3 hours), **Wittenberg** (1-2/hour, 2-3.5 hours, transfer in Leipzig and sometimes also Bitterfeld), **Prague** (every 2 hours, 2.25-2.5 hours), **Hamburg** (4/day direct, 4.5 hours; otherwise about hourly with change in Leipzig or Berlin, 4-4.5 hours), **Frankfurt** (hourly, 4.75 hours), **Nürnberg** (hourly, 4.5 hours, may change in Leipzig), **Munich** (every 2 hours, 6 hours, transfer in Nürnberg), **Vienna** (2/day direct, 7 hours; plus 1 night train/day, 9 hours), **Budapest** (4/day, 9.5 hours; plus 1 night train, 11.5 hours). There are overnight trains from Dresden to Zürich, the Rhineland, and Munich. Train info: Tel. 0180-599-6633, www.bahn.com.

GÖRLITZ

Tucked away in Germany's easternmost corner, the surprisingly beautiful town of Görlitz is a treasure trove of architecture and one of this country's best-kept secrets.

During the Middle Ages, Görlitz (GUR-lits) prospered from trade in cloth and beer. The Old Town was built up as the centuries passed, leaving it a delightful collage of architectural styles. The town escaped most of World War II's bombs, but soon after was split in two along the river—with its downtown in Germany, but a good chunk of its suburbs in Poland. Görlitz's historic buildings were preserved by the East German government, saving the city from the unsightly communist-era blemishes that mark most former East German towns.

After the Wall fell, Görlitz sprang back to life and polished its gorgeous facades. The town offers a unique opportunity to venture to the eastern fringes of Germany, sample Silesian culture and cuisine, and appreciate some fine architecture and a pleasant cityscape. Best of all, although German tourists fill Görlitz on weekends during the summer, it's still virtually undiscovered by foreign tourists—making it a real Back Door experience.

Planning Your Time

Although Görlitz is an ideal day trip from Dresden (hourly trains, 70-90 minutes), the city has inexpensive hotels and its charm warrants an overnight stay. Görlitz opens up on long summer nights, as pubs and cafés spill out into the cobbles. Get lost and wander the back streets and alleys.

Orientation to Görlitz

With a population of about 56,000, Görlitz is the largest city in Saxony east of Dresden, but still small enough to feel sleepy. While a third of the town was given to Poland in 1945, the historic center and most sights of interest to travelers remain in Germany. Most sights are in the compact Old Town (Altstadt), stretching roughly between Marienplatz and the western bank of the Neisse River. The focal points of the Old Town are its twin market squares, Obermarkt and Untermarkt. Modern shopping and services are concentrated in the newer, 19th-century section of downtown, between the Old Town and the train station. Though more modern, this area is considered by many to be no less handsome than the Old Town.

Tourist Information

The TI, called Görlitzinformation, is at the bottom of Obermarkt, the main square inside the Old Town. Free (but very basic) maps are available here. They can arrange guided tours in English and book you a room for free (Easter-Oct Mon-Fri 9:00-18:00, Sat 9:00-17:00, Sun 9:00-16:00; Nov-Easter Mon-Fri 9:30-18:00, Sat-Sun 9:00-14:30, Obermarkt 32, tel. 03581/47570, www.goerlitz.de). Pick up the €1 "Görlitz Experience" brochure, which includes a house-by-house map of the Old Town with brief architectural commentary—more useful than the comprehensive street map (€3). For more detail, look for "Görlitz: A City of Many Faces" (€12, overkill for most visitors).

Festival: Görlitz gets very busy during its annual Old Town Festival (Altstadtfest), on the last weekend in August, with music, stalls on the square, and a medieval market.

Arrival in Görlitz

Görlitz's quiet train station, about a half-mile southwest of the city center, is a sight in itself. Built in 1901, the main hall is a pearl of Prussian *Jugendstil* (Art Nouveau), and the vaguely Neoclassical facade is handsome, too. Lockers are in the passage between the tracks and the main hall (€1.50-2.50). You'll also find handy WCs (€0.50, deposit coin, then wait for buzzer and pull on door) and a *Reisezentrum* for train information and tickets (Mon-Fri 8:00-17:00 except Wed closed 13:00-13:45, Sat 8:00-13:00, closed Sun).

To get into town (a 15-minute **walk**), exit straight through the front entrance and follow Berliner Strasse. At the first large square (Postplatz), the road veers left, and you'll see the former Hertie department store building (marking Marienplatz and the start of my self-guided walk). You can also go three stops on **tram** #2 or #3 to

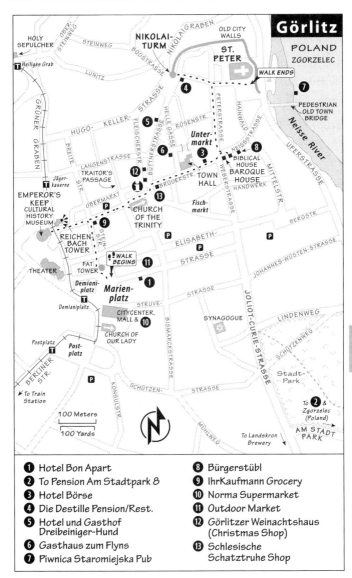

Görlitz

❶ Hotel Bon Apart	❽ Bürgerstübl
❷ To Pension Am Stadtpark 8	❾ IhrKaufmann Grocery
❸ Hotel Börse	❿ Norma Supermarket
❹ Die Destille Pension/Rest.	⓫ Outdoor Market
❺ Hotel und Gasthof Dreibeiniger-Hund	⓬ Görlitzer Weinachtshaus (Christmas Shop)
❻ Gasthaus zum Flyns	⓭ Schlesische Schatztruhe Shop
❼ Piwnica Staromiejska Pub	

Demianiplatz (departs from the platform on your right and across the tracks as you exit the station; €1.30, 4-6/hour, 5 minutes).

Getting Around Görlitz

There are only two tram lines (#2 and #3), plus a few bus lines; most intersect at Demianiplatz. But the Old Town is compact, so unless you're planning to visit the Holy Sepulcher or go out to the

Landeskrone mountain, you may only use public transit to get from the train station into the city center (and even that stretch is walkable without heavy luggage). Buy tickets from the machines on the platforms and trams (coins only) or from bus drivers, and validate them in the little blue box on board (€1.30/ride, *Einzelfahrt Normal;* €3 day pass, *Tageskarte Normal;* €6.50 pass for up to 5 people, *Kleingruppenkarte*). For transit info, see www.zvon.de or www.vgg-goerlitz.de.

Self-Guided Walk

Welcome to Görlitz

The joy of Görlitz is simply wandering the Old Town while appreciating the architecture and history, and poking into shops. Begin this orientation walk at Marienplatz, a square around the corner from the tram stop at Demianiplatz, and just outside the former city walls.

Marienplatz

The unique Art Nouveau **Hertie department store** building (opened in 1913 as the Kaufhaus zum Strauss) has a richly decorated facade concealing an ornate glass-domed interior with intricate staircases and galleries. Though its logo remains on the building, Hertie, a Germany-wide chain, closed and went bankrupt in 2009 (raising worries that Germans will transfer their loyalty from downtown shops to the likes of Wal-Mart and Amazon). To see the amazing interior, pop into the perfume store that now occupies the ground floor. In the entryway are exhibits (in German only) on the history of the building (Mon-Fri 9:00-18:30, Sat 9:00-16:00, closed Sun).

Behind the building is the **Church of Our Lady** (Frauenkirche), a 15th-century late-Gothic church built near the hospital and poorhouse outside the city walls. Although this church seems unremarkable, take a moment to step inside (free, daily 12:00-17:00; Mon-Sat try to catch the *Mittagsrast* prayer and organ music at 12:00).

Imagine being here in the fall of 1989, shortly before the Berlin Wall came down. This church served as a

Görlitz and Silesia

Of the old German province of Silesia ("Schlesien" in German)—which belonged to Prussia, and later to united Germany, from 1742 to 1945—only Görlitz and its surroundings are still part of Germany. The rest is mostly in Poland (where the word for Silesia is "Śląsk"), and a small part is in the Czech Republic ("Slezsko").

The area has always been a melting pot of Germanic and Slavic culture, with more Germans in the towns and Slavs in the countryside. The town of "Gorelec" was first mentioned in 1071, and while the name is Slavic in origin, the town has been predominantly German ever since records began. For most of its early existence, the city technically belonged to Bohemia, which explains why its layout and architecture closely resembles Prague and other Czech towns. But Görlitz was ceded to Saxony after the Peace of Prague in 1635. In 1815, Görlitz fell into Prussian hands at the Congress of Vienna (a punishment for Saxony's support of Napoleon) and with the surrounding towns it was attached to the province of Silesia. After German unification in 1871, Silesia was the finger of the empire that stretched southeastward almost to Kraków.

The city's unusual experience in World War II made it the unique place it is today. First, Görlitz almost miraculously escaped destruction in the war (only its Old Town Bridge was bombed). Then it was split in two by the Potsdam Agreement in 1945. This treaty decreed that the Neisse River—which runs through the center of Görlitz—would be the border between Germany and Poland. The following year, Poland expelled all Germans from its territory, and Poles who had in turn been expelled from eastern Polish lands (now given to Ukraine and Belarus) were resettled in former German homes.

These expulsions created two ethnically distinct halves: the German town of Görlitz on the west side of the river and the Polish town of Zgorzelec in the east. Most Germans of Silesian descent have long since abandoned any hope of reclaiming their lost homeland (just as Poles have given up hopes of reclaiming their eastern territories). But as the "Silesian" shops and museums in Görlitz show, the city is a focal point for Germans wishing to pay homage to their lost roots. (This despite the fact that Görlitz was a latecomer to Silesia and is now once again administered as part of Saxony.) Meanwhile, communities on both sides of the border have gone to great efforts to stress European unity and cooperation by re-establishing cultural connections across the rivers and mountains. Görlitz and Zgorzelec cooperate closely in tourism promotion, planning, and cultural affairs. You'll also hear Polish spoken in the streets of Görlitz and see it on signs.

In 2004, German Görlitz and Polish Zgorzelec completed the reconstruction of a new pedestrian-only Old Town Bridge (Altstadtbrücke) across the Neisse. Locals like to think this largely symbolic gesture makes Görlitz the most European city in Europe. And now that Poland has joined the open-borders Schengen Agreement, anyone can freely cross the bridge without having to flash a passport.

forum for discussions and peace prayers *(Friedensgebete)*. A poster announcing the first prayer meeting was placed in the glass cabinet on the front of the church. Soon, like-minded shopkeepers began to follow suit, and 580 people attended the first meeting. Just two weeks later, 1,300 people showed up, and subsequent meetings swelled to 5,000—so large that they spilled over into other churches. The meetings became a forum for discussing impending political changes, civil rights, and environmental issues. As each participant came forward and voiced his or her concerns, a candle was blown out until the church was dark. Then, as those who had a hopeful or positive experience came forward, a candle was lit until the church was illuminated once again.

The East German secret police, the Stasi, stationed plainclothes police in the buildings across the street to document who was participating in these "acts of civil disobedience." Many people lost their jobs or were otherwise punished. But the hope for democracy and self-determination had already caught on, and today, this church stands as a symbol of peace and solidarity.

On the north side of Marienplatz, the **Fat Tower** (Dicker Turm) is the second-oldest tower in the city's defensive network. Although the tower itself is Gothic (from 1270), it's topped by a copper Renaissance cupola. It's decorated with a sandstone relief of the Görlitz city coat of arms, featuring a Bohemian lion and a Silesian black eagle—representing Görlitz as an independent and free city. A large gate used to stand next to the tower, but it was torn down in the 1840s.

• *Walk down the street to the left of the tower (Steinstrasse) and onto...*

Obermarkt (Upper Market Square)

This 13th-century square is lined with mainly Baroque houses. Like many town squares in east-central Europe, it's long and skinny, with a church at one end.

Reichenbach Tower, dominating the upper (western) end of the square, formed part of the western city wall and dates from the 13th century. The upper portion was added in 1485 and is topped with a Baroque cupola from 1782—take a moment to imagine how the tower looked before this addition. The tower housed city guards and watchmen—who among other things kept a lookout for fires—until the last "tower family" moved out in 1904. Inside is an impressive collection of armaments, early 20th-century photographs, and an interesting exhibit on the daily lives of the tower's occupants (€3, May-Oct Tue-Sun 10:00-17:00, closed

Mon and Nov-April, Platz des 17 Juni, tel. 03581/671-355, www. museum-goerlitz.de). The view from the top is worth the 165 steps.

Across the street with the tram tracks, you'll see a circular building. This bastion was built in 1490 as part of an effort to strengthen the city fortifications. The structure came to be known as the **Emperor's Keep** (Kaisertrutz) when the Swedish troops made their last stand against the imperial Saxon army during the Thirty Years' War. Since then, the Emperor's Keep has been used as an archive, and today it houses the Cultural History Museum, where exhibits run from the Ice Age all the way up to the fall of the Berlin Wall and DDR (€5, Tue-Sun 10:00-17:00, closed Mon, www.museum-goerlitz.de). Next to the building is a statue of Gottlob Demiani, mayor of Görlitz in the early 1800s.

• *At the other end of Obermarkt, the tall tower belongs to the...*

Church of the Trinity (Dreifaltigkeitskirche)

In 1245, Franciscan monks consecrated this church at the southeast corner of Obermarkt. Although originally a Romanesque structure, renovations in 1380 gave the church its current late-Gothic appearance. When the Reformation took hold in Silesia in 1563, the monks surrendered the keys to  the church and monastery—with the condition that the monastery be used as a school. A school operates in the former monastery to this day.

Cost and Hours: Free, daily 12:00-18:00, tel. 03581/643-460.

Visiting the Church: The interior seems austere, but reveals delightful little details. As you enter, go immediately to your left. This is the oldest part of the church. Pillars from the original 13th-century Romanesque chapel are integrated into the walls. The fancy balcony is where the nobility sat. If you've been to Dresden, the high altar will look familiar. Built by artists brought from Dresden, it resembles the crown gate of the Zwinger. The swirly clouds identify this as Rococo. The missing crucifix on the left wall (now in Warsaw) is a reminder of the artifacts that were pillaged from this church during various wars, but the choir stalls, carved in the 1430s, are original.

The church's trophy is in the back chapel: the **Marienaltar,** a beautiful 15th-century carved triptych. It's three works of art in one: Folded up, only the decoration on the outer side of the doors is visible. With these doors open, you can see a grid of eight painted panels on another, inner set of doors. And when these

inner doors are open, you can see
an almost life-size carving of the
Virgin Mary. In the past, only the
eight painted panels were usually
on display, with the Virgin Mary
reserved for high feast days. Today,
the altarpiece is usually fully open,
and reproductions of the outer
doors and the eight interior panels are displayed on an easel to the
right of the altar. The altarpiece is
an eyeful—rich with action and

symbolism. Study the reproductions of the inner doors. The sym-
metry and order of the checked tablecloth is replaced in the other
panels by lots of action and purposefully conflicting lines that create energy and tension. Notice the symbolism—there's a turban-
wearing Ottoman (archenemy of the time) and Jesus wearing a
Franciscan frock (a nod to the church's Franciscan heritage).

Behind you, an exhausted **Jesus,** reminiscent of Auguste Ro-

din's *Thinker,* ponders the fate of man.
This painted wooden statue, from 1910,
used to sit on the grass outside of the
Holy Sepulcher (described under "More
Sights in Görlitz," later)—notice the rot-
ted wood at the base.

The church's **tower** is unusually thin—the locals call it the *Mönch*
("Monk"). The clock doesn't keep very
good time, thanks to one in a series of
Cloth-Maker Rebellions. In the Middle
Ages, Görlitz was run by the powerful
guilds of the cloth trade and the brewers,
who neglected the rights of their workers
and forbade nonmembers from practic-
ing their trades. Finally, in the early 16th
century, the workers rose up against the
corrupt city council, which allowed the guilds to continue their un-
fair practices. The rebels ended their meetings punctually at midnight to avoid the night watchmen, who would be on the other side
of town at that hour. But the city council was one step ahead: They
ordered the church bell to chime seven minutes before midnight to
fool the conspirators out onto the street and into the waiting arms
of the guard. Fourteen of the conspirators were executed, and 25
more banished from the city. To this day, the bell chimes seven
minutes early.

Across the square (starting from the archway at #27) is the

Görlitz Architecture

Although no bombs fell on Görlitz itself during World War II (only on its bridge), the city has experienced its share of de-struction, from the Thirty Years' War to the ravages of three great city fires. Each wave of devastation allowed Görlitz to rebuild in the architectural style of the time. The results are an astonishing collection of exemplary buildings from every architectural era: Gothic, Renaissance, Baroque, *Gründerzeit* (late 19th century), and *Jugendstil* (Art Nouveau). In the late 20th century, the East German government placed the entire city under a protection order, rescuing it from the bleak communist aesthetic of the time. More than 3,700 buildings are registered historical monuments.

Even now, energetic reconstruction efforts continue, partly thanks to the city's secret admirer: Every year since 1993, an unnamed benefactor has donated the equivalent of one million Deutsch Marks (about $665,000) to renovation projects. Nobody knows who this person is, and anyone who attempts to find out is dealt a swift warning from a high-priced Munich lawyer. All of these factors have contributed to making Görlitz the gem that it is today.

Traitor's Passage (Verrätergasse), a dark, sinister alley used by the instigators of the rebellion to sneak in and out of the main mar-ketplace. Walk about halfway down and you'll see the letters *DVRT 1527* carved into the stone next to a gate on the right. This was where the traitors met and stored their weapons. "DVRT" stands for "*die verräterische Rotte Tor*," or "The Gate of the Traitorous Gang"—it's a warning.

• *Return to Obermarkt, then walk down...*

Brüderstrasse

This street, connecting Obermarkt and Untermarkt, is home to a fine collection of Renaissance houses. These houses were the single-family dwellings of Görlitz's rich tradesmen, who lived on the upper floors and stored their goods on the street level. On the left, just down Apothekergasse, is a handy public WC (€0.50, men pee for free).

The orange-and-gray house at the end of Brüderstrasse (#8) claims to be Germany's oldest Renaissance civic building (from 1526) and now houses the **Silesian Museum of Görlitz** (Schlesisches Museum zu Görlitz), a state museum focusing on Silesian history and culture (€5, free English audioguide, Tue-Sun 10:00-17:00, closed Mon, Brüderstrasse 8, tel. 03581/87910, www.schlesisches-museum.de).

• *At the end of Brüderstrasse, you'll reach...*

Untermarkt (Lower Market Square)

This square (which doesn't fully feel like a square, thanks to the four-story buildings in the center) shows just how prosperous the cloth trade made Görlitz.

First, take a look at the buildings that form a sort of traffic island in the middle of the square. The run-down one at #14 (east end of the "island") housed the city **scales;** it was one of the most important commercial buildings because, at its peak, more than 1,000 wagons per day entered Görlitz. Everything had to be weighed and duties paid here. The late-Gothic ground floor, which housed the scales, is topped off with three Renaissance levels. The column-topping busts are a Who's Who of the town's masons and scale-masters.

Around the corner from the scales, on the northern side of the island, the city established a **commodity exchange** *(Börse)* at the beginning of the 18th century. The building was also a kind of department store used to drive simple street vendors away from the financial center. With the rabble banished, the Baroque building with its adorning portal was a favored place for merchants to meet and deal.

• *Now, on the upper side of the square, look at the tall Gothic tower of the...*

Town Hall (Rathaus)

Görlitz had no Town Hall until 1350, when the city purchased this building from a prominent citizen. The tower was extended to 195 feet in 1368. A lightning strike blew the top off the tower on July 9, 1742, prompting the addition of the current Baroque turret. The tower houses two clocks: The upper clock measures the day, month, and phase of the moon, while the lower clock tells the time.

GÖRLITZ

The warrior's head used to stick out his tongue every hour, but now he just seems to open his mouth. The date inscribed on the clock, 1584, commemorates the year when Bartholomäus Sculteus, an astronomer and mathematician, first divided the clock into 12 points. Sculteus also helped develop the Gregorian calendar. The city honored Sculteus, a Görlitz native, by being the first city in Germany to adopt both the new calendar and the clock. The Town Hall stairs represent the height of Görlitz Renaissance sculpture and lead from the street level to the building's then-main entrance. Local officials used the balcony to make public announcements and decrees. Look closely at the statue of Justice (1591): She's not blindfolded—in other words, the city is the highest authority.

• *For evidence that Görlitz is definitely a Protestant town, go to the lower corner of the square and head down Neissstrasse to #29. There you'll find the...*

Biblical House

As the Catholic Church had banned religious depictions on secular buildings, the carvings on the Biblical House made it clear that the Reformation was here to stay. The houses in the Neissstrasse  had all burned to the ground in 1526. Hanz Heinz, a cloth trader, purchased this house and rebuilt it completely in the Renaissance style. The house is named after the sandstone reliefs decorating the facade between the first- and second-floor parapets. The top level represents the New Testament, with (from left to right) the Annunciation, birth of Jesus, Jesus' baptism, the Last Supper, and the Crucifixion. The bottom row depicts the creation of Eve, the Fall of Man, Isaac's sacrifice, Moses receiving the Ten Commandments, and Moses banishing serpents.

• *Next door at #30, step into the...*

Baroque House (Barockhaus)

This museum offers a peek at life in the 17th and 18th centuries, as well as a fine historical library with books and manuscripts dating back to the Middle Ages (€5, Tue-Sun 10:00-17:00, closed Mon, tel. 03581/671-351, www.museum-goerlitz.de).

• *Backtrack to Untermarkt and look right.*

City Apothecary (Ratsapotheke)

The pretty gray-and-pink building at the northeast corner of Untermarkt was once the city pharmacy. The owner attempted to transform a Gothic building into a Renaissance masterpiece, but ended up only combining the two styles. The two sundials on the southern facade were added in 1550. The left dial (Solarium) displays the time using the Arabic, local, Roman, and Babylonian clocks. The dial on the right (*Arachne*, "spider" in Greek) displays the position of the planets and the signs of the zodiac. Today the City Apothecary houses one of the city's nicer cafés, Kretschmer Ratscafé.

• *The street that begins here is called...*

Peterstrasse

Peterstrasse has yet more fine buildings. The house at #6 is a fun example of mixed-up styles: The building is Renaissance, with Gothic doors and windows, Ionic columns, and Baroque decorations.

At the end of Peterstrasse, you can turn either right or left. Left leads to the **Nikolaiturm** (generally closed to the public), the oldest of Görlitz's towers, which marks the site of the original village of Gorelec. The Nikolaiturm, like all of the city-wall towers,

got a facelift in the 18th century that replaced its pointy top with its current round dome. The city walls and gates were destroyed in 1848, and the stones were used to build the Jägerkaserne, a barracks off in the distance to the left of the Nikolaiturm. The only remaining section of the city wall is now a pleasant park that curves around from the base of the Nikolaiturm to the back of the Church of St. Peter. Alternatively, to the right of the park entrance, a small alleyway (Karpfengrund) snakes its way back to Peterstrasse.

• *If you turn right at the end of Peterstrasse, you'll reach the...*

Church of St. Peter (Peterskirche)

The church was completed—after many setbacks, landslides, and Hussite invasions—in 1457, and renovated in restrained Baroque style after fire destroyed the interior in 1691. The spires were added in 1890. Inside, the Silesian-Italian Eugenio Casparini's **Sun Organ** (Sonnenorgel) is a spectacular, one-of-a-kind musical instrument and the center of Görlitz's musical life since 1701. The organ gets its name not from the little golden sun at the center (which spins when air is pushed through the

pipe), but from the 17 groups of circularly arranged pipes that shoot out like the sun's rays. Take in a free 50-minute concert Tuesday, Thursday, or Sunday at noon (Nov-March Sun only). The colorful baptistery, from 1617, is also worth a look (church open Mon-Sat 10:00-18:00, Sun 11:45-18:00—but doors close while lunchtime concerts are underway.)

• *Your walk is finished. Consider visiting some of Görlitz's other sights, or relax with a local Landskron beer.*

More Sights in Görlitz

Holy Sepulcher (Heiliges Grab)—Perhaps Görlitz's most unusual sight, this 500-year-old pilgrimage site is the only complete (and relatively accurate) replica of the garden of Gethsemane and the holy places in Jerusalem as they existed in the 15th century.

After returning from a pilgrimage to Jerusalem, former Görlitz mayor Georg Emmerich (1422-1507) commissioned this site as an offering to those who could not make such a journey themselves. The three structures were completed in 1503. The first is the two-story Chapel of the Holy Cross. Reflecting the traditional belief that Christ was crucified on the site of Adam's grave, the crypt represents the tomb of Adam with the Golgotha Chapel above. Next comes the Salbhaus, a tiny chapel with a statue of Mary anointing Jesus' dead body. Finally, the Church of the Holy Sepulcher itself is a much smaller version of the original. Several decades after this copy was built, the original in Jerusalem was damaged by fire and had to be restored, so Görlitz's Holy Sepulcher is actually more authentic than the buildings in Jerusalem. The Holy Sepulcher was a big deal for medieval pilgrims, who purchased a *Görlitzer Scheckel*—gold, silver, or pewter, according to their means—as payment to the church and a symbol of their pilgrimage.

Cost and Hours: €2; April-Sept Mon-Sat 10:00-18:00, Sun 11:00-18:00; Oct-March Mon-Sat 10:00-16:00, Sun 11:00-16:00; borrow English handout at desk, Heilige-Grab-Strasse 79, www.heiligesgrab-goerlitz.de.

Getting There: Take either tram to Heiliges Grab, two stops past Demianiplatz or five stops from the train station—the entrance is right by the tram stop. You can also walk—from the Nikolaiturm, follow Lunitz for about 10 minutes.

GÖRLITZ

▲**Landskron Brewery**—Beer has been brewed in Görlitz since the 12th century. The last remaining (and best) brewery is Landskron, which brews 12 different beers, including the best *Hefeweizen* (wheat beer) in Germany. It's also one of the last breweries to use open fermentation. The brewery offers tours in German, but the staff tries to be accommodating to English speakers. In the end, it's all about the taste samples anyway. In the summer, the brewery hosts concerts and other events.

Cost and Hours: €7 for the "0.33 Liter Tour" (1.5 hours) or €9.50 for the "0.5 Liter Tour" (2.5 hours), contact the brewery in advance to check the tour schedule and reserve (although it's usually possible to sneak into an already scheduled tour, if you ask Frau Prescher nicely), An der Landskronbrauerei 116, on other side of train tracks from Old Town, ask for public transit directions when you call, tel. 03581/465-100, www.landskron.de, info@landskron.de.

▲**Landeskrone**—On the outskirts of the city is a dormant volcano that stretches 1,376 feet above sea level. The city of Görlitz purchased the Landeskrone from the aristocracy and incorporated it into the city in 1440. The mountainside provided wood for building (especially for rebuilding the town after fires) and basalt for cobblestones, and gave the city a commanding view into three countries at once—helping to defend itself against marauding robber-barons. The observation tower on top, built on the ruins of a Bohemian fort, came in the 18th century, and was followed by a small restaurant and hotel in 1844 (the current version was rebuilt in 1951). The entire area is a park, ideal for short hikes.

Getting There: Take tram #2 to the Biesnitz/Landeskrone stop. It's about a 40-minute hike from the tram stop to the top.

Near Görlitz

Three Silesian towns near Görlitz offer an interesting and diverse glimpse into this unique cultural crossroads.

▲**Zgorzelec**—When everything east of the Neisse River (and, farther north, the Oder River) became a part of Poland, Görlitz lost its eastern suburb. By 1946, Poles transplanted from Belarus and Ukraine eliminated all traces of the German past and created the city of Zgorzelec. On both sides of the river, government and citizenry are making great strides to glue the city back together (at least culturally) in a  united Europe. And since Germany and Poland opened their borders in late 2007, you can stroll freely between the two countries.

A walk into Poland is an interesting experience and offers a stark contrast to wonderfully restored Görlitz. Zgorzelec is obviously the less wealthy part of the city, but offers a fine collection of patrician and burgher houses (along ulica Warszawska). Some have been lovingly renovated, but others are in desperate need of repair.

The main part of Zgorzelec is across the Pope John Paul II Bridge (Neissebrücke), south of the Old Town. Once across the bridge, turn to the right and go up the hill to reach the Upper Lusatian Memorial Hall (nowadays the Dom Kultury, or Civic House of Culture), a memorial to Kaiser Wilhelm I. Wander north through Poland, then cross back into Germany at the pedestrian Old Town Bridge, behind the Church of St. Peter.

Zittau and Oybin Castle (Burg Oybin)—Although Zittau is a splendid city in its own right, with pretty squares and a Town Hall by Karl Friedrich Schinkel, the real reason to come here is to take the narrow-gauge steam railroad to the top of Oybin Mountain to see the castle ruins. Bohemian Emperor Charles IV built the fortress and monastery Burg Oybin in the 14th century. The structure fell into disuse by the 16th century and was repeatedly struck by lightning in the 18th and 19th centuries. Nineteenth-century painters such as Caspar David Friedrich made the castle famous again. The ruins are huge and fun to poke around in, and the views of the unique geological formations of the Zittau Mountains are grand.

Cost and Hours: Castle entry-€5, daily April-Oct 9:00-18:00, Nov-March 10:00-16:00, www.oybin.com.

Getting There: Zittau is an easy train ride from Görlitz. Once in Zittau, to find the steam railroad (Zittauer Schmalspurbahn), exit the train station at the front, walk across the square with the bus stops, and turn left. If you're lucky, one of the steam trains will be puffing away, waiting for you. Trains generally leave Zittau for Oybin Castle every two hours, and may run more frequently on the weekends (€14 round-trip, covered by Lausitz Tageskarte with "historical train supplement"—see "Görlitz Connections," later, tel. 03583/540540, www.soeg-zittau.de.)

Bautzen/Budyšin—This town, about halfway between Dresden and Görlitz, is the cultural capital of the Sorbs (or Wends, as they are known in the US). The Sorbs—not to be confused with the Serbs of the former Yugoslavia, much farther south—are of Slavic descent, and still speak a distinct language that's a hybrid of Polish and Czech. About 20,000 Sorbs live in Germany, making up the country's only indigenous ethnic minority.

Bautzen's dual-language signs and the slightly Mediterranean feel of its spacious squares and public fountains, combined with intact city walls and a tower that's more off-center than Pisa's, make this town a perfect stopover between Dresden and Görlitz.

Bautzen is also home to Germany's only Simultaneous Church, a house of worship shared by Catholics on one side and Protestants on the other. Germany's best spicy mustard comes from Bautzen. For lunch, try **Restaurant Wjelbik,** which serves wonderful Sorbian food (Kornstrasse 7). For more information on the town, see www.bautzen.de.

Shopping in Görlitz

Görlitzer Weinachtshaus celebrates Christmas all year long. Stop here for good deals on traditional holiday craft pieces such as nutcrackers, incense burners shaped like smoking men, and Nativity scenes. Big draws are traditional paper stars from Herrnhut, handblown Sorbian glass eggs, and Thuringian glass (March-Aug Mon-Fri 10:00-17:00, Sat 10:00-16:00, Sun 10:00-15:00; Sept-Dec Mon-Fri 10:00-18:00, Sat 10:00-16:00, Sun 10:00-15:00; closed Jan-Feb; Fleischerstrasse 19, just off Obermarkt—look for the huge nutcracker out front, tel. 03581/649-205).

Schlesische Schatztruhe is a one-stop shop for all your Silesian souvenir needs: books, posters, maps, cookbooks, and more. They have an extensive selection of "Polish pottery" from Bolesławiec (Bunzlau in German). Unfortunately, they don't ship pottery to the US—you'll have to send or carry it yourself (Mon-Sat 9:00-19:00, Sun 10:00-18:00, Brüderstrasse 13, tel. 03581/410-956, www.schlesische-schatztruhe.de).

Sleeping in Görlitz

$$ Hotel Bon Apart is a comfortable hotel that's right by Demianiplatz and easy to reach from the train station by tram. It's a good value, with the best breakfast buffet in town. The 17 rooms and suites have kitchens, and they brew their own beer (Sb-€80-90, Db-€95-130, 1-person suite-€130, 2-person suite-€150, family suites-€170-220, free Wi-Fi and Internet access, Elisabethstrasse 41, tel. 03581/48080, fax 03581/480-811, www.bon-apart.de, hotel@bon-apart.de). Owner François also owns the cheaper **$ Pension Am Stadtpark 8,** with renovated rooms in a gorgeous old building on the edge of the city park, a little farther from the center overlooking the former border crossing (same contact info as Hotel Bon Apart, Am Stadtpark 8).

$$ Hotel Börse, looking right onto Untermarkt, features recently renovated rooms—many of them quite elegant (Sb-€70-75, Db-€109-119, Untermarkt 16, tel. 03581/76420, www.boerse-goerlitz.de, goerlitz-boerse@t-online.de).

$ Die Destille ("The Distillery") is another good value: a clean, friendly, family-run pension with four well-apportioned rooms near

---

Sleep Code

(€1 = about $1.30, country code: 49, area code: 03581)
S = Single, **D** = Double/Twin, **T** = Triple, **Q** = Quad, **b** = bathroom, **s** = shower only. Unless otherwise noted, credit cards
are accepted, English is spoken, and breakfast is included.

To help you sort easily through these listings, I've divided
the accommodations into two categories, based on the price
for a standard double room with bath:

$$ **Higher Priced**—Most rooms €85 or more.
$ **Lower Priced**—Most rooms less than €85.

Prices can change without notice; verify the hotel's cur-
rent rates online or by email.

---

the Nikolaiturm, on the north edge of the Old Town. Breakfast is
served at your table in the recommended ground-floor restaurant.
While renovating the building in the 1990s, workers discovered a
mikveh (ritual Jewish bath) in the basement—they let guests in to
look at it every day at 14:00 (Sb-€55, Db-€70, non-smoking, Wi-Fi
by reception, Nikolaistrasse 6, tel. 03581/405-302, fax 03581/649-
220, www.destille-goerlitz.de, info@destille-goerlitz.de). From the
station, you can take the tram to Demianiplatz, but that only gets
you halfway. Consider taking a taxi all the way (about €8).

$ Hotel und Gasthof Dreibeiniger-Hund ("Three-Legged
Dog"), down the street from Die Destille, is a small, meticulously
restored pension offering 13 cozy and romantic rooms in a 14th-
century shell (Sb-€60, Db-€73-83, cash only, book ahead in sum-
mer, non-smoking, inexpensive Wi-Fi, recommended restaurant,
Büttnerstrasse 13, tel. 03581/423-980, www.dreibeinigerhund.de).

Eating in Görlitz

Local cooking agreeably blends German traditions with Polish and
Czech influences. The Silesian specialty is *Schlesisches Himmelreich*
("Silesian Heaven"), a mix of pork roast and ham with stewed fruit in
a white sauce served with dumplings. For dessert, try *Streuselkuchen,*
a yummy crumb cake available everywhere. Landskron, Görlitz's
ubiquitous brew, is one of the best pilsners in Germany. The first
two places listed here also rent rooms (described earlier).

Die Destille, literally in the shadow of the Nikolaiturm, is
a delightful restaurant oozing comfortable country elegance, with
a friendly staff to boot. They excel at extremely traditional Sile-
sian dishes, including the best *Schlesisches Himmelreich* in town. It's

small, so come early or be prepared to share a table (€8-13 main courses, daily 11:30-14:30 & 17:30-late, Nikolaistrasse 6, tel. 03581/405-302).

Gasthof Dreibeiniger-Hund has a personal and homey restaurant, serving regional cuisine from a changing, seasonal menu. In summer, sit outside under the sprawling oak tree (€7-14 main courses, daily 11:00-23:00, Büttnerstrasse 13, tel. 03581/423-980).

Gasthaus zum Flyns is a small place located down Apothekergasse, off Brüderstrasse near the Town Hall. Named for the Sorbian lion idol that adorns its doorway, the restaurant serves traditional Silesian dishes and solid German cuisine. The highlight is the eponymous Flyns Steak—a grilled pork chop with roasted banana-curry cream sauce (€9-14 plates, Thu-Tue 11:30-14:00 & 18:00-23:00, closed Wed, Langenstrasse 1, tel. 03581/400-697).

Across the Bridge, in Poland: **Piwnica Staromiejska** ("Old Town Pub"), in a former grain mill on the Polish side of the pedestrian Old Town Bridge, serves traditional Polish cuisine, including lavish salads, borscht and *żurek* (Polish soups), and a big selection of main dishes. The lively, largely Polish crowd welcomes visitors from both sides of the city, and the friendly and helpful staff will explain the menu. Don't worry about paying with Polish *złoty*—the restaurant accepts euros and won't cheat you on the exchange (€3-7 main courses, pierogi dumplings and a Żywiec beer-€5, daily 12:00-22:00, ulica Wrocławska 1, Zgorzelec, from Germany dial 00-48-75-775-2692). There's a competing restaurant on the German side of the bridge, the Vierradenmühle, but the Piwnica wins hands down on view, price, service, and food.

Along Peterstrasse and Neissstrasse: Good eateries abound near Untermarkt. The best are on Peterstrasse, between the market and the Church of St. Peter, and on Neissstrasse, stretching from Untermarkt to the river. Almost every building on Neissstrasse was once a brewery. The pick of the litter is the **Bürgerstübl,** which was recently renovated with the help of the Landskron brewery and has a secret *Biergarten* in the back (€8-14 main courses, open Mon-Sat from 18:00, Sat-Sun also 12:00-14:00, Neissstrasse 27, tel. 03581/879-579).

Picnic Supplies: The only grocery store in the Old Town proper is the smallish **IhrKaufmann,** at the corner of Steinstrasse and Obermarkt (Mon-Fri 8:00-18:30, Sat 8:00-16:00, closed Sun). Not far away, in the CityCenter mall behind the Hertie department store and Marienplatz, is the **Norma** discount supermarket (Mon-Fri 8:00-20:00, Sat 8:00-18:00, closed Sun). For fresh fruit and produce, an outdoor market operates on Elisabethstrasse across from Hotel Bon Apart (Mon-Fri 6:00-18:00, Sat 6:00-12:00, closed Sun).

Görlitz Connections

From Görlitz by Train to: Bautzen (about hourly, 30-45 minutes; Bautzen-bound trains continue on to Dresden), **Dresden** (hourly, 1.25-1.75 hours), **Berlin** (hourly, 2.5 hours, transfer in Cottbus to the green-and-yellow ODEG train).

If you're day-tripping from Görlitz to **Zittau** (hourly, 35 minutes) to take the Oybin steam train, you'll save money with the Lausitz Tageskarte day pass (€16), which covers the steam train if you also buy the "historical train supplement" (€5). If Zittau is a stop on a trip into the Czech Republic or Poland, your best bet is the Euro-Neisse Tageskarte day pass (valid for travel as far as Liberec in the Czech Republic and Bolesławiec in Poland): At the ticket machine, choose *Euro-Neisse Tageskarte,* then *1* (€11.50); for groups of up to five adults, choose *Euro-Neisse Kleingruppenkarte,* then *1* (€23).

Train info: Tel. 0180-599-6633, www.bahn.com.

PRACTICALITIES

This section covers just the basics on traveling in Germany (for much more information, see *Rick Steves' Germany*). You can find free advice on specific topics at www.ricksteves.com/tips.

Money

Germany uses the euro currency: 1 euro (€) = about $1.30. To convert prices in euros to dollars, add about 30 percent: €20 = about $26, €50 = about $65. (Check www.oanda.com for the latest exchange rates.)

The standard way for travelers to get euros is to withdraw money from ATMs (which locals call a *Geldautomat*) using a debit or credit card, ideally with a Visa or MasterCard logo. Before departing, call your bank or credit-card company: Confirm that your card(s) will work overseas, find out the PIN code for your credit card, ask about international transaction fees, and alert them that you'll be making withdrawals in Europe. To keep your valuables safe, wear a money belt.

Dealing with "Chip and PIN": Much of Europe is adopting a "chip-and-PIN" system for credit cards, and some merchants rely on it exclusively. European chip-and-PIN cards are embedded with an electronic chip, in addition to the magnetic stripe used on our American-style cards. This means that your credit (and debit) card might not work at automated payment machines, such as those at train and subway stations, toll roads, parking garages, luggage lockers, and self-serve gas pumps. Memorizing your credit card's PIN lets you use it at some chip-and-PIN machines—just enter your PIN when prompted. If a machine won't take your card, look for a machine that takes cash or see if there's a cashier nearby who can process your transaction. The easiest solution is to pay for your purchases with cash you've withdrawn from an ATM using your debit card (Europe's ATMs still accept magnetic-stripe cards).

Phoning

Smart travelers use the telephone to reserve or reconfirm rooms, reserve restaurants, get directions, research transportation connections, confirm tour times, phone home, and lots more.

To call Germany from the US or Canada: Dial 011-49 and then the area code (minus its initial zero) and local number. (The 011 is our international access code, and 49 is Germany's country code.)

To call Germany from a European country: Dial 00-49 followed by the area code (minus its initial zero) and local number. (The 00 is Europe's international access code.)

To call within Germany: If you're dialing within an area code, just dial the local number; but if you're calling outside your area code, you have to dial both the area code (which starts with a 0) and the local number.

To call from Germany to another country: Dial 00 followed by the country code (for example, 1 for the US or Canada), then the area code and number. If you're calling European countries whose phone numbers begin with 0, you'll usually have to omit that 0 when you dial.

Tips on Phoning: A mobile phone—whether an American one that works in Germany, or a European one you buy upon arrival—is handy, but can be pricey. If traveling with a smartphone, switch off data-roaming until you have free Wi-Fi.

To make cheap international calls, you can buy an international phone card in Germany; these work with a scratch-to-reveal PIN code at any phone, allow you to call home to the US for pennies a minute, and also work for domestic calls within Germany. Avoid using international phone cards at pay phones. Because the German phone company slaps on hefty surcharges, you'll get far fewer minutes for your money (for example, 10 minutes instead of 100 on a €5 card) than if you call from your hotel room.

Insertable phone cards, usable only at pay phones, are reasonable for calls within Germany (and work for international calls as well, but not as cheaply as using an international phone card from your hotel-room phone).

Calling from your hotel-room phone is usually expensive, unless you use an international phone card. For much more on phoning, see www.ricksteves.com/phoning.

Making Hotel Reservations

To ensure the best value, I recommend reserving rooms in advance, particularly during peak season. Email the hotelier with the following key pieces of information: number and type of rooms; number of nights; date of arrival; date of departure; and any special requests. (For a sample form, see www.ricksteves.com/

reservation.) Use the European style for writing dates: day/month/ year. For example, for a two-night stay in July, you could request: "1 double room for 2 nights, arrive 16/07/13, depart 18/07/13." Hoteliers typically ask for your credit-card number as a deposit.

Given the economic downturn, hoteliers can be willing and eager to make a deal. I'd suggest emailing several hotels to ask for their best price. Comparison-shop and make your choice.

In general, hotel prices can soften if you do any of the following: offer to pay cash, stay at least three nights, or mention this book. You can also try asking for a cheaper room or a discount, or offer to skip breakfast.

Eating

At mealtime, there are many options beyond restaurants. For hearty, stick-to-the-ribs meals—and plenty of beer—look for a beer hall *(Bräuhaus)* or beer garden *(Biergarten)*. *Gasthaus, Gasthof, Gaststätte,* and *Gaststube* all loosely describe an informal, inn-type eatery. A *Kneipe* is a bar, and a *Keller* (or *Ratskeller*) is a cellar, usually serving traditional food. A *Schnell Imbiss* is a small fast-food take-away stand. Department-store cafeterias are also common and handy.

The classic German dish is sausage. The hundreds of varieties of W*urst* are usually served with mustard *(Senf),* a roll *(Semmel)* or pretzel *(Breze),* and sauerkraut. The various types of *Bratwurst* are grilled *(gebraten).* To enjoy a *Weisswurst*—a boiled white Bavarian sausage made of veal—peel off the skin and eat it with sweet mustard. *Currywurst* comes with a delicious curry-infused ketchup. You'll also find schnitzel everywhere (pork is cheaper than veal). Salads are big, leafy, and good. Germans are passionate about choosing organic products—look for *Bio.*

Ethnic eateries—such as Italian, Turkish, Greek, and Asian—are good values. The Turkish *Döner Kebab*—sliced meat and vegetables served in pita bread—rivals *Wurst* as a German fast-food staple.

In Germany, good service is relaxed (slow to an American). When you want the bill, say, *"Rechnung* (REHKH-noong), *bitte."* To tip for good service, it's customary to round up around 5 to 10 percent. Rather than leave coins on the table, do as the locals do: When you pay, tell the waiter how much you want him to keep, including his tip. For example, for an €8.10 meal, give a €20 bill and say *"Neun Euro"*—"Nine euros"—to include a €0.90 tip and get €11 change.

Germany has both great wine *(Wein)* and beer *(Bier).* Order wine *süss* (sweet), *halb trocken* (medium), or *trocken* (dry). For beer, *dunkles* is dark, *helles* or *Lager* is light, *Flaschenbier* is bottled, and *vom Fass* is on tap. *Pils* is barley-based, and *Weizen, Hefeweizen,* or

Weissbier is yeasty and wheat-based. When you order beer, ask for *eine Halbe* for a half-liter (though it's not always available) or *eine Mass* for a whole liter (about a quart).

Transportation

By Train: German trains—speedy, comfortable, non-smoking, and fairly punctual—cover cities and small towns well. Faster trains (such as the high-speed ICE) are more expensive than slower "regional" trains. To see if a railpass could save you money—which is often the case in Germany—check www.ricksteves.com/rail. If buying point-to-point tickets, note that prices can fluctuate (you can usually save money by booking more expensive train journeys online; tickets are sold up to three months in advance). To research train schedules and fares, visit Germany's excellent online time-table, www.bahn.com.

By Car: It's cheaper to arrange most car rentals from the US. For tips on your insurance options, see www.ricksteves.com/cdw, and for route planning, try www.viamichelin.com. Bring your driver's license. Germany's toll-free autobahn (freeway) system lets you zip around the country in a snap. While there's often no official speed limit, going above the posted recommended speed invalidates your insurance. Many German cities—including Munich, Freiburg, Frankfurt, Köln, Dresden, Leipzig, and Berlin—require drivers to buy a special sticker *(Umweltplakette)* to drive in the city center. These already come standard with most German rental cars; ask when you pick up your car. A car is a worthless headache in cities—park it safely (get tips from your hotel).

Helpful Hints

Emergency Help: To summon the **police** or an **ambulance**, call 112. For passport problems, call the **US Embassy** (in Berlin, tel. 030/83050, consular services tel. 030/8305-1200—Mon–Thu 14:00–16:00 only) or the **Canadian Embassy** (in Berlin, tel. 030/203-120). For other concerns, get advice from your hotel.

Theft or Loss: To replace a passport, you'll need to go in person to an embassy (see above). Cancel and replace your credit and debit cards by calling these 24-hour US numbers collect: Visa—tel. 303/967-1096, MasterCard—tel. 636/722-7111, American Express—tel. 336/393-1111. File a police report either on the spot or within a day or two; you'll need it to submit an insurance claim for lost or stolen railpasses or travel gear, and it can help with replacing your passport or credit and debit cards. Precautionary measures can minimize the effects of loss—back up your photos and other files frequently. For more information, see www.ricksteves.com/help.

Time: Germany uses the 24-hour clock. It's the same through 12:00 noon, then keep going: 13:00, 14:00, and so on. Germany, like most of continental Europe, is six/nine hours ahead of the East/West Coasts of the US.

Business Hours: In Germany, most shops are open from about 9:00 until 18:00 or 20:00 on weekdays, but close early on Saturday (as early as 12:00 and as late as 17:00). Most shops close entirely on Sundays.

Holidays and Festivals: Germany celebrates many holidays, which can close sights and attract crowds (book hotel rooms ahead). For more on holidays and festivals, check Germany's website: www.cometogermany.com. For a simple list showing major—though not all—events, see www.ricksteves.com/festivals.

Numbers and Stumblers: What Americans call the second floor of a building is the first floor in Europe. Europeans write dates as day/month/year, so Christmas is 25/12/13. Commas are decimal points and vice versa—a dollar and a half is 1,50, and there are 5.280 feet in a mile. Germany uses the metric system: A kilogram is 2.2 pounds; a liter is about a quart; and a kilometer is six-tenths of a mile.

Resources from Rick Steves

This Snapshot guide is excerpted from the latest edition of *Rick Steves' Germany,* which is one of more than 30 titles in my series of guidebooks on European travel. I also produce a public television series, *Rick Steves' Europe,* and a public radio show, *Travel with Rick Steves.* My website, www.ricksteves.com, offers free travel information, a Graffiti Wall for travelers' comments, guidebook updates, my travel blog, an online travel store, and information on European railpasses and our tours of Europe. If you're bringing a mobile device on your trip, you can download free information from Rick Steves Audio Europe, featuring podcasts of my radio shows, free audio tours of major sights in Europe, and travel interviews about Germany (via www.ricksteves.com/audioeurope, iTunes, Google Play, or the Rick Steves Audio Europe free smartphone app). You can follow me on Facebook and Twitter.

Additional Resources

Tourist Information: www.cometogermany.com
Passports and Red Tape: www.travel.state.gov
Packing List: www.ricksteves.com/packlist
Travel Insurance: www.ricksteves.com/insurance
Cheap Flights: www.kayak.com
Airplane Carry-on Restrictions: www.tsa.gov/travelers
Updates for This Book: www.ricksteves.com/update

How Was Your Trip?

If you'd like to share your tips, concerns, and discoveries after using this book, please fill out the survey at www.ricksteves.com/feedback. Thanks in advance—it helps a lot.

German Survival Phrases

When using the phonetics, pronounce ī as the long I sound in "light."

Good day.	Guten Tag.	**goo**-tehn tahg
Do you speak English?	Sprechen Sie Englisch?	**shprehkh**-ehn zee **ehng**-lish
Yes. / No.	Ja. / Nein.	yah / nīn
I (don't) understand.	Ich verstehe (nicht).	ikh fehr-**shtay**-heh (nikht)
Please.	Bitte.	**bit**-teh
Thank you.	Danke.	**dahng**-keh
I'm sorry.	Es tut mir leid.	ehs toot meer līt
Excuse me.	Entschuldigung.	ehnt-**shool**-dig-oong
(No) problem.	(Kein) Problem.	(kīn) proh-**blaym**
(Very) good.	(Sehr) gut.	(zehr) goot
Goodbye.	Auf Wiedersehen.	owf **vee**-der-zayn
one / two	eins / zwei	īns / tsvī
three / four	drei / vier	drī / feer
five / six	fünf / sechs	fewnf / zehkhs
seven / eight	sieben / acht	**zee**-behn / ahkht
nine / ten	neun / zehn	noyn / tsayn
How much is it?	Wieviel kostet das?	**vee**-feel **kohs**-teht dahs
Write it?	Schreiben?	**shrī**-behn
Is it free?	Ist es umsonst?	ist ehs oom-**zohnst**
Included?	Inklusive?	in-kloo-**zee**-veh
Where can I buy / find...?	Wo kann ich kaufen / finden...?	voh kahn ikh **kow**-fehn / **fin**-dehn
I'd like / We'd like...	Ich hätte gern / Wir hätten gern...	ikh **heh**-teh gehrn / veer **heh**-tehn gehrn
...a room.	...ein Zimmer.	īn **tsim**-mer
...a ticket to ___.	...eine Fahrkarte nach ___.	ī-neh **far**-kar-teh nahkh
Is it possible?	Ist es möglich?	ist ehs **mur**-glikh
Where is...?	Wo ist...?	voh ist
...the train station	...der Bahnhof	dehr **bahn**-hohf
...the bus station	...der Busbahnhof	dehr **boos**-bahn-hohf
...tourist information	...das Touristen- informationsbüro	dahs too-**ris**-tehn- in-for-maht-see-**ohns**-bew-roh
...toilet	...die Toilette	dee toh-**leh**-teh
men	Herren	**hehr**-rehn
women	Damen	**dah**-mehn
left / right	links / rechts	links / rehkhts
straight	geradeaus	geh-**rah**-deh-**ows**
When is this open / closed?	Um wieviel Uhr ist hier geöffnet / geschlossen?	oom **vee**-feel oor ist heer geh-**urf**-neht / geh-**shloh**-sehn
At what time?	Um wieviel Uhr?	oom **vee**-feel oor
Just a moment.	Moment.	moh-**mehnt**
now / soon / later	jetzt / bald / später	yehtst / bahld / **shpay**-ter
today / tomorrow	heute / morgen	**hoy**-teh / **mor**-gehn

In the Restaurant

I'd like / We'd like...	Ich hätte gern / Wir hätten gern...	ikh **heh**-teh gehrn / veer **heh**-tehn gehrn
...a reservation for...	...eine Reservierung für...	ī-neh reh-zer-**feer**-oong fewr
...a table for one / two.	...einen Tisch für ein / zwei.	ī-nehn tish fewr īn / tsvī
Non-smoking.	Nichtraucher.	nikht-rowkh-er
Is this seat free?	Ist hier frei?	ist heer frī
Menu (in English), please.	Speisekarte (auf Englisch), bitte.	shpī-zeh-kar-teh (owf **ehng**-lish) **bit**-teh
service (not) included	Trinkgeld (nicht) inklusive	trink-gehlt (nikht) in-kloo-**zee**-veh
cover charge	Eintritt	īn-trit
to go	zum Mitnehmen	tsoom **mit**-nay-mehn
with / without	mit / ohne	mit / **oh**-neh
and / or	und / oder	oont / **oh**-der
menu (of the day)	(Tages-) Karte	(**tah**-gehs-) **kar**-teh
set meal for tourists	Touristenmenü	too-**ris**-tehn-meh-**new**
specialty of the house	Spezialität des Hauses	shpayt-see-ah-lee-**tayt** dehs **how**-zehs
appetizers	Vorspeise	**for**-shpī-zeh
bread	Brot	broht
cheese	Käse	**kay**-zeh
sandwich	Sandwich	**zahnd**-vich
soup	Suppe	**zup**-peh
salad	Salat	zah-**laht**
meat	Fleisch	flīsh
poultry	Geflügel	geh-**flew**-gehl
fish	Fisch	fish
seafood	Meeresfrüchte	**meh**-rehs-**frewkh**-teh
fruit	Obst	ohpst
vegetables	Gemüse	geh-**mew**-zeh
dessert	Nachspeise	**nahkh**-shpī-zeh
mineral water	Mineralwasser	min-eh-**rahl**-vah-ser
tap water	Leitungswasser	**lī**-toongs-vah-ser
milk	Milch	milkh
(orange) juice	(Orangen-) Saft	(oh-**rahn**-zhehn-) zahft
coffee	Kaffee	kah-**fay**
tea	Tee	tay
wine	Wein	vīn
red / white	rot / weiß	roht / vīs
glass / bottle	Glas / Flasche	glahs / **flah**-sheh
beer	Bier	beer
Cheers!	Prost!	prohst
More. / Another.	Mehr. / Noch ein.	mehr / nohkh īn
The same.	Das gleiche.	dahs **glīkh**-eh
Bill, please.	Rechnung, bitte.	**rehkh**-noong **bit**-teh
tip	Trinkgeld	**trink**-gehlt
Delicious!	Lecker!	**lehk**-er

For more user-friendly German phrases, check out *Rick Steves' German Phrase Book and Dictionary* or *Rick Steves' French, Italian & German Phrase Book.*

INDEX

INDEX

INDEX

Audio Europe

Join a Rick Steves tour

Enjoy Europe's warmest welcome... with the flexibility and friendship of a small group getting to know Rick's favorite places and people. It all starts with our free tour catalog and DVD.

Great guides, small groups, no grumps.

Start your trip at

Free information and great gear to

▶ Plan Your Trip

Browse thousands of articles and a wealth of money-saving tips for planning your dream trip. You'll find up-to-date information on Europe's best destinations, packing smart, getting around, finding rooms, staying healthy, avoiding scams and more.

▶ Eurail Passes

Find out, step-by-step, if a railpass makes sense for your trip—and how to avoid buying more than you need. Get free shipping on online orders

▶ Graffiti Wall & Travelers Helpline

Learn, ask, share—our online community of savvy travelers is a great resource for first-time travelers to Europe, as well as seasoned pros.

Rick Steves' Europe Through the Back Door, Inc.